SEASONS of the SPIRIT

D1312977

SEASONS of the SPIRIT

READINGS THROUGH THE CHRISTIAN YEAR

selected and edited by

George Every

Richard Harries

Kallistos Ware

TRIANGLE

First published 1984
SPCK, Holy Trinity Church,
Marylebone Road, London NW1 4DU

First Triangle edition 1990

British Library Cataloguing in Publication Data
Seasons of the spirit—New ed.
1. Devotional calendars
I. Every, George   II. Harries, Richard
III. Ware, Kallistos
242A.2   BV4810

ISBN 0-281-0447-3

Filmset by Latimer Trend & Company Ltd, Plymouth
Printed in Great Britain by
BPCC Hazell Books Ltd
Aylesbury, Bucks

Contents

The Editors

George Every became a Roman Catholic in 1973 and is now on the staff of Oscott College, a seminary of the Archdiocese of Birmingham. He was a laybrother of the Anglican Society of the Sacred Mission at Kelham from 1933–1973. There he wrote *Christian Discrimination* (1940), *The Byzantine Patriarchate* and other books on church history and liturgy. His *Christian Mythology* (1970) had a second edition in 1987.

Richard Harries is Bishop of Oxford. He has been Dean of King's College London, a parish priest and a Lecturer in Christian Doctrine on Ethics. He has published fifteen books, including *Christ is Risen* (1988) and *The One Genius: Readings through the year with Austin Farrer* (1987).

Kallistos Ware is Bishop of Diokleia and Spalding Lecturer in Eastern Orthodox Studies in the University of Oxford. He is in charge of the Greek Orthodox parish in Oxford and is a member of the Monastic Brotherhood of St John the Theologian, Patmos. *The Orthodox Way* (1979) has become a classic introduction to the Eastern Orthodox Church for those brought up in the Western tradition.

Introduction

THE PURPOSE of this anthology is to show how time – the sequence of days, months and seasons – can be taken up into Christ, and so be sanctified and transfigured.

Of the three editors one is Roman Catholic, one Anglican and one Orthodox. We have embarked on our task in an ecumenical spirit, hoping that the book will widen the horizon and enrich the prayer of our readers, opening their eyes to unfamiliar treasures in Christian traditions other than their own. We have sought to convey some inkling of the amazing variety that exists within Christianity. Yet this variety is at the same time a diversity in unity. As we made our selection, again and again we were struck by the manner in which the different texts – ancient and modern, Eastern and Western, Catholic and Protestant – do not so much contradict as complement each other. Working together as a team, with each editor suggesting material not only from his own tradition but from that of the other two, we have repeatedly discovered in unexpected ways how much we share in common.

Each month of the year is assigned a chapter of its own, but we have not attempted to provide separate readings for every day. Within each month the material falls into two groups. First, the month has one or more dominant *themes*. The book starts in September with the creation of the world, continuing in October with the potentialities of the human person; later comes the cycle of Christ's incarnation, death and resurrection, leading to Pentecost and the revelation of the Trinity; we end in August with the final glory of the age to come, which is seen anticipated in the persons of our Lord and of his Mother (August 6 and 15). Second, in every month selected *saints* are included. Without attempting to provide a dictionary of saints, we supply brief biographical notes on each person. Where calendars differ, we have adopted what seemed the most appropriate day, without mentioning all the alternatives. Those not yet officially proclaimed as saints, or belonging to traditions that do not observe saints' days, appear usually on the date of their death.

Why have we chosen to start with the month of September? Our present-day practice of beginning the new year on 1 January is not in fact Jewish or Christian in origin, but is inherited from ancient Rome. In a

Christian context it has little to recommend it, introducing as it does an unhappy division between Christmas and Epiphany, which form in reality a single celebration. From the standpoint of sacred time, it is far better to begin the year with either spring or autumn. England observed new year's day in spring, on the feast of the Annunciation (March 25), until the eighteenth century. On the other hand the Jews since Old Testament times have celebrated the new year festival at the end of September, while in the Orthodox Church it falls on September 1. An autumnal starting-point, such as we have preferred, has parallels also in the secular world; in schools and universities throughout the northern hemisphere the year normally begins in September or October and ends in the summer.

Throughout the book it has been our concern to portray a past that remains alive and active in the immediate present – not so much a long line stretched out in time, as the gathering up of time itself into the communion of the living God. 'Jesus Christ is the same yesterday and today and forever' (Hebrews 13.8).

September

CREATION

Nobbut God

First on, there was nobbut God.
Genesis 1.1 (Yorkshire dialect translation)

First on
There was silence.
And God said:
'Let there be clatter.'

The wind, unclenching,
Runs its thumbs
Along dry bristles of Yorkshire Fog.

The mountain ousel
Oboes its one note.

After rain
Water lobelia
Drips like a tap
On the tarn's tight surface-tension.

But louder,
And every second nearer,
Like chain explosions
From furthest nebulae
Light-yearing across space:
The thudding of my own blood.

'It's nobbut me,'
Says God.

NORMAN NICHOLSON

Divine freedom

The world exists. But it *began* to exist. And that means: *the world could have not existed*. There is no necessity whatsoever for the existence of the world. Creaturely existence is not self-sufficient and is not independent. Creation by its very existence witnesses to and proclaims its creaturehood, it proclaims that it has been produced. But unexpectedly it is precisely in its creaturehood and createdness that the stability and substantiality of the world is rooted.

God creates in perfect freedom. This proposition is framed with remarkable precision by the 'subtle doctor' of the western Middle Ages, Duns Scotus: 'The creation of things is executed by God not out of any necessity, whether of essence or of knowledge or of will, but out of a sheer freedom which is not moved – much less constrained – by anything external.' In creation God is determined only by himself. God creates solely out of his goodness. The idea of the world has its basis not in the essence but in the will of God. The might and freedom of God must be defined not only as the power to create and to produce but also as the absolute freedom *not to create*. God creates out of the absolute superabundance of his mercy and love.

FATHER GEORGE FLOROVSKY

Returning the world to God

Contrary to our secular experience of time, the liturgical day begins with Vespers, in the evening. This is, of course, the reminiscence of the biblical 'And the evening and the morning were the first day' (Gen. 1.5).

The vesperal service [in the Orthodox Church] does not begin as a religious 'epilogue' of the day. It begins at the *beginning*, and this means in the 'rediscovery', in adoration and thanksgiving, of the world as God's creation. The Church takes us, as it were, to that first evening on which man, called by God to life, opened his eyes and saw what God in his love was giving to him, saw all the beauty, all the glory of the temple in which he was standing, and rendered thanks to God. And in this thanksgiving he *became himself*.

> Praise the Lord, O my soul. Blessed art thou, O Lord.
> O Lord, how marvellous are thy works: in wisdom hast thou made them all.
> The earth is full of thy riches.
> I will sing unto the Lord as long as I live;
> I will praise my God, while I have any being (Ps. 104).

And it must be so. There must be someone in this world – which rejected God and in this rejection, in this blasphemy, became a chaos of darkness – there must be someone to stand in its centre, and to discern, to see it again as full of divine riches, as the cup full of life and joy, as beauty and wisdom, and to thank God for it. This 'someone' is Christ, the New Adam who restores that 'eucharistic life' which I, the old Adam, have rejected and lost; who makes me again what I am, and restores the world to me. And if the Church *is in Christ*, its initial act is always the act of thanksgiving, of returning the world to God.

FATHER ALEXANDER SCHMEMANN

Pied Beauty

Glory be to God for dappled things —
    For skies of couple-colour as a brinded cow;
      For rose-moles all in stipple upon trout that swim;
Fresh-firecoal chestnut-falls; finches' wings;
    Landscape plotted and pieced — fold, fallow, and
      plough;
      and all trades, their gear and tackle and trim.

All things counter, original, spare, strange;
    Whatever is fickle, freckled (who knows how?)
      With swift, slow; sweet, sour; adazzle, dim;
He fathers-forth whose beauty is past change:
      Praise him.

GERARD MANLEY HOPKINS

From the abyss of nothingness

It is the presence of God that, without cessation, draws each creature from the abyss of its own nothingness above which his omnipotence holds it suspended, lest of its own weight it should fall back therein; and serves as the mortar and bond of connection which holds it together in order that all that it has of its creator should not waste and flow away like water that is not kept in its channel.

God in the heavens is more my heaven than the heavens themselves; in the sun he is more my light than the sun; in the air he is more my air than the air that I breathe sensibly. He works in me all that I am, all that I see, all that I do or can do, as utterly intimate, present, and immanent in me.

LOUIS CHARDON

Divine self-giving

The image of the creation suggested by popular devotion is an image of serene and effortless activity – the activity, one might say, 'of the left hand of God'. 'He spake the word and they were made: He commanded and they were created.' 'By the word of the Lord were the heavens made, and all the hosts of them by the breath of His mouth.' Whatever may have been the original intention of such words, they convey an impression of easy control and limited endeavour, of resources held in reserve and power unused. There is nothing of the giving of self, and therefore nothing of the authenticity of love, in activity so light and easy.

If the work of God in creation is the work of love, then truth demands an imagery which will do justice to the limitless self-giving which is among the marks of authentic love: and the imagery which the head demands may have a new power of appeal to the moral sensitivity of the heart.

As a parenthesis, we may illustrate the kind of imagery which might express the self-giving of God in creation. A doctor tells of an operation which, as a young student, he observed in a London hospital. 'It was the first time that this particular brain operation had been carried out in this country. It was performed by one of our leading surgeons upon a young man of great promise for whom, after an accident, there seemed to be no other remedy. It was an operation of the greatest delicacy, in which a small error would have had fatal consequences. In the outcome the operation was a triumph: but it involved seven hours of intense and uninterrupted concentration on the part of the surgeon. When it was over, a nurse had to take him by the hand, and lead him from the operating theatre like a blind man or a little child.' This, one might say, is what self-giving is like: such is the likeness of God, wholly given, spent and drained in that sublime self-giving which is the ground and source and origin of the universe.

W. H. VANSTONE

God makes the world make itself

When we contemplate the physical creation, we see an unimaginable complex, organized on many planes one above another; atomic, molecular, cellular; vegetable, animal, social. And the marvel of it is that at every level the constituent elements run themselves, and, by their mutual interaction, run the world. God not only makes the world, he makes it make itself; or rather, he causes its innumerable constituents to make it. And this in spite of the fact that the constituents are not for the most part intelligent. They cannot enter into the creative purposes they serve. They cannot see beyond the tip of their noses; they have, indeed, no noses not to see beyond, nor any eyes with which to fail in the attempt. All they can do is blind away at being themselves, and fulfil the repetitive pattern of their existence. When you contemplate this amazing structure, do you wonder that it should be full of flaws, breaks, accidents, collisions and disasters? Will you not be more inclined to wonder why chaos does not triumph; how higher forms of organization should ever arise, or, having arisen, maintain and perpetuate themselves?

Though a thousand species have perished with the mammoth and the dodo, and though all species, perhaps, must perish at the last, it is a sort of miracle that the species there are should have established themselves. And how have they established themselves? Science studies the pattern, but theology assigns the cause: that imperceptible persuasion exercised by creative Will on the chaos of natural forces, setting a bias on the positive and achieving the creatures.

AUSTIN FARRER

Our Lord God showed a ghostly sight of his homely loving; I saw that he is to us everything that is good and comfortable to our help. He is our clothing that for love wrappeth and windeth us, and all becloseth us, hangeth about us for tender love, that he may never leave us, and so in this sight me saw that he is all thing that is good, as to my understanding. And in this he showed a little thing, the quantity of a hazel-nut, lying in the palm of my hand as me seemed; and it was as round as a ball. I looked thereon with the eye of my understanding, and thought 'What may this be?'

And it was answered generally thus, 'It is all that is made.' I marvelled how it could last; for methought it might suddenly have fallen to nought for littleness. And I was answered in my understanding, 'It lasteth, and ever shall, for God loveth it. And so hath all thing being by the love of God.'

And in this little thing I saw three properties; the first is, that God made it. The second is, that God loveth it. The third is, that God keepeth it. But what beheld I therein? Verily the Maker, the Keeper, the Lover. For till I am substancially united to him, I may never have full rest nor very bliss, that is to say that I be so fastened to him, that there be right nought that is made between my God and me.

This little thing that is made, methought it might have fallen to nought for littleness. Of this we need to have knowledge, that making nothing of all that is made, we may love and have God who is unmade. The reason why we are not at ease in heart and soul is that we seek here rest in this thing that is so little, where no rest is; and we do not know our God who is almighty, all wise and all good, for he is very rest.

JULIAN OF NORWICH

Vegetation

O never harm the dreaming world,
the world of green, the world of leaves,
but let its million palms unfold
the adoration of the trees.

It is a love in darkness wrought
obedient to the unseen sun,
longer than memory, a thought
deeper than the graves of time.

The turning spindles of the cells
weave a slow forest over space,
the dance of love, creation,
out of time moves not a leaf,
and out of summer, not a shade.

KATHLEEN RAINE

When I began to pray with all my heart, everything around me seemed delightful and marvellous. The trees, the grass, the birds, the earth, the air, the light seemed to be telling me that they existed for man's sake, that they witnessed to the love of God for man, that everything proved the love of God for man, that all things prayed to God and sang his praise. Thus it was that I came to understand what the *Philokalia* calls 'the knowledge of the speech of all creatures'.

THE WAY OF A PILGRIM

Love all God's creation, the whole of it and every grain of sand in it. Love every leaf, every ray of God's light. Love the animals, love the plants, love everything. If you love everything, you will perceive the divine mystery in things. Once you have perceived it, you will begin to comprehend it better every day, and you will come at last to love the world with an all-embracing love. Love the animals: God has given them the rudiments of thought and untroubled joy. So do not trouble it, do not harass them, do not deprive them of their joy, do not go against God's intent. Man, do not exalt yourself above the animals: they are without sin, while you in your majesty defile the earth by your appearance on it, and you leave the traces of your defilement behind you – alas, this is true of almost every one of us! Love children especially, for like the angels they too are sinless, and they live to soften and purify our hearts, and, as it were, to guide us. Woe to him who offends a child!

My young brother asked even the birds to forgive him. It may sound absurd, but it is right none the less, for everything, like the ocean, flows and enters into contact with everything else: touch one place, and you set up a movement at the other end of the world. It may be senseless to beg forgiveness of the birds, but, then, it would be easier for the birds, and for the child, and for every animal if you were yourself more pleasant than you are now. Everything is like an ocean, I tell you. Then you would pray to the birds, too, consumed by a universal love, as though in an ecstasy, and ask that they, too, should forgive you your sin. Treasure this ecstasy, however absurd people may think it.

FYODOR DOSTOEVSKY
'The Discourses of Father Zossima'

Good

The old man comes out on the hill
and looks down to recall earlier days
in the valley. He sees the stream shine,
the church stand, hears the litter of
children's voices. A chill in the flesh
tells him that death is not far off
now: it is the shadow under the great boughs
of life. His garden has herbs growing.
The kestrel goes by with fresh prey
in its claws. The wind scatters the scent
of wild beans. The tractor operates
on the earth's body. His grandson is there
ploughing; his young wife fetches him
cakes and tea and a dark smile. It is well.

R. S. THOMAS

Every thing that lives is Holy.

If the doors of perception were cleansed, every thing would appear to man as it is, infinite.

He who sees the Infinite in all things, sees God.

To create a little flower is the labour of ages.

'What,' it will be Question'd, 'when the Sun rises, do you not see a round disk of fire somewhat like a Guinea?' O no, no, I see an Innumerable company of the Heavenly host crying, 'Holy, Holy, Holy is the Lord God Almighty.'

For double the vision my Eyes do see,
And a double vision is always with me.

WILLIAM BLAKE

'God saw everything that he had made: and, behold, it was most beautiful' (Gen. 1.31)

God is good; he is goodness itself. God is true; he is truth itself. God is glorious, and his glory is beauty itself.

Beauty is an objective principle in the world, revealing to us the divine glory. The divine source of objective beauty is also the source of the human creation of beauty, that is, of art. God created man in his image, granting to this image three gifts: a will directed towards the good, the gift of reason and wisdom, and the gift of aesthetic appreciation. Man is meant to be the wisdom of the world, just because he participates in the Logos; he is also meant to be the artist of the world, because he can imbue it with beauty. Man must become not only a good and faithful worker in the world; he must not only 'dress and keep it' (Gen. 2.15), as he was commanded in paradise, but he must also become its artist; he must render it beautiful. Because he has been created in the image of God, he is called to create.

Things are transfigured and made luminous by beauty; they become the revelation of their own abstract meaning. And this revelation through beauty of the things of earth is the work of art. The world, as it has been given to us, has remained as it were covered by an outward shell through which art penetrates, as if foreseeing the coming transfiguration of the world.

Man has been called to be a demiurge, not only to contemplate the beauty of the world, but also to express it. Does this not speak of a new service of the Church, one that has not yet been fully revealed in the heart of man and in his history: the service of realizing the work of human participation in the transfiguration of the world? Is it not of this that the words of Dostoevsky speak, 'Beauty will save the world'?

FATHER SERGIUS BULGAKOV

September 3 ST GREGORY THE GREAT *c.547–604*

A loyal subject of the Roman Empire and of the emperor in Constantinople, he was obliged, like other Italian bishops, to make political decisions, in his case not only for his own city and church. He was pope from 590. The next year, in 591, he writes to Bishop Leander of Seville:

Now I am in this place tossed by such billows of this world that I am in no way able to steer into port the old and rotten ship over which, in the hidden dispensation of God, I have assumed the guidance. Now in front of me the billows rush in; now at the side, masses of foam swell up; now from behind, the storm follows on. And in the midst of all this I am sometimes compelled to steer in the very face of the opposing waters, and sometimes by turning aside to avoid the threats of the billows. The rotten planks already sound of shipwreck.

September 7 ST MACARIUS, STARETS OF OPTINO *1788–1860*

In the Orthodox Church the title 'elder' – in Greek *gerōn*, in Russian *starets* – is given to those endowed with the charisma of guiding others. Most commonly they are monk-priests, as was *starets* Macarius, but sometimes they are lay men or women. In nineteenth-century Russia the Optino Hermitage was a particularly influential centre of spiritual direction.

Pray simply. Do not expect to find in your heart any remarkable gift of prayer. Consider yourself unworthy of it. Then you will find peace. Use the empty, cold dryness of your prayer as food for your humility. Repeat constantly: I am not worthy, Lord, I am not worthy! But say it calmly, without agitation. This humble prayer will be acceptable to God.

Remember that the most important thing of all is humility; then, the ability – not the decision only – always to maintain a keen sense of responsibility towards God, towards one's spiritual director, men, and even things. Remember, too, that St Isaac the Syrian warns us that God's wrath visits all who refuse the bitter cross of agony, the cross of active suffering, and who, striving after visions and special graces of prayer, waywardly seek to appropriate the glories of the cross. He also says, 'God's grace comes of itself, suddenly, without our seeing it approach. It comes when the place is clean.' Therefore, carefully, diligently, constantly clean the place; sweep it with the broom of humility.

September 8 NATIVITY OF THE BLESSED VIRGIN

Joachim came in with his flocks and his wife Anna saw Joachim coming. Running to him, she hung on his neck saying, 'Now I know that the Lord has covered me with his blessings, for I was a widow and I am widowed no longer. I was childless, and I am going to conceive in my womb.' And Joachim rested that day in his house.

Anna's months were fulfilled; in the ninth she bore a child. She said to the midwife, 'What have I got?', and she said, 'A daughter.' And Anna said, 'My soul is magnified today', and she took her in her arms. Anna purified herself as her days of purification were accomplished, and gave her breast to the baby. She called her Mary.

Day by day the child grew. When she was six months old her mother put her on the ground to see if she would stand. She walked seven steps and came back to her mother's lap. She picked her up and said, 'By the life of the Lord my God you shall not walk on the ground until the day when I take you to the temple of God.' She set up a sanctuary in her room and would let nothing unclean come through to be near her, and she called in those daughters of the Hebrews who had no other tasks, to play with the baby.

PROTEVANGELION OF JAMES

Thy nativity, O Mother of God,
Has brought joy to all the world:
For from thee has shone forth
The Sun of Righteousness, Christ our God.
He has loosed us from the curse and given the blessing:
He has vanquished death, and bestowed on us eternal life.

By the holy nativity, O most pure Virgin,
Joachim and Anna were set free from the reproach of childlessness,
And Adam and Eve from the corruption of death.
Delivered from the guilt of sin,
Thy people keep the feast and sing:
The barren woman bears God's Mother, the Sustainer of our life.

HYMNS FOR THE FEAST IN THE ORTHODOX CHURCH

September 11   ST SILOUAN, STARETS OF MOUNT ATHOS   *1866–1938*

Brought up in a Russian village, the son of peasants, St. Silouan entered the Russian monastery on the Holy Mountain at the age of twenty-six, remaining there for the rest of his life. Peaceful and humble in character, never ordained priest, he left behind writings – published after his death by his disciple, Archimandrite Sophrony – which testify to a remarkable depth of inner prayer and compassionate love. In his spiritual teaching the *starets* stresses above all the need to love our enemies.

The man who has the Holy Spirit within him, in however slight a degree, sorrows day and night for all mankind. His heart is filled with pity for all God's creatures, and more especially for those who do not know God or who resist him and therefore are bound for the fire of torment. For them, more than for himself, he prays night and day, that all may repent and know the Lord.

I remember a conversation [writes Father Sophrony] between him and a certain hermit who declared with evident satisfaction: 'God will punish all atheists. They will burn in everlasting fire.'

Obviously upset, the *starets* said: 'Tell me, supposing you went to paradise and there looked down and saw somebody burning in hell-fire – would you feel happy?'

'It can't be helped. It would be their own fault,' said the hermit.

The *starets* answered him with a sorrowful countenance.

'Love could not bear that,' he said. 'We must pray for all.'

September 12   ST CYPRIAN   *d. 258*

He became bishop of Carthage in 248 and was martyred ten years later. His treatise *On the Unity of the Church* was addressed to problems arising out of the aftermath of the Decian persecution of 251, the first to cover the whole empire, especially in regard to those who had complied with the demands of the authorities in some degree. He writes:

The episcopate is a single whole, of which each bishop possesses all. So the Church is one, although she be spread around, and multiply with the increase of her progeny: even as the sun's many rays are one light, and the many boughs of the tree have a single source of strength, set deep in the roots under the earth; and as, when many streams flow from one source, although a multiplicity of waters appear to be diffused from the abundant, overflowing bounty, yet in the source itself unity is preserved. By no severance of light can a ray be parted from the sun; a branch broken from a tree cannot bud any more. If a stream be cut off from its source, the dwindling remnant dries. So the Church, flooded with the Lord's light, sends out her rays through the whole world, with one light spread over every place, so long as the unity of the body is not impaired. She stretches her branches over the worldwide earth, rich with her plenty, and pours abroad her bountiful streams, flowing on and on; and yet there is one head, one source, one mother, abounding in the fruitfulness of her fecundity. Of her womb we are born, her milk is our food, her breath gives life to ours.

September 14   THE EXALTATION OF THE CROSS

O cross of Christ, the Christians' hope,
Guide of the wanderers, haven of the storm-tossed,
Victory in warfare, firm foundation of the world,
Physician of the sick, resurrection of the dead,
        Have mercy upon us.

The cross is the guardian of the whole earth,
The cross is the beauty of the Church.
The cross is the strength of kings,
The cross is the support of the faithful.
The cross is the angels' glory, the demons' destruction.

HYMNS FOR THE FEAST IN THE ORTHODOX CHURCH

September 19   ST THEODORE OF TARSUS   *602–690*

He was a Syrian monk sent from Rome to Canterbury in 667. He arrived in 669 and for more than twenty years devoted himself to the organization of the English people into a church that became the seedbed of the nation. His disciples preserved his rulings in a *Penitential* where notice is taken of differences between Greeks and Latins in many practical matters, including the regulation of marriage as well as of feasts and fasts. This elasticity enabled Theodore to make use of practices introduced from Ireland, especially in matters of penitential discipline, but he would not allow women to give penances. As J. R. Green observed in his *Short History of the English People*, 'The policy of Theodore clothed with a sacred form and surrounded with divine sanctions a unity which as yet rested on no basis other than the sword'. This Syrian Greek has some claim to be called the father and founder of the English nation.

September 21   ST MATTHEW THE APOSTLE

'Follow me' (Matt. 4.19): The cost of discipleship

Cheap grace is the deadly enemy of our Church. We are fighting today for costly grace. Cheap grace means grace sold on the market like cheapjack's wares. The sacraments, the forgiveness of sin and the consolations of religion are thrown away at cut prices. Cheap grace is the preaching of forgiveness without requiring repentance, baptism without church discipline, communion without confession, absolution without personal confession. Cheap grace is grace without discipleship, grace without the cross, grace without Jesus Christ, living and incarnate.

Costly grace is the treasure hidden in the field; for the sake of it a man will gladly go and sell all that he has. It is the pearl of great price to buy which the merchant will sell all his goods. It is the kingly rule of Christ, for whose sake a man will pluck out the eye which causes him to stumble; it is the call of Jesus Christ at which the disciple leaves his nets and follows him.

Such grace is *costly* because it calls us to follow, and it is *grace* because it calls us to follow *Jesus Christ*. It is costly because it costs a man his life, and it is grace because it gives a man the only true life.

DIETRICH BONHOEFFER

September 25 ST SERGIUS OF RADONEZH *c. 1314–1392*

> The greatest national saint of Russia, he retired in youth to live as a hermit in the forest; but disciples gathered round him, and eventually he founded a monastery dedicated to the Holy Trinity, which within his own lifetime became the chief religious house in Muscovy. He encouraged his countrymen in their efforts to drive back the Tartars. The following story, recounted by his disciple Epiphanius, indicates the central place of the Eucharist in the saint's spiritual experience.

One day St Sergius was celebrating the divine liturgy, assisted by Simon, one of his disciples; and this Simon beheld a wonderful vision. While the saint was singing the Liturgy, Simon saw a flame hovering over the holy table, surrounding and illuminating it. As the saint was about to receive communion, the divine fire coiled itself together and entered the sacred chalice; and thus the saint received communion. On witnessing this, Simon trembled with fear. The saint, when he moved away from the altar, realized that Simon had been allowed to see this miraculous vision; and, calling him, he said: 'My son, why are you frightened?' And Simon answered: 'My Lord, I have seen a miraculous vision; I have seen the grace of the Holy Spirit co-operating with you.' Then the saint forbade him to speak of it: 'Tell no one of this that you have seen, until the Lord calls me away from this life.'

Lancelot Andrewes was admired in his own time for his learning, holiness and preaching. In the present century he has been appreciated as an English stylist and for his intense but ordered personal spirituality. His large collection of prayers for his own use, *Preces Privatae*, is woven of biblical and liturgical phrases and is arranged according to the days of the week and particular themes.

Commemoration

Blessed art Thou, O Lord,
who didst create the firmament of heaven,
    the heavens and the heavens of heavens;
        the heavenly hosts,
            angels, archangels,
            cherubim, seraphim.

Penitence

Of the Canaanitish woman
    Have mercy on me, O Lord, Thou Son of David:
        Lord, help me:
    yea, Lord, even the whelps eat
      of the crumbs that fall
      from their masters' table.
Of the debtor in ten thousand talents
    Have patience with me, O Lord;
        or rather
        I have not aught to repay, I confess unto
          Thee:
        forgive me all the debt,
          I beseech Thee.

Hope

And now, Lord, what is my hope?
    Truly my hope is even in Thee.
In Thee, O Lord, have I trusted;
    let me never be confounded.

Intercession

    Let us beseech the Lord
for the whole creation:

a supply of seasons { healthful,
fruitful,
peaceful:

for all our race: { not Christians
{ Christians:

for the succour and consolation

    of all, men and women, suffering   { dejection
        hardness in   { sickness
                                   { resourcelessness
                                   { unsettlement:

for the thankfulness and sobriety

    of all, men and women, that are   { cheerfulness
        in good case in   { health
                                   { resourcefulness
                                   { tranquillity:

for those commended to me by
    kindred: brothers, sisters:
        for the blessing of God upon them
            and upon their children:
    friendship:
        for them that love me
            and some even unknown:
    Christian charity:
        for them that hate me
            and some even for the truth and
                righteousness' sake:
    neighbourhood:
        for them that dwell by me quietly and
            harmlessly:
    promise:
        for them I have promised to bear in mind in
            my prayers
    mutual obligation:
        for them that bear me in mind in their
            prayers and beg as much of me:
        much occupation:
    for them that for reasonable causes fail of
            calling upon Thee.

               Blessing
God be merciful unto us
    and bless us:
show us the light of thy countenance
    and be merciful unto us:
God, even our own God,
    God give us thy blessing.

September 27 ST VINCENT DE PAUL *1581–1660*

He founded the Congregation of the Mission in 1625 for the preaching of the gospel in parts of France neglected since the devastations of the religious wars in the century before. In a letter to a priest of the mission on January 15, 1633, he wrote:

During the past few days I have been reading about the simple, normal way of life that our Lord willed to live while he was on earth, and I saw that he loved this ordinary and lowly life so much that he abased himself, so far as lay in his power, to adapt himself to it, and that although he was the uncreated Wisdom of the Eternal Father, yet it was his will to preach his doctrine in a much more commonplace and ordinary style than his apostles did. I ask you to compare his discourses with the letters and sermons of St Peter, St Paul and the other apostles. It would seem that he assumed the style of a man of little learning, while that of the apostles seems to be the style of men with far greater knowledge than he had. What is even more astonishing, it was his will that his sermons should produce much less in the way of results than did those of his apostles; for we may see in the Gospels that he gained his apostles and disciples almost always one by one, and that with trouble and difficulty, and yet by his first sermon St Peter converted five thousand. That, for sure, has given me more light and knowledge, or so it seems, on the marvellous humility of the Son of God than any other reflection on the subject that I have ever made.

September 29 ST MICHAEL AND ALL ANGELS

The Kingdom of God

'In no strange land'

O world invisible, we view thee,
O world intangible, we touch thee,
O world unknowable, we know thee,
Inapprehensible, we clutch thee!

Does the fish soar to find the ocean,
The eagle plunge to find the air –
That we ask of the stars in motion
If they have rumour of thee there?

Not where the wheeling systems darken,
And our benumbed conceiving soars! –
The drift of pinions, would we hearken,
Beats at our own clay-shuttered doors.

The angels keep their ancient places; –
Turn but a stone and start a wing!
'Tis ye, 'tis your estrangèd faces,
That miss the many-splendoured thing.

But (when so sad thou canst not sadder)
Cry; – and upon thy so sore loss
Shall shine the traffic of Jacob's ladder
Pitched betwixt Heaven and Charing Cross.

Yea, in the night, my Soul, my daughter,
Cry, – clinging Heaven by the hems;
And lo, Christ walking on the water
Not of Gennesareth, but Thames!

FRANCIS THOMPSON

The Guardian Angel

Thou angel of God who hast charge of me
From the dear Father of mercifulness,
The shepherding kind of the fold of the saints
To make round about me this night;

Drive from me every temptation and danger,
Surround me on the sea of unrighteousness,
And in the narrows, crooks, and straits,
Keep thou my coracle, keep it always.

Be thou a bright flame before me;
Be thou a guiding star above me,
Be thou a smooth path below me,
And be a kindly shepherd behind me,
Today, tonight, and for ever.

I am tired and I a stranger,
Lead thou me to the land of angels;
For me it is time to go home
To the court of Christ, to the peace of heaven.

CELTIC PRAYER

If you pray truly, you will feel within yourself a great assurance: and the angels will be your companions.

Know this, that as we pray the holy angels encourage us and stand at our side, full of joy and at the same time interceding on our behalf.

EVAGRIUS OF PONTUS

September 30 ST JEROME *c. 345–420*

> He wrote this letter to a family who joined him in Bethlehem after the sack
> of Rome by the Goths in 410.

I am going to write to Demetrias, a virgin of Christ and a lady whose birth
and wealth make her second to none in Roman society. Her grandmother
and her mother are women of distinction, with power to command, faith to
seek and perseverance to get what they want. They want me to lift up my
voice in witness to the virtues of one who, in the words of a famous orator,
is to be praised less for what she is than for what she gives promise of
becoming. With an ardent faith beyond the measure of her years, this lass
has started from a point where others think it a signal virtue to stop.

Some of the holy and highborn ladies who know her best have been
driven by the tempest that has swept over Africa from the shores of Gaul to
take refuge in the holy places. These tell me how night after night,
although no one knew it but the virgins dedicated to God in the retinue of
her mother and grandmother, Demetrias spread a rug of goat's-hair on the
ground and watered her face with tears. Night after night she cast herself at
the Saviour's knees and begged him to accept her choice and fulfil her
aspirations. She put back in their cases her necklaces, pearls and glowing
gems. Then, dressing herself in a coarse tunic and throwing over herself a
still coarser cloak, she came in and threw herself suddenly down at her
grandmother's knees, and there with tears and sobs showed what she really
was. That staid and holy woman was amazed. Her mother was totally
overcome for joy. Both women could hardly believe that to be true which
they had longed to be true.

Then Italy put off her mourning, and the ruined walls of Rome resumed
in part their ancient splendour; for they believed the full conversion of
their foster-child to be a sign of God's favour towards them.

October

THE HUMAN PERSON

It is meet and right, just and right, here and everywhere to give you thanks, O Lord, holy Father, eternal God, who brought us up from perpetual death and the deep darkness of the underworld, and endowed our mortal body, composed out of fragile clay, with your Son and eternity. Who is fit to tell the tale of your praise, or eloquent enough to display the wholeness of your works, for at these every tongue marvels, as all your priests extol your glory?

In the chaos of confused beginnings, and the everlasting darkness of floating objects, you imposed wonderful forms on the wondering elements, when the young world blushed at the sun's fire, and the raw earth marvelled at the moon doing her business. That all this might not be uninhabited, and an empty space serve only things, your hands fashioned a figure of clay, animated with holy fire, as the swift spirit quickened the slow parts. The inwardness of this, O Father, we are not allowed to examine.

You alone know the greatness of your work, how human limbs first stirred as the earth began to move and the blood in the veins to flow, and as the body was freed the nerves came into action, and the bones about the inner organs grew strong. Why should we be given these gifts, the wretches that we are? We are made like to you and your Son, and from lumps of clay into eternal beings. But we forgot the commands of your blessedness and, being mortal, sank again into the earth from whence we came. We wept, having lost the eternal comfort of your presence.

GALLICAN PRAYER

Unfallen Man

Several of the early Fathers envisage man, at his first creation, as being in a state of simplicity and innocence, not of fully realized sanctity and knowledge. As they see it, original sin was not a fall from exalted heights of wisdom and glory, but a failure to grow in the right way.

God set man in paradise, giving him the opportunity to advance, so that by growing and becoming mature, and by sharing in the divine life, he might thus ascend to heaven. For man was created in an intermediate state, neither entirely mortal nor wholly immortal, but capable of becoming either.

THEOPHILUS OF ANTIOCH

He was a little child, and it was necessary that he should grow and so come to his perfection.

ST IRENAEUS

Man has no Body distinct from his Soul; for that call'd Body is a portion of Soul discern'd by the five Senses.

> The pride of the peacock is the glory of God.
> The lust of the goat is the bounty of God.
> The wrath of the lion is the wisdom of God.
> The nakedness of woman is the work of God.

WILLIAM BLAKE

Microcosm and mediator

Wishing to form a single creature from the two levels of creation – from both invisible and visible nature – the Creator Logos fashioned man. Taking a body from the matter which he had previously created, and placing in it the breath of life that comes from himself, which Scripture terms the intelligent soul and the image of God (cf. Gen. 1.27; 2.7), he formed man as a second universe, great in his littleness. He set him on earth as a new kind of angel, adoring God with both aspects of his twofold being, overseer of the material creation and initiate into the spiritual creation; king of all upon earth, but subject to the King above; earthly yet heavenly; temporal yet immortal; visible yet spiritual; midway between majesty and lowliness; a single person, yet both spirit and flesh – spirit by grace, flesh because of his pride; spirit, that he may continue in existence and glorify his benefactor; flesh, that he may suffer, and through suffering may be reminded and chastened when he grows conceited because of his greatness; a living creature guided in this world by God's providence, and then translated to another realm; and, as the culmination of the mystery, deified through his obedience to God. So God in his splendour has bound together soul and body; and, though he separates them at death, he will hereafter bind them together again in a yet more exalted way.

ST GREGORY OF NAZIANZUS

Within reality there are five divisions. The first is between uncreated nature and the created nature that acquires existence through coming into being. Second, the created nature that receives its existence from God is divided into the intelligible and the sensible. Third, within sensible or visible nature there is a division between heaven and earth. Fourth, earth is divided into paradise and the world. Fifth, man is divided into male and female. Now man is, as it were, a workshop that contains everything in an all-inclusive way; and so by virtue of his nature he acts as mediator, endowed with full power to link and unify the extreme points at the five different levels of division, because in the various aspects of his nature he is himself related to all these extremes. It is thus his vocation to make manifest in his person the great mystery of the divine intention – to show how the divided extremes in created things may be reconciled in harmony, the near with the far, the lower with the higher, so that through gradual ascent all are eventually brought into union with God. That is why man was introduced last of all into the creation, as a natural bond of unity, mediating between all divided things because related to all through the different aspects of his own self, drawing them all to unity within himself, and so uniting them all to God their cause, in whom there is no division.

Through dispassion he transcends the division between male and female. Through the holiness of his life he unites paradise and the world, thus producing a single earth. Through his angelic life of virtue, so far as this is possible for human beings, he unites heaven and earth, integrating the visible creation. Then, through his equality with the angels in spiritual knowledge, he unifies the intelligible and the sensible, making all created things into one single creation. Finally, in addition to all this, through love he unites created nature with the uncreated, rendering them one through the state of grace that he has attained. With the fullness of his being he coinheres fully in the fullness of God, becoming everything that God himself is, save for identity of essence.

ST MAXIMUS THE CONFESSOR

Priest and King of the Creation

We shall only understand the character of the world when we think of it as a gift or present.

The whole world ought to be regarded as the visible part of a universal and continuing sacrament, and all man's activities as a sacramental, divine communion.

Because man is unable to give God anything except that which he has already received from God, man learns to perceive the world as gift and sacrament by sacrificing something in this world for God's sake, as a sign of his grateful love, and as the vehicle of this love. God for his part returns to man what man has sacrificed in the form of fresh gifts, containing a new manifestation of his love, in a new and repeated blessing. 'Grace for grace.' And so an unbroken interchange between God and man in man's use of the world takes place, an ever-renewed and growing mutuality of love. The more man discovers the beauty and the higher use of created things, and the greater the gratitude and love with which he responds to God, the more God responds with still greater love and blessing, because man is in the position to receive it.

Man puts the seal of his understanding and of his intelligent work on to creation, thereby humanizing it and giving it humanized back to God. He actualizes the world's potentialities. Thus the world is not only a gift but a task for man. Man is able to mark the world with his seal because the world as the gift of God's love for man is not the fruit of necessity but the fruit of divine freedom. If it were the fruit of necessity there would be no freedom in it, and it would develop as an inexorable causal process. But it is so constituted that divine freedom and human freedom can manifest themselves in an unbroken dialogue.

FATHER DUMITRU STANILOAE

The Fall of the Angels

Many words spake
The angel of presumption:
'Why should I toil?' said he;
'To me it is no whit needful
To have a superior:
I have great power to form
A diviner throne.'
Then was the Mighty angry,
The highest ruler in heaven
Hurled him from the lofty seat.

The fiend with all his comrades
Fell then from heaven above
through as long as three nights and days,
the angels from heaven into hell;
There they have at even
immeasurably long,
each of all the fiends,
renewal of fire;
then cometh ere dawn
the eastern wind,
frost bitter-cold,
ever fire or dart.

CAEDMON

He trusted to have equall'd the most High,
If he oppos'd; and with ambitious aim
Against the Throne and Monarchy of God
Rais'd impious War in Heav'n and Battle proud
With vain attempt. Him the Almighty Power
Hurl'd headlong flaming from th' Ethereal Sky
With hideous ruin and combustion down
To bottomless perdition, there to dwell
In Adamantine Chains and penal Fire,
Who durst defy th' Omnipotent to Arms.

JOHN MILTON

The Lament of Adam

Banished from the joys of paradise, Adam sat outside and wept, and beating his hands upon his face he said: 'I am fallen, in thy compassion have mercy upon me.'

When Adam saw the angel drive him out and shut the door of the divine garden, he groaned aloud and said: 'I am fallen, in thy compassion have mercy upon me.'

O paradise, share in the sorrow of thy master who is brought to poverty, and with the sound of thy leaves pray to the Creator that he may not leave thy gate closed for ever. I am fallen, in thy compassion have mercy upon me.

HYMN ON THE SUNDAY OF FORGIVENESS
(the Sunday before Lent in the Orthodox Church)

Corruption

Sure, it was so. Man in those early days
    Was not all stone and earth;
He shin'd a little, and by those weak rays
    Had some glimpse of his birth.
He saw heaven o'er his head, and knew from whence
    He came, condemnèd, hither;
And, as first love draws strongest, so from hence
    His mind sure progress'd thither.
Things here were strange unto him; sweat and till;
    All was a thorn or weed;
Nor did those last, but – like himself – died still
    As soon as they did seed;
They seem'd to quarrel with him; for that act,
    That fell him, foil'd them all;
He drew the curse upon the world, and crack'd
    The whole frame with his fall.
This made him long for home, as loth to stay
    With murmurers and foes;
He sigh'd for Eden, and would often say
    'Ah! what bright days were those!'

Nor was heav'n cold unto him; for each day
    The valley or the mountain
Afforded visits, and still Paradise lay
    In some green shade or fountain.
Angels lay leiger here; each bush, and cell,
    Each oak, and highway knew them;
Walk but the fields, or sit down at some well,
    And he was sure to view them.
Almighty Love! where art thou now? mad man
    Sits down and freezeth on;
He raves, and swears to stir nor fire, nor fan,
    But bids the thread be spun.
I see, thy curtains are close-drawn; thy bow
    Looks dim too in the cloud;
Sin triumphs still, and man is sunk below
    The centre, and his shroud.
All's in deep sleep and night: thick darkness lies
    And hatcheth o'er thy people –
But hark! what trumpet's that? what angel cries
    'Arise! thrust in thy sickle'?

HENRY VAUGHAN

Wonder

How like an angel came I down!
How bright are all things here!
When first among his works I did appear,
Oh, how their Glory me did crown!
The world resembled his Eternity,
In which my soul did walk;
And every thing that I did see
Did with me talk.

The skies in their magnificence,
The lively, lovely air;
Oh, how divine, how soft, how sweet, how fair!
The stars did entertain my sense,
And all the works of God so bright and pure,
So rich and great did seem
As if they ever must endure
In my esteem.

A native health and innocence
Within my bones did grow,
And while my God did all his glories show,
I felt a vigour in my sense
That was all spirit. I within did flow
With seas of life, like wine;
I nothing in the world did know,
But 'twas divine.

The streets were paved with golden stones,
The boys and girls were mine;
Oh, how did all their lovely faces shine!
The Sons of Men were Holy Ones,
Joy, Beauty, Welfare did appear to me,
And every thing which here I found,
While like an angel I did see,
Adorned the ground.

THOMAS TRAHERNE

One foot in Eden

One foot in Eden still, I stand
And look across the other land.
The world's great day is growing late,
Yet strange these fields that we have planted
So long with crops of love and hate.
Time's handiworks by time are haunted,
And nothing now can separate
The corn and tares compactly grown.
The armorial weed in stillness bound
About the stalk; these are our own.
Evil and good stand thick around
In the fields of charity and sin
Where we shall lead our harvest in.

Yet still from Eden springs the root
As clean as on the starting day.
Time takes the foliage and the fruit
And burns the archetypal leaf
To shapes of terror and of grief
Scattered along the winter way.
But famished field and blackened tree
Bear flowers in Eden never known.
Blossoms of grief and charity
Bloom in these darkened fields alone.
What had Eden ever to say
Of hope and faith and pity and love
Until was buried all its day
And memory found its treasure trove?
Strange blessings never in Paradise
Fall from these beclouded skies.

EDWIN MUIR

Freedom

God can do everything, except compel a man to love him.

Man is free, for he is in the image of divine liberty; and that is why he has the power to choose.

PAUL EVDOKIMOV

It was only when the idea of human freedom developed and was brought into relation with divine providence that the doctrine of predestination arose, and had to arise in trying to solve this problem. It solves the riddle by denying one of the concepts and consequently explains nothing.

The most tremendous thing granted to man is choice, freedom. And if you want to save it and keep it, there is only one way: in the very same second to give it back to God, and yourself with it. If the sight of what is granted to you tempts you, and you give way to the temptation and look with desire of your own on your freedom to choose, you lose your freedom.

SØREN KIERKEGAARD

Some have called me the philosopher of freedom, and a reactionary Russian bishop once said of me that I was 'the captive of freedom'. I do indeed love freedom above all else. Man came forth out of freedom and issues into freedom. Freedom is a primordial source and condition of existence, and, characteristically, I have put freedom, rather than being, at the basis of my philosophy. I do not think any other philosopher has done this in such a radical and thoroughgoing way. The mystery of the world abides in freedom: God desired freedom and freedom gave rise to tragedy in the world. Freedom is at the beginning and at the end. I might say that all my life I was engaged in hammering out a philosophy of freedom. I was moved by the basic conviction that God is truly present and operative only in freedom. Freedom alone should be recognized as possessing a sacred quality, while all the other things to which a sacred character has been assigned by men since history began ought to be made null and void.

I found strength to renounce many things in life, but I have never renounced anything in the name of duty or out of obedience to precepts and prohibitions: I renounced for the sake of freedom, and, maybe, also out of compassion. Nothing could ever tie me down, and this, no doubt, has to some extent weakened my efficiency and diminished my possibilities of self-realization. I always knew, however, that freedom gives birth to suffering, while the refusal to be free diminishes suffering. Freedom is not easy, as its enemies and slanderers allege: freedom is hard; it is a heavy burden. Men often renounce freedom to ease their lot.

All things in human life should be born of freedom and pass through freedom and be rejected whenever they betray freedom. The true meaning and origin of the fallen condition of man is to be seen in the primordial rejection of freedom.

NICOLAS BERDYAEV

October 4 ST FRANCIS OF ASSISI *1182–1226*

He was the first of the 'little brothers' who became the Friars, and this is from the opening poem in his *Canticles*:

Praise to my Lord for Sister Water be;
Most useful, humble, precious, chaste is she.
Praise to my Lord for Brother Fire, so bright;
By whom thou dost illuminate the night;
For he is lively, and most beautiful;
And most robust withal, and powerful.
Praised be my Lord and God for Mother Earth,
Who governs and sustains us; who gives birth
To all the many fruits and herbs that be;
And coloured flowers in rich variety.
Praised be my Lord for those who pardon wrong
For love of thee: enduring sorrow long;
Bearing their woes in peace. – Blessed are they!
By the Most High they shall be crown'd one day.
Praised be my Lord for Sister Death, from whom
No living soul escapes. She brings the doom
Of endless woe to all who pass away
In guilt of mortal sin. But blessed they
Who die in doing thy most holy will.
To them the Second Death can bring no ill.
O praise and bless my Lord right thankfully,
And serve ye him with great humility.

October 6 WILLIAM TYNDALE *?1494–1536*

Translator of the Bible and reformer.

The kings ought, I say, to remember that they are in God's stead, and ordained of God, not for themselves, but for the wealth of their subjects. Let them remember that their subjects are their brethren, their flesh and blood, members of their own body, and even their own selves in Christ. Therefore ought they to pity them, and to rid them from such wily tyranny, which increaseth more and more daily. And though that the kings, by the falsehood of the bishops and abbots, be sworn to defend such liberties; yet ought they not to keep their oaths, but to break them; forasmuch as they are unright and clean against God's ordinance, and even but cruel oppression, contrary unto brotherly love and charity.

And let the kings put down some of their tyranny, and turn some unto a common wealth. If the tenth part of such tyranny were given the king yearly, and laid up in the shire-towns, against the realm had need, what would it grow to in certain years? Moreover one king, one law, is God's ordinance in every realm. Therefore ought not the king to suffer them to have a several law by themselves, and to draw his subjects thither. It is not meet, will they say, that a spiritual man should be judged of a worldly or temporal man. O abomination! see how they divide and separate themselves: if the lay-man be of the world, so is he not of God! If he believe in Christ, then is he a member of Christ, Christ's brother, Christ's flesh, Christ's blood, Christ's spouse, coheir with Christ, and hath his Spirit in earnest, and is also spiritual.

October 15 ST TERESA OF AVILA *1515–1582*

She began the reform of her order, the Carmelites, in 1560 with the help of St John of the Cross. In and after 1567 she was able to make a number of new foundations in Spain. In addresses to her nuns she has much to say of the prayer of quiet:

Now, daughters, I still want to describe this prayer of quiet to you, in the way I have heard it talked about, and as the Lord has been pleased to teach it to me, perhaps in order that I might describe it to you. It is in this kind of prayer, as I have said, that the Lord seems to me to begin to show us that he is hearing our petition; he begins to give us his Kingdom on earth so that we may truly praise him and hallow his name and strive to make others do likewise.

This is a supernatural state, and however hard we try, we cannot reach it for ourselves; for it is a state in which the soul enters into peace, or rather in which the Lord gives it peace through his presence, as he did to that just man Simeon. In this state all the faculties are stilled. The soul, in a way which has nothing to do with the outward senses, realizes that it is now very close to its God, and that, if it were but a little closer, it would become one with him through union.

This is not because it sees him either with its bodily or with its spiritual eyes. The just man Simeon saw no more than a poor little child, who, to judge from the swaddling clothes in which he was wrapped, might well have been the son of these poor people rather than the Son of his heavenly Father. But the child himself revealed to him who he was. Just so, though less clearly, does the soul know who he is. It cannot understand how it knows him, yet it can only understand that it is in the Kingdom (or at least near to the King who will give it the Kingdom), and it feels such reverence that it dares to ask nothing. It is, as it were, in a swoon both inwardly and outwardly, so that the outward man does not wish to move, but rests, like one who has almost reached the end of his journey, so that it may better start again upon its way, with redoubled strength for the task.

October 18 ST LUKE

By tradition the evangelist was a physician.

> Saviour, who didst healing give,
>   Still in power go before us;
> Thou through death didst bid men live,
>   Unto fuller life restore us;
> Strength from thee the fainting found,
>   Deaf men heard, the blind went seeing;
> At thy touch was banished sickness,
>   And the leper felt new being.
>
> Thou didst work thy deeds of old
>   Through the loving hands of others;
> Still thy mercies manifold
>   Bless men by the hands of brothers;
> Angels still before thy face
>   Go, sweet health to brothers bringing;
> Still, hearts glow to tell his praises
>   With whose name the Church is ringing.
>
> Loved physician! for his word
>   Lo, the Gospel page burns brighter,
> Mission servant of the Lord,
>   Painter true, and perfect writer;
> Saviour, of thy bounty send
>   Such as Luke of Gospel story,
> Friends to all in body's prison
>   Till the sufferers see thy glory.

H. D. RAWNSLEY

October 19 FR JOHN OF KRONSTADT *1829–1908*

In the Orthodox Church very few of the married parish clergy have been recognized as saints. Father John, who served at the naval base of Kronstadt close to St Petersburg, forms a notable exception: although his official proclamation has so far taken place only in certain parts of the Russian Church, he is deeply loved and venerated by the Orthodox people both in Russia and elsewhere. He is remembered above all as a 'praying priest', deeply devoted to the liturgy, and with an intense power of intercession. An eloquent preacher, he had the capacity to move the most hardened of his hearers to repentance, and huge crowds flocked from all parts of Russia to listen to him. He possessed gifts of healing, insight and prophecy. Here are a few of the maxims found in his spiritual diary *My Life in Christ*.

The Lord has become everything to you, and you must become everything to the Lord.

Prayer is a state of continual gratitude.

It ought to be as easy to pray as to think.

During divine service be trustful, as a child trusts his parents. Be simple, trustful, undoubting. Cast all your care upon the Lord, and be entirely free from sorrow.

Do not confuse man, the image of God, with the wickedness that is in him, for the wickedness is only accidental, his misfortune, a sickness, an illusion of the devil; but his being, the image of God, still remains.

October 28 ST SIMON AND ST JUDE, APOSTLES

The patron saints of revolutionaries.

The Church condemns violence, but it condemns indifference more harshly. Violence can be the expression of love, indifference never.

GRAHAM GREENE

October 30   THE SPIRITUALITY OF THE REFORMATION

> Martin Luther (1485–1546), more than any other man, represents the Reformation. This extract is from a letter to a friend of his, Matthias Weller, who was suffering from depression. He was a musician, so Luther advises him to find solace in music.

Honourable, kind, good friend:

Your dear brother has informed me that you are deeply distressed and afflicted with melancholy. He will undoubtedly tell you what I have said to him.

Dear Matthias, do not dwell on your own thoughts, but listen to what other people have to say to you. For God has commanded men to comfort their brethren, and it is his will that the afflicted should receive such consolation as God's very own. Thus our Lord speaks through Saint Paul: 'Comfort the fainthearted.'

When you are sad, therefore, and when melancholy threatens to get the upper hand, say: 'Arise! I must play a song unto the Lord on my regal (be it the Te Deum laudamus or the Benedictus), for the Scriptures teach us that it pleases him to hear a joyful song and the music of stringed instruments.' Then begin striking the keys and singing in accompaniment, as David and Elisha did, until your sad thoughts vanish. If the devil returns and plants worries and sad thoughts in your mind, resist him manfully and say: 'Begone, devil! I must now play and sing unto my Lord Christ.'

The best thing you can do is to rap the devil on the nose at the very start. Act like that man who, whenever his wife began to nag and snap at him, drew out his flute from under his belt and played merrily until she was exhausted and let him alone.

When good people comfort you, my dear Matthias, learn to believe that God is speaking to you through them. Pay heed to them and have no doubt that it is most certainly God's word, coming to you according to God's command through men, that comforts you.

November

DEATH AND THE COMMUNION OF SAINTS

Preparation for Death

Death is the touchstone of our attitude to life. People who are afraid of death are afraid of life. It is impossible not to be afraid of life with all its complexity and dangers if one is afraid of death. This means that to solve the problem of death is not a luxury. If we are afraid of death we will never be prepared to take ultimate risks; we will spend our life in a cowardly, careful and timid manner. It is only if we can face death, make sense of it, determine its place and our place in regard to it, that we will be able to live in a fearless way and to the fullness of our ability. Too often we wait until the end of our life to face death, whereas we would have lived quite differently if only we had faced death at the outset.

Most of the time we live as though we were writing a draft for the life which we will live later. We live, not in a definitive way, but provisionally, as though preparing for the day when we really will begin to live. We are like people who write a rough draft with the intention of making a fair copy later. But the final version never gets written. Death comes before we have had the time or even generated the desire to make a definitive formulation.

The injunction 'be mindful of death' is not a call to live with a sense of terror in the constant awareness that death is to overtake us. It means rather: 'Be aware of the fact that what you are saying now, doing now, hearing, enduring or receiving now may be the *last* event or experience of your present life.' In which case it must be a crowning, not a defeat; a summit, not a trough. If only we realized whenever confronted with a person that this might be the last moment either of his life or of ours, we would be much more intense, much more attentive to the words we speak and the things we do.

Only awareness of death will give life this immediacy and depth, will bring life to life, will make it so intense that its totality is summed up in the present moment. All life is at every moment an ultimate act.

METROPOLITAN ANTHONY OF SOUROZH

42

When it is time for sleep and you approach your bed, say: 'Bed, perhaps this night you will become my grave. I do not know.'

In your heart be always ready for the moment of your departure. If you are wise, you will expect it at every hour. Each day say to yourself: 'Perhaps the messenger who comes to fetch me has already reached the door. What am I doing sitting here? I must depart for ever, I cannot cannot come back again.'

Go to sleep with these thoughts every night, and reflect on these things every day. And when the messenger arrives, go joyfully to meet him, saying: 'Come in peace. I knew you would come, and I have not neglected anything that could help me on my journey.'

ST ISAAC THE SYRIAN

Death is often nearer than you imagine and many who promised themselves a long life have been cut off.
    Are you so ready, that when death comes, it will be no surprise?
    Do not live in such a state, in which you dare not die.
    Learn every day the art of dying well.
    Defer not doing penance till the hour of death. At that time the pains of your body, and anguish of mind, will take up all your thoughts.
    Live, as you intend to die, for you will die as you live. If you forget God in your lifetime, you will be forgotten at the hour of death.
    The death of the wicked is miserable, the death of the just is precious in the sight of God.

THOUGHTS FOR WEDNESDAY, THURSDAY AND FRIDAY,
ST OMER'S, 1726

The royal doors are opening! The great Liturgy is about to begin.

DYING WORDS OF PRINCE EUGENE TRUBETSKOY

Give rest, O Lord, to thy servant . . .

The choir of saints has found the fountain of life
And the door of paradise;
May I also find the way through repentance.
I am the lost sheep:
Call me back and save me, O Saviour.

I am an image of thine ineffable glory,
Even though I bear the marks of sin.
Take pity on thy creature, O Master,
And cleanse me in thy lovingkindness.
Grant me the homeland of my heart's desire,
Making me once more a citizen of paradise.

Of old thou hast created me from nothing
And honoured me with thy divine image;
But when I disobeyed thy commandment,
Thou hast returned me to the earth whence I was taken.
Lead me back again to thy likeness,
Refashioning my ancient beauty.

Give rest, O God, to thy servant
And establish him in paradise,
Where the choirs of the saints and the righteous
Shine as the stars of heaven.
Give rest to thy servant who has fallen asleep,
And overlook all his offences.

Blessed is the road on which you go today: for there is made ready for you a place of repose.

May Christ give you rest in the land of the living, and open for you the gates of paradise; may he receive you as a citizen of the Kingdom, and grant you forgiveness of your sins: for you were his friend.

FROM THE FUNERAL SERVICE OF THE ORTHODOX CHURCH

I admire thee, master of the tides,
    Of the Yore-flood, of the year's fall;
The recurb and the recovery of the gulf's sides,
    The girth of it and the wharf of it and the wall;
Stanching, quenching ocean of a motionable mind;
Ground of being, and granite of it: past all
    Grasp God, throned behind
Death with a sovereignty that heeds but hides, bodes but abides;

    With a mercy that outrides
    The all of water, an ark
For the listener; for the lingerer with a love glides
    Lower than death and the dark;
A vein for the visiting of the past-prayer, pent in prison,
The-last-breath penitent spirits – the uttermost mark
    Our passion-plungèd giant risen,
The Christ of the Father compassionate, fetched in the storm of
    his strides.

GERARD MANLEY HOPKINS

Every day call this prayer to mind, and repeat it to yourself as often as possible: 'Lord, have mercy upon all who appear before thee today.' For at every hour and every moment thousands of people depart from this earthly life and their souls appear before God – and how many of them depart in loneliness, unknown to anyone, sad and dejected because no one feels sorrow for them or even cares whether they are alive or not! And then, perhaps, from the other end of the earth your prayer for the repose of their souls will rise up to God, although you never knew them nor they you. How deeply moving it must be for a man's soul, as he stands in fear and trembling before the Lord, to know at that very instant that there is someone to pray even for him, that there is still a fellow creature left on earth who loves him! And God will look on both of you more favourably, for if you have had so much pity on him, how much greater will God's pity be, for God is infinitely more loving and merciful than you! And he will forgive him for your sake.

FYODOR DOSTOEVSKY
'The Discourses of Father Zossima'

God in his love separates us from one another temporarily, in order once more to unite us all in Christ for eternity. Let us keep silent, and devoutly reverence this love which surrounds us on every side. In him we live and move and have our being. Whether alive or dead, we are all in him. It would be more true to say: We are all alive in him, for in him there is no death. Our God is not a God of the dead but of the living. He is your God, he is the God of her who has died. There is only one God, and in that one God you are both united. Only you cannot see each other for the time being. But this means that your future meeting will be all the more joyful; and then no one will take your joy from you. Yet even now you live together: all that has happened is that she has gone into another room and closed the door.

Spiritual love is not conscious of visible separation.

ARCHIMANDRITE MACARIUS (GLUKHAREV)

Go forth upon thy journey from this world, O Christian soul,
In the peace of him in whom thou hast believed,
In the name of God the Father, who created thee,
In the name of Jesus Christ, who suffered for thee,
In the name of the Holy Ghost, who strengthened thee.
May angels and archangels, and all the armies of the heavenly host, come to meet thee,
May all the saints of God welcome thee,
May thy portion this day be in gladness and peace and thy dwelling in paradise.
Go forth upon thy journey, O Christian soul.

THE GELASIAN SACRAMENTARY

God is love, and in the saints the Holy Spirit is love. Dwelling in the Holy Spirit, the saints behold hell and embrace it, too, in their love.

ST SILOUAN OF MOUNT ATHOS

I do not believe that after the happiness of those who enjoy glory there can be a joy like that of those in purgatory. This happiness ever increases by a continual influx of God into them, which increases in proportion as it destroys the hindrances to these blessed communications which arise from the stain and rust of their sins. It is this rust that is consumed in such a manner by these purifying flames that the soul becomes more and more open to the love of God.

When a body is hidden from the sun by a cover which hinders it from receiving light, the more the cover is withdrawn, the more the sun becomes present to the body which had been in the shade. The rust and the remains of sin are like this strange body which hides for a time from these souls the presence of God, who is their sun.

ST CATHERINE OF GENOA

O lady, root of my hope, who for me
And my salvation did endure to see
Hell, I have seen upon the sterile shore
The footprints of your virtue and your power.
I recognize the wonder of your ways
To draw me from my prison in the maze
Of servile fear to freedom. Pray you keep
My soul, that when my body fall asleep
And my unloosed spirit seek release
It please you give me peace.

DANTE TO BEATRICE

November 1 ALL SAINTS' DAY

Let no man think that because those blessed souls are out of sight, far distant in another world, and we are here toiling in a vale of tears, we have therefore lost all mutual regard to each other. No; there is still, and ever will be, a secret but unfailing correspondence between heaven and earth. The present happiness of these heavenly citizens cannot have abated ought of their knowledge and charity, but must needs have raised them to a higher pitch of both. They, in a generality, retain the notice of the sad condition of us poor travellers here below. As for us wretched pilgrims that are yet left here below to tug with many difficulties, we cannot forget that better half of us that is now triumphant in glory. It is abundant comfort to us that some part of us is in the fruition of that glory, whereto we, the other poor labouring part, desire and strive to aspire; that our head and shoulders are above water, while the other limbs are yet wading through the stream.

JOSEPH HALL

The saints in each generation, joined to those who have gone before and filled like them with light, become a golden chain, in which each saint is a separate link, united to the next by faith and works and love. So in the one God they form a single chain which cannot quickly be broken.

ST SYMEON THE NEW THEOLOGIAN

The spiritual powers of the cherubim glorify thee with hymns that are never silent.

The six-winged seraphim exalt thee with unceasing voices.

All the hosts of angels praise thee with thrice-holy songs.

O most holy Virgin Mother of God,

And the witnesses and ministers of the Word,

All the choirs of the prophets and the martyrs, who possess immortal life:

Intercede earnestly for all of us, for we are all in great distress,

That we may be delivered from the error of the evil one

And so may sing the angel's song:

Holy, holy, holy, thrice-holy Lord,

Have mercy upon us and save us. Amen.

FROM GREAT COMPLINE IN THE ORTHODOX CHURCH

The joy of all who sorrow,
The champion of all who suffer wrong,
Food to the hungry,
Comfort to strangers,
A staff for the blind,
Visitor of the sick,
Protection and aid to all in trouble,
Helper of orphans:
Most pure Mother of the most high God,
We pray thee, make haste to deliver thy servants.

ORTHODOX HYMN TO THE BLESSED VIRGIN MARY

The Church visible and invisible

The Church is one. Her unity follows of necessity from the unity of God; for the Church is not a multitude of persons in their separate individuality, but a unity in the grace of God, a living unity manifested in a multitude of rational creatures who freely submit themselves to grace.

The Church is one, notwithstanding her apparent division from the viewpoint of a man still living on earth. It is only in relation to man that it is possible to recognize a division of the Church into visible and invisible; her unity is, in reality, true and absolute. Those who are alive on earth, those who have finished their earthly course, those who, like the angels, were not created for a life on earth, those in future generations who have not yet begun their earthly course – all are united together in one Church, in one and the same grace of God; for the creation of God which has not yet been manifested is already manifest to him; and God hears the prayers and knows the faith of those whom he has not yet called out of non-existence into existence. The Church, the Body of Christ, reveals and fulfils herself in time without changing her essential unity or inward life of grace. And therefore, when we speak of the 'Church visible and invisible', we so speak only in relation to man.

The Church visible, or upon earth, lives in complete communion and unity with the whole body of the Church, of which Christ is the head.

We know that when any one of us falls, he falls alone; but no one is saved alone. He who is saved is saved in the Church, as a member of her and in union with all her other members. If anyone believes, he is in the communion of faith; if he loves, he is in the communion of love; if he prays, he is in the communion of prayer. No one, then, can rest his hope on his own prayers alone, but everyone who prays should ask for the intercession of the whole Church – not as though doubting the intercession of Christ, the one Advocate, but in the assurance that the whole Church ever prays for all her members. All the angels pray for us, the apostles, martyrs and patriarchs, and above them all, the Mother of our Lord; and this holy unity is the true life of the Church.

ALEXIS KHOMIAKOV

November 3   RICHARD HOOKER   *1554–1600*

He was born at Heavitree, near Exeter, and educated at the local grammar school as the Elizabethan settlement was taking root. He became a scholar and then a fellow of Corpus Christi College, Oxford, and from 1585 was Master of the Temple in the Strand, where he contended before lawyers in defence of traditional institutions:

And as it cometh to pass in a kingdom rightly ordered, that after a law is once published, it presently takes effect far and wide, all states framing themselves thereunto; even so let us think it fareth in the natural course of the world; since the time that God did first proclaim the edicts of his law upon it, heaven and earth have hearkened unto his voice, and their labour has been to do his will: he 'made a law for the rain'; he gave his 'decree unto the sea, that the waters should not pass his commandment'. Now if nature should intermit her course, and leave altogether, though it were but for a while, the observation of her own laws; if those principal and mother elements of the world, whereof all things in this lower world are made, should lose the qualities which now they have; if the frame of that heavenly arch erected over our heads should loosen and dissolve itself; if celestial spheres should forget their wonted motions, and by irregular volubility turn themselves any way as it might happen; if the prince of the lights of heaven, which now as a giant doth run his unwearied course, should, as it were, through a languishing faintness begin to stand and to rest himself; if the moon should wander from her beaten way, the times and seasons of the year blend themselves by disordered and confused mixtures, the fruits of the earth pine away as children at the withered breasts of their mother no longer able to yield them relief: what would become of man himself, whom these things now do all serve? See we not that obedience of creatures unto the law of nature is the stay of the whole world?

November 8   THE ARCHANGELS MICHAEL AND GABRIEL AND ALL THE OTHER BODILESS POWERS OF HEAVEN

On this day the Orthodox Church commemorates the Holy Angels.

Captains and leaders of the dread hosts of heaven enthroned on high,
Ministers of the divine glory,
Michael and Gabriel the chief commanders,
Who serve the Master with all the spiritual powers:
Make intercession, without ceasing, for the world,
Asking that we may receive forgiveness of our sins
And grace and mercy in the day of judgement.

HYMN FOR THE FEAST IN THE ORTHODOX CHURCH

When anyone prays, the angels that minister to God and watch over mankind gather round about him and join with him in his prayer. Nor is that all. Every Christian – each of the 'little ones' who are in the Church – has an angel of his own, who 'always beholds the face of our Father which is in heaven' (Matt. 18.10), and who looks upon the Godhead of the Creator. This angel prays with us and works with us, as far as he can, to obtain the things for which we ask.

'The angel of the Lord', so it is written, 'encamps beside those who fear the Lord and delivers them' (Ps. 33.8), while Jacob speaks of 'the angel who delivers me from all evils' (Gen. 48.16): and what he says is true not of himself only but of all those who set their trust in God. It would seem, then, that when a number of the faithful meet together genuinely for the glory of Christ, since they all fear the Lord, each of them will have, encamped beside him, his own angel whom God has appointed to guard him and care for him. So, when the saints are assembled, there will be a double Church, one of men and one of angels.

ORIGEN

November 9 ST NEKTARIOS OF PENTAPOLIS *1846–1920*

The child of very poor parents, he was ordained priest and then bishop in Alexandria. Falsely accused by others who were jealous of his rapid promotion, he was deposed and expelled from Egypt, but he refused to defend himself against slander. Travelling to Greece, at first he found all doors closed to him; but after a time he was made a diocesan preacher in the provinces, and then for fourteen years he served as director of the Rizareion theological school in Athens. His last years were spent on the nearby island of Aegina, as spiritual father of the women's monastery of the Holy Trinity which he had founded.

The best-loved saint of modern Greece, he has caught the imagination of the Orthodox people through his meekness, humility and warm compassion. A lover of study and a gifted writer, at the same time he willingly accepted the most menial tasks. When the school cleaner at the Rizareion fell ill, for months St Nektarios rose in the early hours of the morning to sweep out the passages and the lavatories, so that the man's post would not be given to anyone else, but would be waiting for him when he recovered. At the monastery he watered the garden and mended the nuns' shoes. Here is an account by Fr Philotheos Zervakos, Abbot of Longovarda, of his first meeting with the saint. He approached the monastery in the mid-day heat, during the hour of rest.

Outside the walls I saw an old man with a white beard, wearing a straw hat, with his cassock tucked into his belt, carrying earth and stones in a wheelbarrow. Thinking it was a workman or novice, I said: 'Is Bishop Nektarios here?' 'Yes,' he answered, 'he is here. Why do you want him?' 'Please tell him that there's someone to see him,' I replied. The old man took me to the guesthouse and left me. A few minutes later, he returned wearing his outer cassock and his tall black hat, and I realized — what had never entered my head — that the person I had taken for a workman and treated with contempt was in fact the Bishop himself.

November 10   ST LEO   *400–461*

Leo I was elected pope in 440. He played a prominent part in ordering the practice of the Western Churches in the crisis produced by barbarian invasions. In a letter to bishops in Africa he wrote:

Rightly did the Fathers whose views we venerate, in speaking of the choice of priests, reckon those men fit for the administration of the sacraments who had been slowly advanced through several grades, and had given good proof of themselves in those, that in each one of them their practices bore witness to the character of their lives. It is unfair and preposterous that the inexpert should be preferred to the expert, the young to the old, the raw recruits to those who have seen much service.

November 11   ST MARTIN   *316–397*

He was chosen as bishop of Tours in 371. According to Sulpicius Severus:

He so fulfilled, with authority and grace, the office of a bishop that he never forsook his original purpose of living the holy life of a monk. And so at one time he used a cell next door to his church; but because of the unendurable turmoil of those who came in crowds to him there, he set himself up in a monastery two miles out of the city, at a spot so hidden and retired as to suit a hermit's solitude. On one side a high mountain rose up in a sheer cliff, and on the other the river Loire made a slight bend and enclosed a level space that could be approached only by one very narrow path. Martin had a small cell of logs made for himself, and some of the brothers did the same, but several had made themselves retreats in caves cut from the rock of the overhanging mountain. There some eighty disciples of his in all lived and followed their master's example. None of them had anything of his own, but they had everything in common. No art but that of a scribe was practised there. All broke their fast at the same time; no one tasted wine unless sickness made it necessary. Many of them were of noble birth and had lived a different kind of life before they constrained themselves to humility and patience; and many of these afterwards became bishops.

November 13 CHARLES SIMEON *1759–1836*

Leader of the Evangelical Revival, he spent most of his ministry as vicar of Holy Trinity Church, Cambridge, where his pastoral zeal broke down the initial hostility to his preaching. He was a leading figure in the missionary movement and a founder of the Church Missionary Society (CMS).

Sermon on the excellency of the Liturgy.

The whole Christian world has from time to time been agitated with controversies of different kinds; and human passions have grievously debased the character and actions even of good men in every age. But it should seem that the compilers of our Liturgy were inspired with a wisdom and moderation peculiar to themselves. They kept back no truth whatever, through fear of giving offence; yet were careful so to state every truth as to leave those inexcusable who should recede from the Church on account of any sentiments which she maintained. In this, they imitated the inspired penmen; who do not dwell on doctrines after the manner of human systems, but introduce them incidentally, as it were, as occasion suggests, and bring them forward always in connection with practical duties. The Godhead of Christ is constantly asserted, and different prayers are addressed to him; but nothing is said in a way of contentious disputation. The influences of the Holy Spirit, from whom all holy desires, all good counsels, and all just works do proceed, are stated; and the inspiration of the Holy Spirit is sought; but all is conveyed in a way of humble devotion, without reflection on others, or even a word that can lead to controversy of any kind.

November 15   ST PAISIUS VELICHKOVSKY   *1722–1794*

Born in south Russia, he went as a young man to the Holy Mountain of
Athos, remaining there for seventeen years and then spending the last thirty
years of his life in Romania. He gathered round him more than a thousand
disciples, and worked with them especially on the translation of Greek
ascetic and mystical texts into Slavonic. In his teaching he insisted upon the
importance of inner prayer, and also upon the need for strict obedience by
each monk to his spiritual father or elder (*starets*). Here is his answer to the
brethren of a nearby monastery who, misinterpreting the meek and humble
manner of their abbot, thought him unsuitable to be their superior.

Monks should give over all their will to their superior and should submit to
him in everything as to the Lord himself. Receive from his lips as from the
lips of God the word that is for the profit of your souls. In every
undertaking, for every work, always seek his blessing and counsel, with full
humility and trust. And if in any matter some brother might think that
there is no need to ask the Father, since 'I know and am able to do it myself'
– this is from the enemy. But from God and the holy Fathers this is what
we have received: that in every matter, even if a brother might be very
skilled in it, first he must ask the superior. And if the superior should reply
of his own accord, 'Do as you think best', then with the fear of God and
trusting in the prayers of the superior, you should begin as God will
instruct you. Having completed the obedience, again go to the Father, and
having confessed in detail what you have done, fall down at his feet,
begging forgiveness for whatever sins you have committed in holy
obedience.

November 17 ST HILDA *614–680*

She was nobly born, being the daughter of Hereric, nephew to King Edwin, with whom she embraced the faith and mysteries of Christ, at the preaching of Paulinus, the first bishop of the Northumbrians.

Resolving to leave the life of the world she went away into the province of the East Angles, intending to pass from there into the land of the Franks, and so live as an exile for our Lord in the monastery of Cale, that she might more easily attain to the eternal Kingdom in heaven; because her sister Heresuid, the mother of Aldwulf, king of the East Angles, was at that time living in the same monastery under regular discipline, awaiting her eternal reward. Led by her sister's example, she continued a year in the same province, intending to go abroad. But afterwards, Bishop Aidan gave her the land of a family on the north side of the Wear, where for a year she lived a monastic life with very few companions.

After this she was made abbess in the monastery called Heruteu. She began immediately to reduce all things to a regular system, according to the instruction she had received from learned men. Her prudence was so great that even kings and princes, as occasion offered, asked and received her advice. She obliged those under her direction to give so much attention to reading the holy Scriptures, and so to exercise themselves in works of justice, that many of them might be found fit for ecclesiastical duties. In short we afterwards saw five bishops come out of that monastery.

BEDE

November 21 THE ENTRY OF THE MOST HOLY MOTHER OF GOD INTO THE TEMPLE

In the Orthodox Church this is observed as one of the twelve great feasts in the annual calendar. According to tradition, at the age of three the blessed Virgin Mary was taken by her parents Joachim and Anna to the temple in Jerusalem, to be dedicated to the Lord. She lived there for nine years, in preparation for her future task of bearing God incarnate.

> The all-pure temple of the Saviour,
> The precious bridal-chamber and Virgin,
> The sacred treasure-house of the glory of God,
> Is led today into the Lord's house,
> And with her she brings the grace of the Holy Spirit.
> Of her God's angels sing in praise:
> She is indeed the heavenly tabernacle.

HYMN FOR THE FEAST IN THE ORTHODOX CHURCH

November 22   ST CECILIA

She is a Roman martyr of the second or third century who became the patroness of church music. Dryden writes in his 'Song for St Cecilia's Day':

> From harmony, from heavenly harmony,
>   This universal frame began:
> When nature underneath a heap
>   Of jarring atoms lay,
>   And could not heave her head,
> The tuneful voice was heard from high
>   'Arise, ye more than dead.'
> Then cold, and hot, and moist, and dry
> In order to their stations leap,
>   And Music's power obey.
> From harmony, from heavenly harmony
>   This universal frame began;
>   From harmony to harmony
> Through all the compass of the notes it ran,
> The diapason closing full in man.

November 23   ST COLUMBAN   *d. 615*

He was an Irish monk who came to Gaul in 585 and founded a monastery at Luxueil. Crossing the Alps into Lombardy he founded another monastery at Bobbio, where he died. A disciple writes of him:

In his love of solitude the man of God was walking through a dense undergrowth of bushes bearing berries, on the hillside close to us, when he found the carcass of a deer, slaughtered by a wolf pack, and a bear wanting to eat it, who had already, in lapping up the blood, devoured a small portion of the flesh. The man of God came up to her and told her not to hurt the hide, which was needed for the use of those who make sandals. The beast forgot her fierceness, began to be tame and, contrary to her nature, caressed him. Submitting her neck to be patted, she left the carcass.

The man of God went back to his brothers and told them to go to the spot and get the hide. They noticed birds of prey on all sides, who did not dare to approach the forbidden carcass, but watched at a distance, to see if any wild beast or bird would dare to try and take the forbidden food.

November 25 ST CLEMENT OF ROME

> He comes third after Linus and Cletus in the traditional Roman list of successors of St Peter. He was in charge of the church's foreign correspondence in AD 96 and rather later. He wrote to the Corinthians:

Let us consider, beloved, how the Master continually proves to us that there will be a resurrection in the future, of which he has given us first-fruits by raising the Lord Jesus Christ from the dead. Look, beloved, at the resurrection now happening at the proper seasons. Day and night display resurrection. The night sleeps, the day rises: day departs, night comes on. Look at the crops; how and in what way are they sown? 'The sower went forth', and cast each of the seeds into the earth; they fell on the ground, parched and bare, and decayed there; then from their decay the magnitude of the Master's providence raises them up, and from one grain more grow and bear fruit.

November 30 ST ANDREW THE APOSTLE

From *The Acts of Peter and Andrew*:

Peter, Andrew, Alexander, Rufus and Matthias went to a city of the barbarians. As they came near, Andrew asked Peter, 'Father Peter, are we going to have the same trouble in this city as we had in the country of the cannibals?' Peter replied, 'I don't know, but look, over there is an old man in his field. Let us go up to him and say "Will you give us bread?", and if he gives it to us, we may know that in this city we will not suffer. But if he says "We have no bread", we shall know that trouble is coming to us.'

When they came up to the old man, Peter said, 'Have you bread to give, for we have been in want.' The old man said, 'Wait a bit, and look after the oxen, the plough and the land, that I may go into the town and get you loaves.' Peter said, 'If you give us hospitality, we will look after the oxen and the field.' He asked, 'Are the oxen yours?' The old man said, 'No, they are hired', and the old man went into the city.

Peter got up and girded his cloak and his undergarment, and said to Andrew, 'It is not right for us to rest and be idle, especially when the old man has left his work and is working for us.' Then Peter took hold of the plough and sowed the wheat, and Andrew was behind the oxen. He took the plough out of Peter's hand and sowed the wheat, saying, 'O seed cast into the ground in the field of the righteous, let the young men of the city therefore come forth, for the apostles of Christ are coming, pardoning the sins of those who believe, and healing every disease.'

November 30 ST ANDREW THE APOSTLE

When Andrew had found Jesus, he called his brother Simon to be partaker of his joys, which (as it happens in accidents of greatest pleasure) cannot be contained within the limits of the possessor's thoughts. But this calling of Peter was not to a beholding, but to a participation of his felicities; for he is strangely covetous, who would enjoy the sun, or the air, or the sea, alone; here was treasure for him and all the world; and by lighting on his brother Simon's taper he made his own light the greater and more glorious. And this is the nature of grace, to be diffusive of its own excellencies; for here no envy can inhabit; the proper and personal ends of holy persons in the contact, and transmissions of grace, are increased by the participation and communion of others. For our prayers are more effectual, our aids increased, our encouragement and examples more prevalent, God more honoured, and the rewards of glory have accidental advantages by the superaddition of every new saint and beatified person; the members of the mystical body, when they have received nutriment from God, and his holy son, supplying to each other the same which themselves received and live on, in the communion of saints. Every new star gilds the firmament and increases its first glories: and those, who are instruments of the conversion of others, shall not only introduce new beauties, but when themselves shine like the stars in glory, they shall have some reflections from the light of others, to whose fixing in the orb of heaven themselves have been instrumental.

JEREMY TAYLOR

December

ADVENT:
THE COMING OF CHRIST IN HUMILITY
AND IN GLORY

The end draws near, my soul, the end draws near;
Yet you do not care or make ready.
The time grows short, rise up: the Judge is at the door.
The days of our life pass swiftly, as a dream, as a flower.
Why do we trouble ourselves over what is all in vain?

I am deprived of the bridal chamber, of the wedding and the supper;
For want of oil my lamp has gone out;
While I slept the door was closed;
The supper has been eaten;
I am bound hand and foot, and cast out.

ST ANDREW OF CRETE

Most gracious Lord, by whose direction this time is appointed for renewing the memory of thy infinite mercy to man in the incarnation of thy only Son; grant that we may live, this holy time, in the spirit of thanksgiving, and every day raise up our hearts to thee in the grateful acknowledgement of what thou hast done for us.

Besides this, we ask thy grace, O God, that we may make a due use of this holy time, for preparing our souls to receive Christ our Lord coming into the world at the approaching solemnity of Christmas.

Christ came into the world to do good to all. Grant, O God, we may thus prepare to meet him. Grant we may be watchful at this time above all others, in avoiding every thing that can be injurious to our neighbour, whether in afflicting him, or giving him scandal, or drawing him into sin, or casting any blemish on his reputation; but in all things, O God, may we follow the spirit of charity, being forward in bringing comfort and relief to all, as far as their circumstances shall require, and ours permit.

Grant, O Lord, that thus we may prepare to meet our redeemer.

JOHN GOTER

Watching

Year passes after year, silently; Christ's coming is ever nearer than it was. O that, as he comes nearer earth, we may approach nearer heaven! O my brethren, pray him to give you the heart to seek him in sincerity. Pray him to make you in earnest. You have one work only, to bear your cross after him. Resolve in his strength to do so. Resolve to be no longer beguiled by 'shadows of religion', by words, or by disputings, or by notions, or by high professions, or by excuses, or by the world's promises or threats. Pray him to give you what Scripture calls 'an honest and good heart', or 'a perfect heart', and, without waiting, begin at once to obey him with the best heart you have. Any obedience is better than none, – any profession which is disjoined from obedience, is a mere pretence and deceit. Any religion which does not bring you nearer to God is of the world. You have to seek his face; obedience is the only way of seeking him. All your duties are obediences. If you are to believe the truths he has revealed, to regulate yourselves by his precepts, to be frequent in his ordinances, to adhere to his Church and people, why is it, except because *he* has bid you? And to do what he bids is to obey him, and to obey him is to approach him. Every act of obedience is an approach, – an approach to him who is not far off, though he seems so, but close behind this visible screen of things which hides him from us. He is behind this material framework; earth and sky are but a veil going between him and us; the day will come when he will rend that veil, and show himself to us. And then, according as we have waited for him, will he recompense us. If we have forgotten him, he will not know us; but 'blessed are those servants whom the Lord, when he cometh, shall find watching . . . he shall gird himself, and make them sit down to meat, and will come forth and serve them. And if he shall come in the second watch, or come in the third watch, and find them so, blessed are those servants'. May this be the portion of every one of us! It is hard to attain it; but it is woeful to fail. Life is short; death is certain; and the world to come is everlasting.

JOHN HENRY NEWMAN

Human progress and the coming glory

Expectation – anxious, collective and operative expectation of an end of the world, that is to say, of an issue for the world – that is perhaps the supreme Christian function and the most distinctive characteristic of our religion. Historically speaking, that expectation has never ceased to guide the progress of our faith like a torch. We persist in saying that we keep vigil in expectation of the Master. But in reality we should have to admit, if we were sincere, *that we no longer expect anything*. The flame must be revived at all costs. At all costs we must renew in ourselves the desire and the hope for the great coming. But where are we to look for the source of this rejuvenation? From the perception of *a more intimate connection* between the victory of Christ and the outcome of the work which our human effort here below is seeking to construct.

Let us look at the earth around us. What is happening under our eyes within the mass of peoples? What is the cause of this disorder in society, this uneasy agitation, these swelling waves, these whirling and mingling currents and these turbulent and formidable new impulses? Mankind is visibly passing through a crisis of growth. Mankind is becoming dimly aware of its shortcomings and its capacities; it sees the universe growing luminous like the horizon just before sunset. It has a sense of premonition and of expectation.

The progress of the universe, and in particular of the human universe, does not take place in competition with our God, nor does it squander energies that we rightly owe to him. The greater man becomes, the more humanity becomes united, with consciousness of, and mastery of, its potentialities, the more beautiful creation will be, the more perfect adoration will become, and the more Christ will find, for mystical extensions, a body worthy of resurrection. The world can no more have two summits than a circumference can have two centres. The star for which the world is waiting, without yet being able to give it a name, or rightly appreciate its true transcendence, or even recognize the most spiritual and divine of its rays, is, necessarily, Christ himself, in whom we hope. To desire the parousia, all we have to do is to let the very heart of the earth, as we Christianize it, beat within us.

TEILHARD DE CHARDIN

THE BIBLE

In the Anglican Church, the second Sunday in Advent is traditionally known as Bible Sunday.

If you do not love the blessed and truly divine words of Scripture, you are like the beasts that have neither sense nor reason.

In our natural desire for life we eat and drink, we talk and listen; and in the same way with an insatiable thirst we should devote ourselves to reading the words of God.

ST NILUS OF ANCYRA

Constant meditation upon the holy Scriptures will perpetually fill the soul with incomprehensible ecstasy and joy in God.

ST ISAAC THE SYRIAN

He who is humble in his thoughts and engaged in spiritual work, when he reads the holy Scriptures, will apply everything to himself and not to his neighbour.

ST MARK THE MONK

The only pure and all-sufficient source of the doctrines of faith is the revealed word of God, contained now in the holy Scriptures.

Every thing necessary to salvation is stated in the holy Scriptures with such clearness, that every one, reading it with a sincere desire to be enlightened, can understand it.

Every one has not only a right, but it is his bounden duty to read the holy Scriptures in a language which he understands, and edify himself thereby.

METROPOLITAN PHILARET OF MOSCOW

December 2 NICHOLAS FERRAR *1592–1637*

In 1626 Nicholas Ferrar settled at Little Gidding. Soon he began to organize his whole household (some thirty people) into a regular life of prayer and work under a strict rule. Offices were said through the day and much of the night was kept for a vigil of prayer. This is part of a letter he wrote to his parents when he thought he was dying:

And you, my most dearest parents, if God shall take me from you now, I beseech you be of good comfort and be not grieved at my death, which I undoubtedly hope shall be to me the beginning of eternal happiness. And to you no loss, for you shall with inestimable joy receive me in the Kingdom of heaven to reign there with you and my dearest brother Erasmus and your other children that are departed in the Lord. If I go before you you must come shortly after; think it is but a little forbearance of me. It was God that gave me to you and if he take me from you be not only content but most joyful that I am delivered from this vale of misery and wretchedness. I know that through the infinite mercy of my gracious God it shall be my happiness, for I shall then, I know, enjoy perpetual quietness and peace and be delivered from those continual combats and temptations which afflict my poor soul. Oh Lord, thou knowest, I may truly say, *from my youth up, thy terrors have I suffered with a troubled mind.* My soul hath been almost rent through violent temptations that have assaulted it, for to thy glory, oh Lord, will I confess my own weaknesses and the great dangers which thou hast delivered me from. It was the Lord that kept me, else had they devoured my soul and made it desolate; and this God that hath kept me ever since I was born, ever since I came out of your womb, my most dear mother, will preserve me to the end, I know, and give me grace that I shall live in his faith and die in his fear and favour, and rest in his peace, and rise in his power and reign in his glory.

December 2   BLESSED JOHN RUYSBROECK   *1293–1381*

An Augustinian canon, living in what is today Belgium, he wrote his chief
works not in Latin but in the vernacular Flemish. In his mystical theology
he is influenced by the German Dominican Meister Eckhart; but
Ruysbroeck's teaching is less speculative and less open to misunderstand-
ing, keeping closer to the traditional Christian understanding of union with
God. Following Dionysius the Areopagite and others, he holds that on the
higher levels of inner prayer the aspirant transcends images and discursive
thinking, and experiences the divine mystery through direct and un-
mediated 'feeling' or intuition.

If above all things we would taste God, and feel eternal life in ourselves, we
must go forth into God with our feeling, above reason; and there we must
abide, onefold, empty of ourselves, and free from images, lifted up by love
into the simple bareness of our intelligence. For when we go out in love
beyond and above all things, and die to all observation in ignorance and in
darkness, then we are wrought and transformed through the Eternal
Word, who is the image of the Father. In this idleness of our spirit, we
receive the Incomprehensible Light, which enwraps us and penetrates us,
as the air is penetrated by the light of the sun. And this Light is nothing
else than a fathomless staring and seeing. What we are, that we behold; and
what we behold, that we are: for our thought, our life and our being are
uplifted in simplicity, and made one with the Truth which is God. And
therefore in this simple staring we are one life and one spirit with God: and
this I call a contemplative life.

December 3 ST FRANCIS XAVIER *1505–1552*

He was one of the original members of the Society of Jesus who were students in Paris with St Ignatius Loyola. He became a pioneer in missions to India and the Far East, and died on the way to China. In this letter, written in 1550 to his superiors in India, he gives his first impressions of Japan:

The Japanese are in all matters naturally curious, eager to learn as much as they possibly can; and so they never cease to ply us with one question or another, and to inquire further about our answers. Especially they seek most eagerly to hear what is new about religion. We are told that before our arrival they were perpetually at strife among themselves, each contending that his own sect was best. But after hearing us they dropped their disputations over their own disciplines and all began to dispute over the Christian law. It is astonishing to find in so large a city every house and place resounding with celebration of the divine law in the conversation of everybody. If I wished to pursue researches into these, I would never come to an end of writing. The Japanese have a high opinion of the wisdom of the Chinese, in the mysteries of religion, in moral questions, and in the institutions of society. And so what impresses them most is that, if things are as we preach, the question arises how is it that the Chinese do not know it?

After many inquiries and disputations the Amangucians have begun to attach themselves to the Church of Christ, some of them from the working class, and some from the nobility. In the space of two months at least 500 have become Christians, and this number increases from day to day. We must be glad and thank the Lord that so many embrace the Christian religion, who tell us of the fallacies of the Bonzes and of their books, and the mysteries of their sects, for those who have joined themselves to Christ were following the discipline of another. The most learned among their number each and all explain to us the institutes and precepts of their previous discipline. If it were not for my study of these I would not know enough of the false religions of the Japanese to be able to oppose them. How much the Christians love us is past believing. They come constantly to our house and do anything that is in their power as we want. All Japanese seem to be naturally courteous. The Christians indeed, certainly – bless them – show themselves most kind and obliging to us. God in his mercy reward and grant us the same happiness in heaven.

December 4 ŚT AMBROSE *c. 340–397*

He was elected bishop of Milan in 374 and baptized directly after. This is from his *De Mysteriis*, addressed to candidates for baptism:

If a human blessing had power to change nature, what can we say of the divine consecration where the very words of our Lord and Saviour act? The sacrament that you receive is consecrated by the word of Christ. If the word of Elijah had power to draw down fire from heaven, will not the word of Christ be powerful enough to change the character of the elements?

You have read of the work of creating all things that he spoke the word, and they were made; he commanded, and they were created. The word of Christ which then could make what is out of nothing, can it not change the things that are into what they were not? To give new natures to things is no less wonderful than to change their natures.

But why do we use arguments? Let us give more immediate examples, and by the instance of the incarnation show the truth of the mystery. Did the use of nature proceed when the Lord Jesus was born of Mary? If we look to the order of generation, it normally results from the union of a woman with a man. It is then clear that the virgin gave birth outside the order of nature. This body that we consecrate is virgin-born. Why then do you seek the natural order in the case of the Body of Christ, since the Lord himself was born of a virgin in a way beyond nature? In truth it was the true flesh of Christ that was crucified and buried; indeed, therefore, the sacrament is of his flesh.

December 6 ST NICOLAS

Little is known for certain about the life of St Nicolas, bishop of Myra in Lycia (Asia Minor). It is believed that he suffered imprisonment during the last major persecution of the Church under Diocletian in the early fourth century, and that he attended the first Ecumenical Council at Nicaea in 325. Christian tradition has come to regard him, in the words of an Orthodox hymn, as 'an example of faith and an icon of gentleness'. His place in the Church's conscience is explained by a contemporary Russian Orthodox icon-painter, Leonid Ouspensky:

The quite exceptional veneration of St Nicolas is well known. He is revered not only by Christians but often also by Muslims. In the weekly liturgical cycle of the Orthodox Church, among the days of the week dedicated to the Saviour and to different orders of heavenly and earthly sanctity, only three persons are singled out by name: the Mother of God, John the Forerunner and St Nicolas. The reason for the special veneration of this bishop, who left neither theological works nor other writings, is evidently that the Church sees in him the personification of a shepherd – of one who protects and intercedes. According to his *Life*, when St Nicolas was raised to the dignity of bishop he said: 'This office demands a different type of conduct, so that one may live no longer for oneself but for others.' This 'life for others' is his characteristic feature and is manifested by the great variety of forms of his solicitude for men: his care for their preservation, their protection from the elements, from human injustice, from heresies and so forth. This solicitude was accompanied by numerous miracles both during his life and after his death. Indefatigable intercessor, steadfast, uncompromising fighter for Orthodoxy, he was meek and gentle in character and humble in spirit.

December 12 ST JANE FRANCES DE CHANTAL *1572–1641*

Jane Frances Fremyot was married to the Baron de Chantal. In 1601 she was left a widow with six children. St Francis de Sales became her spiritual director, and together they founded the Order of the Visitation, with an emphasis on active works not found before among nuns. In this deposition to support the canonization of St Francis she delicately describes his dealings with herself:

I have often noticed how gladly he left the Holy Spirit to do his work freely in souls, and he himself followed the attraction of that divine Spirit, and guided them as they were led by God, leaving them to follow the divine inspirations, rather than his own instructions. I have observed this in my own case, and I have also been told of it by others with whom he dealt in the same manner; and, if I am not mistaken, he showed, by thus acting, great enlightenment in the discerning of spirits.

He was absolutely admirable and incomparable in his method of training minds according to their various capacities, without ever urging them on unduly: indeed he gave and imprinted upon the hearts of his penitents a certain liberty which set them free from all scruples and difficulties, and raised the soul to such a tender love of God, that every hindrance to the devout life vanished. To this fact all his books bear ample testimony, and I know that there was an inexpressible sweetness in obeying his counsels; indeed, as regards myself, my only trouble was that he did not give me commands enough.

December 12 ST HERMAN OF ALASKA *d. 1837*

> Originally a member of Valamo monastery in Finland, in 1794 he joined a group of Russian monks who travelled as missionaries to Alaska. His later life was spent as a hermit on the remote Spruce Island. American Orthodox honour him as 'apostle of Alaska'.

His great object in life was to help and uplift the native Aleuts, whom he regarded as mere children in need of protection and guidance. He was ever pleading for them with the officers of the Russian–American Company. 'I, the lowest servant of these poor people,' he wrote to Yanovsky, 'with tears in my eyes ask this favour: be our father and protector. I have no fine speeches to make, but from the bottom of my heart I pray you to wipe the tears from the eyes of the defenceless orphans, relieve the suffering of the oppressed, and show them what it means to be merciful.'

Father Herman was a nurse of the natives in a literal as well as a figurative sense. When an epidemic broke out in Kodiak and carried off scores of people, he never left the village, but went from house to house, nursing the sick, comforting the afflicted and praying with the dying. It is no wonder that the natives loved him and came from afar to hear him tell the story of Christ.

One day the captain and officers of a Russian man-of-war invited Father Herman on board to dine with them. In the course of the conversation he put this question to them: 'What do you, gentlemen, regard as most worthy of love?' Each answered in his own way. Finally Father Herman said: 'Let me beseech you, my friends, that from this day forth, from this hour, from this minute, you will love God above all.'

December 14 ST JOHN OF THE CROSS *1542–1591*

Juan de Yepes became a Carmelite in 1562. Involved with St Teresa in the reform of his order, he suffered much from the suspicions of those who regarded the negative element in his mysticism as heretical. He speaks here of 'the dark night of the soul':

Why does the soul call the divine light which enlightens the soul and purges it of its ignorances, the dark night? I reply that the divine wisdom is for two reasons not night and darkness only, but pain and torment also to the soul. The first is that divine wisdom is so high that it transcends the capacity of the soul, and therefore is, in that respect, darkness. The second reason is based on the meanness and impurity of the soul, and in that respect the divine wisdom is painful to it, and dark also.

In another chapter of *The Ascent of Mount Carmel* he writes of interior wisdom:

Because this interior wisdom is so simple, general, and spiritual, that it enters not into the understanding under any form or image subject to sense, the imagination therefore and the senses cannot account for it, or any conception of it, so as to speak in any degree correctly about it, though the soul be distinctly conscious that it feels and tastes this sweet and strange wisdom.

December 20 ST IGNATIUS OF ANTIOCH *d. c.107*

> Bishop of Antioch in Syria, he is known to us from his seven letters written on the way to Rome, where he suffered martyrdom. Here he writes to the Roman Christians, begging them not to try to save his life.

To all the churches I write, and I wish you all to know, that of my own free will I am dying for God's sake, provided you do not prevent me. I beg you, do not show me ill-timed kindness. Let me be thrown to the wild beasts, for through them I shall come to God. I am God's wheat, ground by the teeth of the wild beasts so as to be made pure bread.

Until now I am a slave. But if I suffer, I shall become the freedman of Jesus Christ, and I shall rise free in him. Now that I am a prisoner in bonds, I am learning to lay aside all desire.

Now I am beginning to be a disciple. May nothing visible or invisible out of envy try to stop me reaching Jesus Christ. Fire, cross, attacks of wild beasts, bones wrenched apart, limbs hacked, my whole body crushed, cruel, diabolical tortures – let them all be inflicted to me, only let me come to Jesus Christ.

I seek him who died for us; I long for him who rose on our account. The pangs of a new birth are upon me. Bear with me, brothers. Do not prevent me from living, do not wish for my death. Allow me to receive the pure light. When I come there, I shall be truly human. Suffer me to be an imitator of the Passion of my God.

My love is crucified.

THE LAST DAYS OF ADVENT

The Great 'O's

O Wisdom, which camest out of the mouth of the Most High, and reachest from end to another, mightily and sweetly ordering all things: Come and teach us the way of prudence.

O Adonai, the leader of the house of Israel, who appearedst in the bush to Moses in a flame of fire, and gavest him the law in Sinai: Come and deliver us with an outstretched arm.

O Root of Jesse, which standest for an ensign of the people, at whom kings shall shut their mouths, and to whom the Gentiles shall seek: Come and deliver us, and tarry not.

O Key of David, and Sceptre of the house of Israel; that openest, and no man shutteth, and shuttest, and no man openeth: Come and bring the prisoner out of the prison-house, and him that sitteth in darkness, and the shadow of death.

O Dayspring, Brightness of Light everlasting, and Sun of Righteousness: Come and enlighten him that sitteth in darkness, and the shadow of death.

O King of the nations, and their Desire, the Cornerstone, who makest both one: Come and save mankind, whom thou formedst of clay.

O Emmanuel, our King and Lawgiver, the Desire of all nations, and their Salvation: Come and save us, O Lord our God.

O Virgin of virgins, how shall this be? For neither before thee was any like thee, nor shall there be after. Daughters of Jerusalem, why marvel ye at me? The thing which ye behold is a divine mystery.

December 25 CHRISTMAS DAY

Come, let us greatly rejoice in the Lord
As we tell of this present mystery.
The middle wall of partition has been destroyed;
The fiery sword turns back,
The cherubim withdraw from the tree of life,
And I partake of the delight of paradise
From which I was cast out through disobedience.
For the express image of the Father,
The imprint of his eternity,
Takes the form of a servant,
And without suffering change comes forth
From a Virgin Mother.
What he was, he has remained – true God;
What he was not, he has taken on himself,
Becoming man from love for humankind.
To him let us cry aloud:
God born of a Virgin, have mercy upon us.

What shall we offer thee, O Christ,
Who for our sakes hast appeared on earth as man?
Every creature made by thee offers thee thanks.
The angels offer thee a hymn;
The heavens, a star;
The Magi, gifts;
The shepherds, their wonder;
The earth, a cave;
The wilderness, a manger;
And we offer thee a Virgin Mother.
God before all ages, have mercy upon us.

HYMNS FOR THE FEAST IN THE ORTHODOX CHURCH

Christ is born: glorify him. Christ comes from heaven: go out to meet him. Christ descends to earth: let us be raised on high. Let all the world sing to the Lord; let the heavens rejoice and let the earth be glad, for his sake who was first in heaven and then on earth. Christ is here in the flesh: let us exult with fear and joy – with fear, because of our sins; with joy, because of the hope that he brings us.

Once more the darkness is dispersed; once more the light is created. Let the people that sat in the darkness of ignorance now look upon the light of knowledge. The things of old have passed away; behold, all things are made new. He who has no mother in heaven is now born without father on earth. The laws of nature are overthrown, for the upper world must be filled with citizens. He who is without flesh becomes incarnate; the Word puts on a body; the Invisible is seen; he whom no hand can touch is handled; the Timeless has a beginning; the Son of God becomes Son of Man – Jesus Christ, the same yesterday, today and for ever.

Light from light, the Word of the Father comes to his own image, man. For the sake of my flesh he takes flesh; for the sake of my soul he is united to a rational soul, purifying like by like. In every way he becomes man, except for sin. O strange conjunction! The Self-existent comes into being; the Uncreated is created. He shares in the poverty of my flesh, that I may share in the riches of his Godhead.

ST GREGORY OF NAZIANZUS

The divine humility

In his prose poem *Khristos* (1878), Turgenev dreams that he is in a village church together with the peasant congregation. A man comes to stand beside him: 'I did not turn towards him, but immediately I felt that this man was Christ.' However, when eventually he turns towards him he perceives 'a face like everyone's face. A face like all men's faces . . . And the clothes on him like everyone else's.' Turgenev is astonished: 'What sort of a Christ is this then? . . . Such an ordinary, ordinary man.' But he concludes: 'Suddenly I was afraid – and came to my senses. Only then did I realize that it is just such a face – a face like all men's faces – that is the face of Christ.'

FATHER SERGEI HACKEL

All greatness grows great by self-abasement, and not by exalting itself.

NESTORIUS

The fact that the omnipotent nature should have been capable of descending to the humiliated condition of humanity provides a clearer proof of power than great and supernatural miracles. His descent to our lowliness is the supreme expression of his power.

ST GREGORY OF NYSSA

Incarnation

There came, at a predetermined moment, a moment in time and of time,
A moment not out of time, but in time, in what we call history: transecting, bisecting the world of time, a moment in time but not like a moment of time,
A moment in time, but time was made through that moment: for without the meaning there is no time, and that moment of time gave the meaning.
Then it seemed as if men must proceed from light to light, in the light of the Word,
Through the Passion and Sacrifice saved in spite of their negative being;
Bestial as always before, carnal, self-seeking as always before, selfish and purblind as ever before,
Yet always struggling, always reaffirming, always resuming their march on the way that was lit by the light;
Often haltering, loitering, straying, delaying, returning, yet following no other way.

T. S. ELIOT
Chorus from 'The Rock'

December 26 ST STEPHEN

St Stephen, being brought by false accusations before the tribunal, with great courage and liberty of spirit gave an account of his faith; but the evidence of miracles or reason could not satisfy them, who thirsted not for truth, but for his blood; and therefore seeing themselves hitherto disappointed, they hurry him with violence out of Jerusalem, and there discharge their malice against him, in stoning him to death. And as a little before his execution, he had the comfort of seeing heaven open before him, and Jesus standing at the right hand of his father; so he gave proof of being his disciple, in praying for those that stoned him; they had malice in their hearts, and he perfect charity in his; they threw stones and death at him, he sent up prayers to heaven for them; he kneel'd down and cried with a loud voice, *Lord, lay not this sin to their charge,* and so expir'd.

This was the wonderful charity of this first martyr: 'Tis this the Church prays for in the collect of this festival, and ought to be the subject of every one's prayer in particular.

All these: I say, I look on as evil Christians, who live without charity, and are in evident danger of dying so. These have not learnt St Stephen's lesson, in receiving the stones thrown at them with his patience and charity, but still endeavour to throw them back again with the passion of that hand, with which they were cast at them; and truly, considering the great number of Christians that thus, in rendring evil for evil, are throwing stones at one another, 'tis to be fear'd, so many lose the patronage of Jesus, who thus unduly undertake to vindicate themselves.

JOHN GOTER

December 27 ST JOHN THE EVANGELIST

'Beloved, let us love one another' (1 John 4.7).

Imagine a circle marked out on the ground. Suppose that this circle is the world, and that the centre of the circle is God. Leading from the edge of the circle to its centre are a number of lines, and these represent the paths or ways of life that men can follow. In their desire to come closer to God, the saints move along these lines towards the middle of the circle, so that the further they advance, the nearer they approach both to God and to one another. The closer they come to God, the closer they come to one another; and the closer they come to each other, the closer they come to God.

Such is the nature of love. The nearer we draw to God in our love for him, the more we are united together by love for our neighbour; and the greater our union with our neighbour, the greater is our union with God.

ST DOROTHEUS OF GAZA

The Lord bestows such grace on his chosen that they embrace the whole earth, the whole world, with their love, and their souls burn with longing that all men should be saved and behold the glory of the Lord.

Blessed is the soul that loves her brother, for *our brother is our life*.

ST SILOUAN OF MOUNT ATHOS

December 28   THE HOLY INNOCENTS

This execution was sad, cruel and universal: no abatements made for the dire shriekings of the mothers, no tender-hearted soldier was employed, no hard-hearted person was softened by the weeping eyes, and pity-begging looks of those mothers, that wondered how it was possible any person should hurt their pretty sucklings; no connivances there, no protections, or friendships, or consideration, or indulgences, but Herod caused that his own child which was at nurse in the coasts of Bethlehem should bleed to death; which made Augustus Caesar to say, that in Herod's house it were better to be a hog than a child, because the custom of the nation did secure a hog from Herod's knife, but no religion could secure his child.

Jesus, when himself was safe, could also have secured the poor babes of Bethlehem, but yet it did not so please God. He is Lord of his creatures, and hath absolute dominion over our lives, and he had an end of glory to serve upon these babes, and an end of justice upon Herod; and to the children he made such compensation, that they had no reason to complain that they were so soon made stars, when they shined in their little orbs and participations of eternity, for so the sense of the Church hath been that they having died the death of martyrs, though incapable of making the choice, God supplied the defects of their will, by his own entertainment of the thing; that as the misery and their death, so also their glorification might have the same author in the same manner of causality; even by a peremptory and unconditioned determination in these particulars.

JEREMY TAYLOR

January

January 1

On 1 January 1745 and on almost every New Year's Day thereafter, Dr Johnson composed a prayer for himself. He did this in the small hours, and although he was normally a speedy writer he seems to have taken two or three hours over these little prayers.

1773

JAN 1. MANE 1.33′. Almighty God, by whose mercy my life has been yet prolonged to another year, grant that thy mercy may not be vain. Let not my years be multiplied to encrease my guilt, but as age advances, let me become more pure in my thoughts, more regular in my desires, & more obedient to thy laws. Let not the cares of the world distract me, nor the evils of age overwhelm me. But continue and encrease thy loving kindness towards me, and when thou shalt call me hence, receive me to everlasting happiness, for the sake of Jesus Christ, our Lord. Amen.

January 1   THE NAMING OF JESUS

'*You shall call his name* JESUS: *for he shall save his people from their sins*' (Matt. 1.21).

Ah! Ah! that wonderful Name! Ah! that delectable Name! This is the Name that is above all names, the Name that is highest of all, without which no man hopes for salvation. This Name is sweet and joyful, giving veritable comfort to the heart of man. Verily the Name of Jesus is in my mind a joyous song and heavenly music in mine ear, and in my mouth a honeyed sweetness. Wherefore no wonder I love that Name which gives comfort to me in all my anguish. I cannot pray, I cannot meditate, but in sounding the Name of Jesus. I savour no joy that is not mingled with Jesus. Wheresoever I be, wheresoever I sit, whatsoever I do, the thought of the savour of the Name of Jesus never leaves my mind. I have set it in my mind, I have set it as a token upon my heart. What can he lack who desires to love the Name of Jesus unceasingly?

RICHARD ROLLE

January 1 ST BASIL THE GREAT *c. 330–379*

One of the three Cappadocian Fathers, he was the brother of St Gregory of Nyssa (10 January) and the close friend of St Gregory of Nazianzus (25 January). Educated in the best pagan and Christian culture of the day, he turned at the age of twenty-seven to the monastic life, and in 370 was consecrated archbishop of Caesarea. Upholding the full divinity of the Son and the Holy Spirit, during a period of intense controversy he played a decisive role in clarifying Christian faith in the Trinity. Much of his energy was devoted to reorganizing monasticism in Asia Minor. He preferred life in community to the hermit way, because of the greater opportunities that it offers for mutual love and obedience. 'Whose feet will you wash,' he asked, 'or whom will you serve, how can you be last of all, if you are alone?' Around his episcopal residence in Caesarea he formed a vast complex of charitable institutions, hospitals, orphanages and hostels for the poor, since he regarded active, loving compassion as man's highest vocation: 'Who does not know that man is a tame and sociable animal, not solitary and wild? For nothing is so characteristic of our nature as to communicate with one another, and to need one another, and to love our own kind.'

January 2 ST SERAPHIM OF SAROV *1759–1833*

A monk-priest, after twenty years spent in solitude he became towards the end of his life a *starets* or spiritual guide, visited daily by scores or even hundreds from all parts of Russia. In these words, to the nuns of the convent of Diveyevo which was under his care, he insists that the bond between the spiritual father and his children continues unbroken by death:

Now you lack nothing, but when I am gone you will have many, many troubles. You will need patience. Pray constantly. Thank God for everything. Always be joyful. Do not let the spirit of discouragement overwhelm you. When I am with you no longer, come to my grave, and the more often the better. Whatever is on your heart, all your sorrow, prostrate on the ground tell it all to me, speaking as to one alive. And I will hear you and take away all your bitterness. For to you I am alive, and I shall be so always.

January 6 EPIPHANY

At the Manger from *For the Time Being: A Christmas Oratorio*

First Wise Man	Led by the light of an unusual star,
	We hunted high and low.
Second Wise Man	Have travelled far,
	For many days, a little group alone
	With doubts, reproaches, boredom, the unknown.
Third Wise Man	Through stifling gorges.
First Wise Man	Over level lakes,
Second Wise Man	Tundras intense and irresponsive seas.
Third Wise Man	In vacant crowds and humming silences,
First Wise Man	By ruined arches and past modern shops,
Second Wise Man	Counting the miles,
Third Wise Man	And the absurd mistakes.
The Three Wise Men	O here and now our endless journey stops.
Wise Men	Our arrogant longing to attain the tomb,
Shepherds	Our sullen wish to go back to the womb,
Wise Men	To have no past,
Shepherds	No future,
Tutti	Is refused.
	And yet without our knowledge, Love has used
	Our weakness as a guard and guide.
	– We bless –
Wise Men	Our lives' impatience,
Shepherds	Our lives' laziness,
Tutti	And bless each other's sin, exchanging here
Wise Men	Exceptional conceit
Shepherds	With average fear.
Tutti	Released by Love from isolating wrong,
	Let us for Love unite our various song,
	Each with his gift according to his kind
	Bringing this child his body and his mind.

W. H. AUDEN

Helena, the mother of Constantine, discovers the relics of the cross of Christ, and reflects on the three kings:

'Like me,' she said to them, 'you were late in coming. The shepherds were here long before; even the cattle. They had joined the chorus of angels before you were on your way. For you the primordial discipline of the heavens was relaxed and a new defiant light blazed amid the disconcerted stars.

'How laboriously you came, taking sights and calculating, where the shepherds had run barefoot! How odd you looked on the road, attended by what outlandish liveries, laden with such preposterous gifts!

'You came at length to the final stage of your pilgrimage and the great star stood still above you. What did you do? You stopped to call on King Herod. Deadly exchange of compliments in which began that unended war of mobs and magistrates against the innocent!

'Yet you came, and were not turned away. You too found room before the manger. Your gifts were not needed, but they were accepted and put carefully by, for they were brought with love. In that new order of charity that had just come to life, there was room for you, too. You were not lower in the eyes of the holy family than the ox or the ass.

'You are my especial patrons,' said Helena, 'and patrons of all late-comers, of all who have a tedious journey to make to the truth, of all who are confused with knowledge and speculation, of all who through politeness make themselves partners in guilt, of all who stand in danger by reason of their talents.

'Dear cousins, pray for me,' said Helena, 'and for my poor overloaded son. May he, too, before the end find kneeling-space in the straw. Pray for the great, lest they perish utterly. And pray for Lactantius and Marcias and the young poets of Trèves and for the souls of my wild, blind ancestors; for their sly foe Odysseus and for the great Longinus.

'For his sake who did not reject your curious gifts, pray always for all the learned, the oblique, the delicate. Let them not be quite forgotten at the throne of God when the simple come into their kingdom.'

EVELYN WAUGH

Lord, when the wise men came from far,
Led to thy cradle by a star,
Then did the shepherds too rejoice,
Instructed by thy angel's voice.
Blest were the wise men in their skill,
And shepherds in their harmless will.

Wise men, in tracing Nature's laws,
Ascend unto the highest cause;
Shepherds with humble fearfulness
Walk safely, though their light be less.
Though wise men better know the way,
It seems no honest heart can stray.

There is no merit in the wise
But love, the shepherds' sacrifice.
Wise men, all ways of knowledge passed,
To the shepherds' wonder come at last.
To know can only wonder breed,
And not to know is wonder's seed.

SIDNEY GODOLPHIN

Epiphany commemorates not only the coming of the three wise men but also the baptism of Christ in the Jordan. This second aspect of the feast is much emphasized by the Christian East, especially at the Great Blessing of the Waters, often celebrated on a river bank or the seashore. Christ's baptism at the hands of John is seen as anticipating our own, and is given at the same time a cosmic significance: the Saviour, himself sinless, enters the streams of the Jordan, thereby cleansing the waters and so imparting grace and redemption to the entire material creation.

Magnify, O my soul, one of the Trinity who bowed his head and
  received baptism.
Today the Master buries in the waters the sin of mortal man.
Today the Master has come to sanctify the nature of the waters.

At thine appearing in the body,
The earth was sanctified,
The waters blessed,
The heaven enlightened,
And mankind set free from the bitter tyranny of the enemy.

O marvellous gifts! O divine grace,
Forbearance past speech!
For see, the Creator and Master now wears
My nature in the Jordan, yet without sin;
He cleanses me through water,
Illumines me through fire,
And makes me perfect through the Holy Spirit.

The true Light has appeared,
And grants enlightenment to all.
Christ who is above all purity is baptized with us;
He sanctifies the water
And it becomes a cleansing for our souls.
The outward sign is earthly,
The inward grace is higher than the heavens.
Salvation comes through washing,
And through water the Spirit:
Descending into the water we ascend to God.
Wonderful are thy works, O Lord: glory to thee.

HYMNS FOR THE FEAST IN THE ORTHODOX CHURCH

Today the grace of the Holy Spirit in the form of a dove descended upon the waters.

Today the Sun that never sets has risen and the world is filled with splendour by the light of the Lord.

Today the moon shines upon the world with the brightness of its rays.

Today the glittering stars make the earth fair with the radiance of their shining.

Today the clouds drop down upon mankind the dew of righteousness from on high.

Today the Uncreated of his own will accepts the laying on of hands from his own creature.

Today the waters of the Jordan are transformed into healing by the coming of the Lord.

Today the transgressions of men are washed away by the waters of the Jordan.

Today the blinding mist of the world is dispersed by the Epiphany of our God.

Today things above keep feast with things below, and things below commune with things above.

Today earth and sea share in the joy of the world, and the world is filled with gladness.

At thine Epiphany the whole creation sang thy praises.

FROM THE GREAT BLESSING OF THE WATERS

See, Fire and Spirit in the womb that bore you:
See, Fire and Spirit in the river where you were baptized.
   Fire and Spirit in our baptism:
In the Bread and the Cup, Fire and Holy Spirit.

In your Bread is hidden a Spirit not to be eaten,
In your Wine dwells a Fire not to be drunk.
   Spirit in your Bread, Fire in your Wine,
A wonder set apart, yet received by our lips.

How wonderful your footsteps, walking on the waters!
You subdued the great sea beneath your feet.
   Yet to a little stream you subjected your head,
Bending down to be baptized in it.

The stream was like John who performed the baptism in it,
In their smallness each an image of the other.
   To the stream so little, to the servant so weak,
The Lord of them both subjected himself.

ST EPHREM THE SYRIAN

As the name of the Trinity is invoked, the candidate is immersed three times in the water and then three times rises up from the water once more: and immediately he enters into possession of all that he seeks. He is born and created; he receives the good seal; he is granted all the happiness that he desires; darkness before, he now becomes light; non-existent before, he now receives existence. God claims him for his own and adopts him as a son. From prison and utter enslavement he is led to a royal throne.

The water of baptism destroys one life and reveals another: it drowns the old man and raises up the new.

To be baptized is to be born according to Christ; it is to receive existence, to come into being out of nothing.

ST NICOLAS CABASILAS

Adult Baptism

After this you were led to the holy pool of divine baptism, as Christ was carried from the cross to the sepulchre that is before our eyes. Each of you was asked whether he believed in the name of the Father, and of the Son, and of the Holy Spirit, and you made this confession and descended into the water three times, and ascended again; here again quietly pointing by way of a figure to the burial of Christ for three days. For as our Saviour passed three days and nights in the heart of the earth, so you in your first coming out of water represented the first day of Christ under the earth, and by your descent, the night; for as he who is the night sees no more, but he who is in the day stays in the light, so in descending you saw nothing, as in the night, but in coming up again you were as in the day. At one and the same moment you died and were born; the water of salvation was your grave and your mother at once. What Solomon spoke of others may be applied to you. He said: 'There is a time to bear and a time to die' (Eccles. 3.2); but to you on the other hand the time of death is also the time to be born. One and the same season brings both of these about; and your birth and your death go hand in hand.

O what a strange and inconceivable thing it is! We did not really die, we were not really buried; we were not crucified and raised again; our imitation of Christ was but in a figure, while our salvation is truth. Christ actually was crucified and buried, and truly rose again; and all these things have been transmitted to us, that we might by imitation participate in his sufferings, and so gain salvation in truth.

ST CYRIL OF JERUSALEM

God loves infinitely an infinite goodness; the Son loves it in the Father whence it comes, the Father loves it in the Son in whom he places it, and upon whom he pours it out: 'This is my Son, my only beloved, in whom I am well-pleased.'

The Father's unqualified delight, his outpouring of his Holy Spirit, comes down with Christ from heaven to earth.

When St John came to write the story of Christ's baptism, he connected it with Jacob's dream of the ladder from heaven to earth, on which the angels of God ascended and descended (John 1.32, 51; Gen. 28.12). And certainly the baptism has so many levels of meaning in it, that without ever going outside it we can run up as though by steps from earth to heaven and down again. At the height of it is the bliss of the Trinity above all worlds, in the midst is the sonship of Jesus to his heavenly Father; at the foot of it (and here it touches us) is the baptism of any Christian.

We cannot be baptized without being baptized into his baptism: and the unity we have with him both in receiving baptism and afterwards in standing by it, brings down on us the very blessing and the very Spirit he received. In so far as we are in Christ, we are filled with Holy Ghost, and the Father's good pleasure rests upon us; infinite Love delights in us.

AUSTIN FARRER

Baptismal grace, the presence within us of the Holy Spirit – inalienable and personal to each one of us – is the foundation of all Christian life.

VLADIMIR LOSSKY

The aim of the Christian life is to return to that perfect grace of the most holy and life-giving Spirit, which was originally conferred upon us through divine baptism.

ST KALLISTOS AND ST IGNATIOS XANTHOPOULOS

January 10 ST GREGORY OF NYSSA *c. 330–c. 395*

The younger brother of St Basil and his devoted supporter in the doctrinal controversies of the day, in character he was gentler and more retiring, and in his theology more mystical and speculative. Here is his account of the last moments of St Macrina, the elder sister who had a profound influence upon both himself and Basil.

At evening her bed was turned to the east, and ceasing to talk with us she now spoke to God in prayer, her hands outstretched, murmuring in a low voice so that we could just catch what she was saying:

'O Lord, you have freed us from the fear of death. You have made the end of our life here into the beginning of true life for us. You give rest to our bodies for a time in sleep, and then you awaken them again with the sound of the last trumpet. Our earthly body, formed by your hands, you consign in trust to the earth, and then once more you reclaim it, transfiguring with immortality and grace whatever in us is mortal or deformed. You have opened for us the way to resurrection, and given to those that fear you the sign of the holy cross as their emblem, to destroy the enemy and to save our life.

'Eternal God, on you have I depended from my mother's womb, you have I loved with all the strength of my soul, to you have I dedicated my flesh and my soul from my youth until now. Set by my side an angel of light, to guide me to the place of repose, where are the waters of rest, among the holy Fathers. You have broken the fiery sword and restored to paradise the thief who was crucified with you and implored your mercy: remember me also in your Kingdom, for I too have been crucified with you. Let not the dread abyss separate me from your elect. Let not the envious one bar the way before me. But forgive me and accept my soul into your hands, spotless and undefiled, as incense in your sight.'

Ending this prayer, she made the sign of the cross on her eyes, mouth and heart. The fever increased, and she could speak no more.

January 13 ST HILARY *c. 315-367*

He was elected bishop of Poitiers in 353, but spent five years from 356 in exile for his opposition to the condemnation of St Athanasius. There he learnt much and became an important link between East and West. On his return he wrote on the Trinity and the incarnation:

How can we make a fitting recompense for so great a condescension? The one only-begotten God, born of God in an unutterable way, is enclosed in the shape of a tiny human embryo in the womb of the Virgin and grows in size. He who contains all things and in whom and through whom everything came into existence is brought forth according to the law of human birth; and he at whose voice the archangels tremble, and the heavens, the earth and all the elements of the world dissolve is heard in the cries of a baby. He who is invisible and incomprehensible and is not to be judged by estimates of sight, sense and touch, is covered up in a cradle. If anyone considers these conditions unfitting for a God, he will have to admit that his indebtedness to such generosity is all the greater, the less they are suited to the majesty of God.

It was not necessary for him through whom man was made to become man, but it was necessary for us that God should be made flesh and dwell with us, that is to say, dwell within all flesh by assuming one fleshly body. His abasement is our glory. What he is, while appearing in the flesh, that we have in turn become: restored to God.

January 13 GEORGE FOX *1624-1691*

Apprenticed in youth to a shoemaker, at the age of nineteen he felt the call to give up all ties of family and friendship. After a period of doubt and searching, he became an itinerant preacher, teaching that the truth is to be found in the 'inner light', the hidden voice of God speaking to the soul. In this way he founded what has become the Society of Friends (the Quakers). Because of his opposition to institutional religion he suffered frequent imprisonment, but showed remarkable patience and perseverance in the face of persecution. The following extract comes from the early part of his *Journal*:

I was still under great temptations sometimes, and my inward sufferings were heavy; but I could find none to open my condition to but the Lord alone, unto whom I cried night and day. I went back into Nottinghamshire, and there the Lord showed me that the natures of those things which were hurtful without, were within, in the hearts and minds of wicked men. I cried to the Lord, saying, 'Why should I be thus, seeing I was never addicted to commit those evils?' and the Lord answered that it was needful I should have a sense of all conditions, how else should I speak to all conditions; and in this I saw the infinite love of God. I saw also that there was an ocean of darkness and death, but an infinite ocean of light and love which flowed over the ocean of darkness. In that also I saw the infinite love of God; and I had great openings.

January 17 ST ANTONY OF EGYPT *c. 251–356*

The chief founder of Christian monasticism, he withdrew as a young man into the utter solitude of the desert. In his later life a loosely organized group of hermits gathered round him, while thousands of others – not under his immediate direction, but inspired by his example – went into the wilderness to become monks. In the words of his friend and biographer, St Athanasius (2 May), 'The desert became a city'. Antony acted also as the spiritual guide of countless lay people, 'a physician given by God to Egypt', as Athanasius puts it.

The following incident, recorded by Athanasius, comes from Antony's early days in solitude. It surely applies also to many who, although living in the 'world', have likewise to undergo the dark night of God's seeming absence:

After a long period of struggle against temptation, when he was brought close to madness and despair, Antony saw the roof opened, as it seemed, and a ray of light descending towards him. Suddenly the demons vanished and the pain in his body ceased instantly. 'Where were you, Lord?' he said. 'Why did you not appear at the beginning and put an end to my distress?' And a voice came to him: 'I was here, Antony, but I waited to see you fight.'

January 19 ST MACARIUS OF EGYPT *c. 300–c. 390*

A Coptic monk living in the desert of Scetis, originally a camel-driver, he was abrupt and rugged in character, rigorously ascetic, but with a shrewd understanding and an unexpected gentleness. The *Homilies* attributed to him are certainly not his work, and were probably written in Syria in the late fourth or early fifth century. The stories that follow come from the early monastic collection, *The Sayings of the Desert Fathers*:

They said of Abba Macarius that if a brother came to see him with fear, thinking that he was coming to a great and holy elder, the old man refused to say anything to him. But if one of the brethren spoke to him in a familiar and contemptuous way, 'Abba, when you were a camel-driver, and stole the natron and sold it, and the keepers caught you, they beat you, didn't they?' – then the old man would gladly talk with him about whatever he asked.

One day Abba Macarius returned to his cell to find a man with a donkey, stealing all his possessions. As if he was a stranger, he helped the thief to load his animal and in deep peace sent him on his way. 'We brought nothing into the world,' he said, 'and it is certain that we can take nothing out of it. The Lord gave, let it be as he wishes; blessed be the Lord in all things.'

Some people asked Abba Macarius, 'How should we pray?' 'There is no need to use a lot of words,' he replied. 'Just stretch out your hands and say, "Lord, as you will and as you know best, have mercy on me." And if the conflict grows fierce, say, "Lord, help me." He knows what we need and will show mercy to us.'

They said of Abba Macarius the Great that he became, as it is written, a god upon earth. Just as God shelters the world, so Abba Macarius covered up the faults of others: what he saw, it was as if he saw it not; what he heard, as if he heard it not.

January 21   ST MAXIMUS THE CONFESSOR   *c. 580–662*

> A monk, first near Constantinople and then in North Africa, he insisted
> upon the full humanity of Jesus Christ, maintaining that the Saviour, who
> was 'tempted in everything just as we are' (Heb. 4.15), possesses a human as
> well as a divine will. For this uncompromising defence of Christ's human
> freedom he was persecuted during his lifetime, dying in exile from
> maltreatment, although vindicated after his death. In his ascetic and
> mystical writings he assigns supreme importance to love, and underlines the
> intrinsic goodness of all created things.

Nothing created by God is evil. It is not food that is evil but gluttony, not
the begetting of children but unchastity, not material things but avarice,
not esteem but self-esteem. It is only the misuse of things that is evil, not
the things themselves.

January 24   ST FRANCIS DE SALES   *1567–1622*

> He was bishop of Geneva from 1602, but had to administer the Catholic part
> of his diocese from the family estate at Annecy in Savoy, for the city itself
> was the capital of Calvinism. He exercised a pastoral ministry to many in
> France, especially to intelligent women. This letter is addressed to an
> expectant mother:

My dearest daughter, we have at Annecy a Capuchin painter who, as you
may think, only paints for God and his temple: and though while working
he has to pay so close an attention that he cannot pray at the same time, and
though this occupies, and even fatigues his spirit, still he does this work
with good heart for the glory of our Lord, and the hope that these pictures
will excite many faithful to praise God, and to bless his goodness.

Well, my dear daughter, your child will be a living image of the divine
majesty; but while your soul, your strength, your natural vigour is
occupied with this work, it must grow weary and tired, and you cannot at the
same time perform your ordinary exercises so actively and so gaily; but
suffer lovingly this lassitude and heaviness, in consideration of the honour
which God will receive from your work. It is your image which will be
placed in the eternal temple \of the heavenly Jerusalem, and will be
eternally regarded with pleasure by God, by angels and by men; and the
saints will praise God for it, and you also will praise him when you see it
there; and so meanwhile take courage, though feeling your heart a little
torpid and sluggish, and with the superior part attach yourself to the holy
will of our Lord, who has so arranged for it according to his eternal
wisdom.

January 25   THE CONVERSION OF ST PAUL

St John Chrysostom writes in his book *On the Priesthood*:

No one loved Christ more than Paul; no one showed greater zeal than he did, no one was thought more worthy of grace. Still, in spite of all these advantages, he fears and trembles for his government and for his subjects. 'I fear,' he said, 'that as the serpent beguiled Eve, so your thoughts may be corrupted from simplicity towards Christ' (2 Cor. 11.3), and again, 'I was with you in fear and much trembling' (1 Cor. 2.3). Yet this was a man caught up into the third heaven, who shared in the unspeakable mysteries of God (2 Cor. 12.2–4), and endured deaths every day (1 Cor. 15.36) after he came to believe; he was a man who did not wish to use even authority given him by Christ, lest any of those who believed should be made to stumble (1 Cor. 9.14).

If, then, he who went beyond the commands of God, and nowhere sought his own advantage (1 Cor. 10.33), but that of those he governed, was so filled with fear when he looked on the greatness of his office, what shall we fear who often seek our own, who not only fail to go beyond the commands of Christ but oftener fall short of them. 'Who is weak,' he says, 'and I am not weak? Who is made to stumble, and I burn not?' (2 Cor. 11.29).

January 25   ST GREGORY OF NAZIANZUS *329–389*

St Gregory 'the Theologian', as he is known in Eastern Christendom — an indication of his crucial importance as a religious thinker – is the third of the Cappadocian Fathers, the close friend and collaborator of St Basil and St Gregory of Nyssa. An eloquent preacher, poet as well as theologian, he was consecrated bishop in 372 and presided during part of the second Ecumenical Council (Constantinople, 381).

The whole of man's life is but a single day, to those who labour with love.

January 27 ST JOHN CHRYSOSTOM *354–407*

His reputation as a preacher at Antioch led to his promotion to be archbishop of Constantinople in 397. There he fell out with the court and had eventually to go into exile in 404. The reasons for this are explained by a contemporary historian, Socrates:

Because of the rectitude of his life he was free from anxiety about the future, and the simplicity of his character rendered him open and ingenuous; nevertheless, the liberty of speech that he allowed himself was offensive to many. In his public teaching the great end that he proposed was the reformation of the morals of his auditors, but in private conversation he was frequently thought haughty and assuming by those who did not know him.

January 28 ST THOMAS AQUINAS *1225–1274*

He is chiefly known for his introduction to theology for those who had received a philosophical education, in his own Dominican Order and at universities in Paris, Oxford and elsewhere. But he was also a hymn-writer and a powerful preacher. This sermon on the Eucharist was probably preached in 1264:

This is the banquet at which Christ ministered to those who on earth were his companions and sat with him at table. It is the supper to which the householder invited his son on his return from the feast of the prefiguring lamb. O cleansing waters foreshadowed in earlier springs! This Pasch in which Christ is offered requires that virtue supersede vice, and makes free those who are spiritually Hebrews. This food satisfies the hunger of the devout heart. Faith is the seasoning, devotion and love of the brethren the relish. The teeth of the body break this food, but only an unfaltering faith can savour it. What a ration this is for the march that brings the traveller as far as the mountain of virtue. O living bread, begotten in heaven, fermented in the womb of the Virgin, baked in the furnace of the cross, brought to the altar hidden under the cover of the wafer; strengthen my heart to good, make it steadfast on life's path, make my mind glad, my thoughts pure.

January 30 CHARLES THE MARTYR *1600–1649*

King Charles I was a man of sensitive intelligence, a patron of the arts who made an important collection of paintings and was among the first to appreciate the genius of Shakespeare. He fell out with the Presbyterian party in Scotland and their friends in England and Ireland, partly because of his attitude to Catholic powers, to France and Spain, and to some of his Catholic subjects. The Long Parliament, elected in 1640 while the Scots were occupying the north of England, consolidated the power of their friends in local and central government. When this provoked rebellion in Ireland the King was not trusted to put it down and more guarantees were required of him by those in control of the offices of state. Against·these he raised his own following.

During the four years of war that followed, the Westminster Assembly of Divines prepared to impose upon England and Ireland a complete scheme of Presbyterian government and discipline after the Scottish model. This was resented not only by Royalists but by officers of the parliamentary army who would have wished the King to join them in setting up a military dictatorship. But he preferred to work for a compromise that would submit the scheme of government and discipline to revision at a later date by a more representative body. This would have made it possible to disband the army, who purged Parliament and brought the King to trial to save themselves from arrest for their war crimes. He was generally regarded as a martyr for constitutional government, not only in the Church of England, and not only by Royalists, until in the nineteenth century Liberal historians saw the seeds of parliamentary reform in proposals made by the army leaders, and of the French Revolution in the execution of a king.

January 31 ST JOHN BOSCO *1815–1888*

He did much for street boys in Turin, the capital of Piedmont, when this was the centre of movements for the unification of Italy, opposed by the Pope and therefore by the Bishop of Turin, who was in exile. This passage from his life shows him protesting against the conduct of the police at his home for boys:

'If these letters and proofs exist, why does not your excellency produce them? I demand justice for so many poor children who, alarmed by the repeated investigations and by the appearance of police officers in their usually peaceful home, weep and tremble for their future. It grieves me to see them in such a state, held up to public reprobation, even by the press. For them, therefore, I demand justice and honourable amends, so that they may not suffer the loss of their daily bread.'

At these last words, Farini seemed much moved and disturbed. Rising from his seat, he began to pace the room in silence. After a few minutes, the door opened, and Count Camillo Cavour, Minister of Foreign Affairs and President of the Ministry, made his appearance. Smiling and rubbing his hands, he asked: 'What is the matter?' as if he knew nothing. 'What is the matter?' he repeated, taking him [Don Bosco] by the hand and leading him to a chair.

At the sight of Cavour, and from his friendly words, Don Bosco anticipated a favourable ending to this affair. Therefore, with renewed courage, he answered: 'The house at Valdocco which you, Count Cavour, have so often visited, praised and benefited, is now doomed to destruction; those poor children trained to a life of honest labour are to be cast out and exposed to danger. In addition, morality, religion and the sacraments have been made subjects of derision by the agents of the Government in my house and in the presence of the boys, who were greatly scandalized.'

'Calm yourself, dear Don Bosco,' rejoined Cavour, 'and rest assured that none of us wish you any harm. But you have been deceived, and others, taking advantage of your kindness, have induced you to adopt an attitude in politics which can only lead to evil consequences.'

February

PRAYER

God's Breath in Man

Prayer the Churches banquet, Angels age,
    Gods breath in man returning to his birth,
    The soul in paraphrase, heart in pilgrimage,
The Christian plummet sounding heav'n and earth;
Engine against th' Almightie, sinners towre,
    Reversed thunder, Christ-side-piercing spear,
    The six-daies world transposing in an houre,
A kind of tune, which all things heare and fear;
Softnesse, and peace, and joy, and love, and blisse,
    Exalted Manna, gladnesse of the best,
    Heaven in ordinarie, man well drest,
The milkie way, the bird of Paradise,
    Church-bels beyond the starres heard, the souls bloud,
    The land of spices; something understood.

GEORGE HERBERT

Prayer as action

Prayer is action; to pray is to be highly effective.

Prayer is the science of scientists and the art of artists. The artist works in clay or colours, in words or tones; according to his ability he gives them pregnancy and beauty. The working material of the praying person is living humanity. By his prayer he shapes it, gives it pregnancy and beauty: first himself and thereby many others.

Man is created for prayer just as he is created to speak and to think.

TITO COLLIANDER

The flower of gentleness

Prayer is the flower of gentleness and of freedom from anger.

Prayer is the fruit of joy and thankfulness.

Prayer is the remedy for gloom and despondency.

Do not pray that your own will may be done, for your will may not accord with the will of God. But pray as you have been taught, saying: *Thy will be done in me*. Pray to him in this way about everything – that his will be done. For he desires what is good and profitable for your soul, whereas you do not always ask for this.

Often in my prayers I have asked for what I thought was good, and persisted in my petition, stupidly trying to force the will of God, instead of leaving it to him to arrange things as he knows best. But afterwards, on obtaining what I asked for, I was very sorry that I did not pray rather for God's will to be done; because the thing turned out to be different from what I had expected.

What is good, except God? Then let us leave all our concerns to him, and all will be well.

If you long for prayer, renounce all to gain all.

At the time of trials and temptations, use a brief but intense prayer.

When you are in the inner temple, pray not as the Pharisee but as the publican.

Strive never to pray *against* anyone.

If when you are praying no other joy can attract you, then truly you have found prayer.

EVAGRIUS OF PONTUS

Degrees of prayer

The principal thing is to stand before God with the intellect in the heart, and to go on standing before him unceasingly day and night until the end of life.

There are various degrees of prayer. The first degree is bodily prayer, consisting for the most part in reading, in standing and in making prostrations.

The second degree is prayer with attention: the intellect becomes accustomed to collecting itself in the hour of prayer, and prays consciously throughout, without distraction. The intellect is focused upon the written words to the point of speaking them as if they were its own.

The third degree is prayer of feeling: the heart is warmed by concentration, so that what hitherto has only been thought now becomes feeling. Where first it was a contrite phrase now it is contrition itself; and what was once petition in words is transformed into a sensation of entire necessity. Whoever has passed through action and thought to true feeling will pray without words, for God is God of the heart.

When the feeling of prayer reaches the point where it becomes continuous, then spiritual prayer may be said to begin. This is the gift of the Holy Spirit praying for us, the last degree of prayer that our intellects can grasp.

But there is, they say, yet another kind of prayer which cannot be comprehended by the intellect, and which goes beyond the limits of consciousness.

ST THEOPHAN THE RECLUSE

Pray without ceasing

Public prayer may be measured; its hours can be counted; *private* prayer is immeasurable, for it may be at all times; when in company, as well as when alone; amid conversation, as when silent; 'when thou sittest in the house, and when thou walkest by the way, and when thou liest down, and when thou risest up'; in the midst of business and employment, as when unoccupied; in short intervals, when for the moment thou seemest to have nothing else to do, or when most employed, that thou mayest do what thy hand findeth to do with all thy might, and 'as unto the Lord, not unto men'. 'Most businesses', says a good Doctor of our Church, 'have wide gaps, all have some chinks, at which devotion may slip in. Be we never so urgent, or closely intent upon any work (be we feeding, be we travelling, be we trading, be we studying) nothing can forbid but that we may together wedge in a thought concerning God's goodness, and bolt forth a word of praise for it; but that we may reflect on our sins, and spend a penitential sigh on them; but that we may descry our need of God's help, and dispatch a brief petition. A "God be praised", a "Lord have mercy", a "God bless" or "God help me", will no wise interrupt or disturb our proceedings.'

He then cannot be said to have any care about continual prayer, who passes any day, between morning and evening, without it; who lets his thoughts run on through the day on his daily business, without checking them to offer at least some brief prayer to God; who begins a work without asking God to bless it; who receives a mercy, or his daily food, without blessing him; who comes into his daily temptations without asking God to deliver him from them; who is beset by any care, and casts it not on God; who does not labour to fix his heart, like David, upon God, that he may praise him; who does not consider prayer (whatever he may yet have come up to) as the main business of life, as it will be of life eternal, and so does not wish and strive at least to interpose it at all intervals he may have; who does not, at least, divide each day into portions, and begin, at least, each such portion with some prayer.

E. B. PUSEY

The Jesus Prayer

As a way of fostering the continual sense of God's presence and making prayer more inward, many Christians practise the Invocation of the Holy Name or the Jesus Prayer. In the Orthodox tradition this usually takes the form, 'Lord Jesus Christ, Son of God, have mercy on me', sometimes with 'the sinner' added at the end. In the West the name of Jesus is often invoked on its own.

The invocation of the name may be practised anywhere and at any time. We can pronounce the name of Jesus in the streets, in the place of our work, in our room, in church, etc. We can repeat the name while we walk. Besides that 'free' use of the name, not determined or limited by any rule, it is good to set apart certain times and certain places for a 'regular' invocation of the name. One who is advanced in that way of prayer may dispense with such arrangements. But they are an almost necessary condition for beginners.

Before beginning to pronounce the name of Jesus, establish peace and recollection within yourself and ask for the inspiration and guidance of the Holy Ghost. 'No man can say that Jesus is the Lord, but by the Holy Ghost' (1 Cor. 12.3). The name of Jesus cannot really enter a heart that is not being filled by the cleansing breath and the flame of the Spirit. The Spirit himself will breathe and light in us the name of the Son.

Then simply begin. In order to walk, one must take a first step; in order to swim, one must throw oneself into the water. It is the same with the invocation of the name. Begin to pronounce it with adoration and love. Cling to it. Repeat it. Do not think that you are invoking the name; think only of Jesus himself. Say his name slowly, softly and quietly.

Continue this invocation for as long as you wish or as you can. The prayer is naturally interrupted by tiredness. Then do not insist. But resume it at any time and wherever you may be, when you feel again so inclined. In time you will find that the name of Jesus will spontaneously come to your lips and almost continually be present to your mind, though in a quiescent and latent manner. Even your sleep will be impregnated with the name and memory of Jesus. 'I sleep, but my heart waketh' (Song of Songs 5.2).

A MONK OF THE EASTERN CHURCH

Prayer as waiting

The attitude which brings about salvation is not like any form of activity. The Greek word which expresses it is *hypomene*, and *patientia* is rather an inadequate translation of it. It is the waiting or attentive and faithful immobility which lasts indefinitely and cannot be shaken. The slave, who waits near the door so as to open immediately the master knocks, is the best image of it. He must be ready to die of hunger and exhaustion rather than change his attitude. It must be possible for his companions to call him, talk to him, hit him, without his even turning his head. Even if he is told that the master is dead, and even if he believes it, he will not move. If he is told that the master is angry with him and will beat him when he returns, and if he believes it, he will not move.

Attention animated by desire is the whole foundation of religious practices.

SIMONE WEIL

Prayer as silence

When you pray, you yourself must be silent. You do not pray to have your own earthbound desires fulfilled, but you pray: Thy will be done. It is not fitting to wish to use God as an errand boy. You yourself must be silent; let the prayer speak.

TITO COLLIANDER

A mutual relationship

First of all, it is very important to remember that prayer is an encounter and a relationship, a relationship which is deep, and this relationship cannot be forced either on us or on God. The fact that God can make himself present or can leave us with the sense of his absence is part of this live and real relationship. If we could mechanically draw him into an encounter, force him to meet us, simply because we have chosen this moment to meet him, there would be no relationship and no encounter. We can do that with an image, with the imagination, or with the various idols we can put in front of us instead of God; we can do nothing of the sort with the living God, any more than we can do it with a living person. A relationship must begin and develop in mutual freedom. If you look at the relationship in terms of *mutual* relationship, you will see that God could complain about us a great deal more than we about him. We complain that he does not make himself present to us for the few minutes we reserve for him, but what about the twenty-three and a half hours during which God may be knocking at our door and we answer 'I am busy, I am sorry' or when we do not answer at all because we do not even hear the knock at the door of our heart, of our minds, of our conscience, of our life. So there is a situation in which we have no right to complain of the absence of God, because we are a great deal more absent than he ever is.

METROPOLITAN ANTHONY OF SOUROZH

Inner simplicity

He to whom all things are one, and who draweth all things to one, and seeth all things in one, can be steadfast in heart and abide at peace in God. O God, who art truth, make me one with thee in everlasting love. I am oftentimes weary of reading and hearing many things. In thee is all that I will and desire. Let doctors all hold their peace, and all creatures keep silent in thy sight; do thou speak to me alone.

THOMAS À KEMPIS

But now thou askest me and sayest: 'How shall I think on himself, and what is he?' Unto this I cannot answer thee, except to say: 'I know not.'

For thou hast brought me with thy question into that same darkness, and into that same *cloud of unknowing*, that I would thou wert in thyself. For of all other creatures and their works – yea, and of the works of God himself – may a man through grace have fullness of knowing, and well can he think of them; but of God himself can no man think. And therefore I would leave all that thing that I can think, and choose to my love that thing that I cannot think. For why, he may well be loved, but not thought. By love may he be gotten and holden; but by thought never. And therefore, although it be good sometime to think on the kindness and worthiness of God in special, and although it be a light and a part of contemplation: nevertheless in this work it shall be cast down and covered with a *cloud of forgetting*. And thou shalt step above it stalwartly, but listily, with a devout and a pleasing stirring of love, and try to pierce that darkness above thee. And smite upon that thick *cloud of unknowing* with a sharp dart of longing love; and go not thence for aught that befalleth.

THE CLOUD OF UNKNOWING

And also our good Lord showed, that it is full great pleasure to him that a simple soul come to him naked, plainly and homely. For this is the natural dwelling of the soul by the touching of the Holy Ghost, as by the understanding I have in this showing.

God of thy goodness give me thyself, for thou art enough for me; and I may ask nothing that is less, that may full worship of thee; and if I ask any thing that is less, ever me wanteth. But only in thee I have all.

And these words of the goodness of God be full lovesome to the soul, and full near touching the will of our Lord; for his goodness fulfilleth all his creatures, and all his blessed works without end. For he is the endless head, and he made us only for himself; and restored us by his precious Passion, and ever keepeth us in his blessed love; and all this is of his goodness.

JULIAN OF NORWICH

Prayer for the beginning of the day

To thee, O Master that lovest all men, I hasten on rising from sleep; by thy mercy I go forth to do thy work, and I pray to thee: help me at all times, in everything; deliver me from every evil thing of this world and from every attack of the devil; save me and bring me to thine eternal Kingdom. For thou art my Creator, the Giver and Provider of everything good; in thee is all my hope, and to thee I ascribe glory, now and ever, and to the ages of ages. Amen.

ATTRIBUTED TO ST MACARIUS OF EGYPT

Blessing of the Kindling

I will kindle my fire this morning
In presence of the holy angels of heaven,
In presence of Ariel of the loveliest form,
In presence of Uriel of the myriad charms,
Without malice, without jealousy, without envy,
Without fear, without terror of any one under the sun,
But the Holy Son of God to shield me.
    Without malice, without jealousy, without envy,
    Without fear, without terror of any one under the sun,
    But the Holy Son of God to shield me.

God, kindle thou in my heart within
A flame of love to my neighbour,
To my foe, to my friend, to my kindred all,
To the brave, to the knave, to the thrall,
O Son of the loveliest Mary,
From the lowliest thing that liveth,
To the Name that is highest of all.

CELTIC PRAYER

The Moment of Exhaustion

The simplest thing to be done at this moment is to 'let go' deliberately. In traditional language it was expressed in words like 'Into thy hands I commend my spirit'. If words like these help you to pray at such moments, use them as fully as you can. If you are not accustomed to them or helped by them, find the shortest phrase that expresses for you the entire act of putting yourself into the keeping of the Other. It may be done with such words as 'I/we are in your hands', 'we are yours' or simply reflecting 'let go' while you permit your body to relax. It is probable that we should learn to do this regularly and not just leave it to the times of exhaustion, but if we are going to learn to do it at all, we can begin with those desperate moments.

But it is not easily learned: all of us carry to the point of exhaustion the accumulations of problems and difficulties. Yet praying is a necessary part of truly living, and nowhere is this more true than in respect of the tired, beaten condition which active people find themselves in again and again. To be able to pray 'let go' is so important a part of our life that it deserves all the practice that it requires to become part of our maturing way of living, and its connection with final letting go should not be forgotten.

ALAN ECCLESTONE

Prayer for the acceptance of God's will

O Lord, I know not what to ask of thee. Thou alone knowest what are my true needs. Thou lovest me more than I myself know how to love. Help me to see my real needs which are concealed from me. I dare not ask either a cross or consolation. I can only wait on thee. My heart is open to thee. Visit and help me, for thy great mercy's sake. Strike me and heal me, cast me down and raise me up. I worship in silence thy holy will and thine inscrutable ways. I offer myself as a sacrifice to thee. I put all my trust in thee. I have no other desire than to fulfil thy will. Teach me how to pray. Pray thou thyself in me. Amen.

METROPOLITAN PHILARET OF MOSCOW

February 2 PRESENTATION OF CHRIST IN THE TEMPLE

Simeon blessed them both, but turned from the one who appeared to be the father to speak to his mother, Mary. He said: 'See, he will be for falling and rising to many in Israel' (Luke 2.33). He speaks of the fall of those who fail to believe, the resurrection of believers; or in another way the Lord is a wrecker of evil in our hearts, but a renewer of the good; lust decays, prudence rises. Or this can be understood in yet another way, that Christ is ordained for ruin, for he is going to suffer and fall into death, and many will rise at the time of his dying. Stay where you are, for a fall; go on, for the resurrection of many. The cross is a sign of contradiction for this time, since unbelievers will not receive it. The incarnation of the Lord is called a sign, and a sign of wonder, for God became man, and a virgin a mother. This sign, I mean the incarnation of Christ, is contradicted; for some say the body was from heaven, and others that it was imaginary.

THEOPHYLACT OF BULGARIA

February 6 ST VARSANUPHIUS THE GREAT *early sixth century*

> Spiritual father in a monastery close to Gaza, he lived as a recluse, receiving no visitors and answering questions only in writing. The following extracts from his letters show how the obedience rendered by the spiritual child does not involve the suppression of his freedom, and how the spiritual father does not merely offer advice but out of love carries the burdens of his children and takes responsibility for their sins.

As for the rule of life which you ask me to give you: you are following far too many roundabout ways in order to delay entering through the narrow gate that leads to eternal life. See, Christ tells you briefly how to enter. Leave men's rules, and listen to what he says: 'He who endures to the end will be saved' (Matt. 10.22). Do not ask me to give you orders, for I want you to be 'not under the law but under grace' (Rom. 6.14).

Do not force men's free will, but sow in hope. For our Lord never used compulsion on anyone, but preached the Good News; and whoever wished listened to him.

Next to God himself, I have stretched out my wings over you up to this day. I am carrying your burdens and your faults, your negligence and your contempt for my words of advice. Awaiting your repentance, I have seen and covered up all your failings, just as God also sees and covers up our sins. If you do as I ask, I will take upon myself the condemnation passed against you, and by the grace of Christ I will not abandon you either in this world or the next. I have taken from you your burden and load and debt, and you have become a new man, innocent and pure.

February 14 ST CYRIL *d. 869*   ST METHODIUS *d. 885*

Constantine and his brother Methodius were citizens of Salonica. In their own country of Macedonia they met the Slavs. Constantine, who at the end of his life took Cyril as his monastic name, was employed on diplomatic missions to the Arabs and to the Khazars north of the Black Sea, who lived among other Slavs. He and his brother devised liturgical books in a language that has come to be called Old-Slavonic, based on the speech of the Macedonian Slavs whom they met in their youth, but understood also in Moravia, a country whose boundaries correspond to those of the modern Czechoslovakia, where they went in 863 from Constantinople to preach the gospel at the invitation of the Moravian king. They had trouble there with other missionaries coming from lands where Latin and Greek were the only known liturgical languages, but their books in Slavonic were approved at Rome where Constantine was professed as a monk under the name of Cyril and died in 869. Methodius continued to have trouble with missionaries coming from the Franks. Slavonic books continued to be in use in some places in Croatia and Dalmatia, but their future lay in Serbia and Bulgaria, close to the lands where Old Slavonic really was the vernacular speech, and above all in Russia, where it was used to translate not only liturgical books, but sermons, lives of the saints and other theological works. There and in Bulgaria and Serbia it became the basis of a rich and varied culture. The Old Slavonic liturgy is still in use in these lands, and in some places by emigrants from them in Western Europe and America.

February 21   SAINTS AND MARTYRS OF AFRICA

During the last hundred years many Christians in Africa have died for their faith. One of these was Archbishop Janani Luwum of Uganda who was killed in 1977 while in the hands of the security forces of Idi Amin.

The preaching of both churches, Anglican and Catholic, now became more direct. 'Uganda is killing Uganda,' Janani told the men at the police barracks at Nsambya during an official visit at the end of August. 'We look to you to uphold the laws of our land. Do not abuse this privilege.' Afterwards some thanked him for speaking so openly, and showing them so clearly their responsibility. But others were afraid his words would annoy the President, whose anger might fall on them.

Janani continued to attend government functions. 'Even the President needs friends,' he would say. 'We must love the President. We must pray for him. He is a child of God.' He feared no one but God who was the centre of his life. But his wish that the Church of Uganda should have a guiding influence upon the government misled some people, who complained that he lived a comfortable life and was on the government side. When the Archbishop met one of his critics in December, he made clear the truth. In words that proved prophetic, he told him: 'I do not know for how long I shall be occupying this chair. I live as though there will be no tomorrow. I face daily being picked up by the soldiers. While the opportunity is there, I preach the gospel with all my might, and my conscience is clear before God that I have not sided with the present government, which is utterly self-seeking. I have been threatened many times. Whenever I have the opportunity I have told the President the things the churches disapprove of. God is my witness.'

February 26 ST POLYCARP *c. 70–155*

He was Bishop of Smyrna. He prayed at his martyrdom:

'O Lord God Almighty, the Father of your beloved and blessed Son Jesus Christ, through whom we have received the knowledge that you are the God of angels and powers and of all created beings, and of the whole company of the righteous who live in your sight, I thank you for making me worthy of this day and hour, that I should be given a part in the number of the martyrs, a share in the cup of your Christ and of resurrection to eternal life in soul and body through the incorruption that comes to us from the Holy Spirit.

'May I be accepted this day before you as a rich and acceptable sacrifice, as you, the God of all truth, foreordained, prophesied to me, and now fulfil in me. Therefore I praise you for all things, I bless you, I glorify you, together with the eternal and heavenly Christ, your beloved child, through whom be glory to you with him and the Holy Spirit, now and to ages of ages. Amen.'

When he had said Amen to his prayer, the men in charge of the fire lit it, and a great flame blazed up. And we, to whom the vision was given, saw a marvel. We have been preserved alive to report the event to others.

The fire made something like a room, or the sail of a vessel filled with wind, and surrounded the body of the martyr like a kind of wall. Inside it he was not like burning flesh, but like bread being baked, or gold and silver refined in the fire. Moreover we smelt a fragrant scent like incense or other costly spices.

THE MARTYRDOM OF POLYCARP

February 27   GEORGE HERBERT   *1593–1633*

Of Welsh extraction, he gave up his desire to be a courtier and was ordained to a small country parish. He is among the finest poets of the Church of England, of whose spirit and teaching he is an authentic representative.

The Flower

How fresh, O Lord, how sweet and clean
Are thy returns! ev'n as the flowers in spring;
To which, besides their own demean,
The late-past frosts tributes of pleasure bring.
Grief melts away
Like snow in May,
As if there were no such cold thing.

Who would have thought my shrivel'd heart
Could have recover'd greennesse? It was gone
Quite under ground; as flowers depart
To see their mother-root, when they have blown;
Where they together
All the hard weather,
Dead to the world, keep house unknown.

These are thy wonders, Lord of power,
Killing and quick'ning, bringing down to hell
And up to heaven in an houre;
Making a chiming of a passing-bell.
We say amisse,
This or that is:
Thy word is all, if we could spell.

And now in age I bud again,
After so many deaths I live and write;
I once more smell the dew and rain,
And relish versing: O my onely light,
It cannot be
That I am he
On whom thy tempests fell all night.

February 29 ST JOHN CASSIAN *c. 360–c. 430*

After twelve years in the Egyptian desert, where he was a disciple of
Evagrius, Cassian settled in later life near Marseilles, founding twin
monasteries, one for men and one for women. He is an important 'bridge
figure', transmitting Eastern monastic teaching to the West; and his two
main works, the *Institutes* and the *Conferences*, exercised a deep influence on
St Benedict. (See March 14.) In the passage below Cassian recommends the
frequent repetition of a verse from the Psalms as a help in maintaining
unceasing remembrance of God. Many Christians today use the Jesus
Prayer for this purpose.

To preserve the continual recollection of God, keep these holy words
always before you: *O God, make speed to save me; O Lord, make haste to help
me* (Ps. 70:1).

I am attacked by the passion of gluttony: I must say at once, *O God,
make speed to save me; O Lord, make haste to help me.* I try to read but am
overcome by a headache: I must call out, *O God, make speed to save me; O
Lord, make haste to help me.* I am afflicted by insomnia: as I sigh and
groan, I must pray, *O God, make speed to save me; O Lord, make haste to
help me.* I have gained the grace of humility and simplicity: to keep myself
from growing conceited, I must cry with all my strength, *O God, make
speed to save me; O Lord, make haste to help me.*

This verse should be our constant prayer: in adversity that we may be
delivered, in prosperity that we may be kept safe and may not fall victim to
pride. Let this verse be the unremitting occupation of your heart. At work,
in every task, on a journey, do not cease to repeat it. Meditate on these
words as you drop off into slumber; through incessant use, grow
accustomed to repeat them even when asleep; let them be your first
thought as you awake; let them accompany you all the day long.

PREPARATION FOR LENT

Mutual forgiveness

The Sunday immediately before Lent is known in the Orthodox Church as the 'Sunday of Forgiveness'. Before renewing our relationship with Christ through the Lenten fast, we renew our relationship with each other by asking and giving forgiveness; for a fast without mutual love would be the fast of demons.

However hard I try, I find it impossible to construct anything greater than the three words, 'Love one another' – only to the end, and without exceptions: and then all is justified and life is illumined, whereas otherwise it is an abomination and a burden.

MOTHER MARIA

In 1979 the son of Bishop Dehqani-Tafti, of the Anglican Church in Iran, was shot and killed. This is part of his father's prayer:

O God,
We remember not only Bahram but also his murderers.

O God,
Bahram's blood has multiplied the fruit of the Spring in
    the soil of our souls;
So when his murderers stand before thee on the day of
    judgement
Remember the fruit of the Spirit by which they have
    enriched our lives,
And forgive.

Fasting

Do not limit the benefit of fasting merely to abstinence from food, for a true fast means refraining from evil. Loose every unjust bond, put away your resentment against your neighbour, forgive him his offences. Do not let your fasting lead only to wrangling and strife. You do not eat meat, but you devour your brother; you abstain from wine, but not from insults. So all the labour of your fast is useless.

ST BASIL THE GREAT

The most searching and profound prayer any of us can make is to eat our dinner. To eat at all is to recognize – if we are humble enough to admit it – our total dependence.

The trouble is that, in the West, something frightful has happened to our attitude to food. For all sorts of economic and other reasons our appetite for food is grossly overstimulated, with the result that many of us over-consume it.

I find that there are three levels on which I need to tackle the problem.

On the first level I need to 'tune in' much more patiently and attentively to what my body is saying to me about its hunger or lack of it. Over the years I have developed the dangerous trick of using food to achieve other ends apart from fulfilling simple physical needs – to tranquillize me when I am anxious, to cheer me when I am sad, to pep me up still further when I am jolly. In the end it is hard to know any longer whether I am hungry or not, hard too to break out of 'automatic' eating at regular times.

The next level is what we actually *do* about reforming our eating habits. I recently decided that I wanted to shake up my ideas about food from top to bottom, trying to throw modish ideas about slimming out of the window but to cherish the cross little infant inside me whose fierce rebellion has stymied more than one sensible eating plan; working mainly from the idea of what my body *needs*, in terms of nutrition, but also respecting what it *likes*.

The third level on which we have to care about food, that most crucial of twentieth-century questions after the Bomb itself, is on the political level. What has to be redeemed here is the uncaringness, the cynicism, the blind commercialism which affects on the one hand the hungry millions but also the way food is prepared, marketed and advertised here. In this area, as in others, our need to learn to love matter is part of the kit for survival.

To fast is to learn to love and appreciate food, and one's own good fortune in having it.

MONICA FURLONG

To keep a true Lent

Is this a Fast, to keep
    The Larder leane?
    And cleane
From fat of Veales and Sheep?

Is it to quit the dish
    Of Flesh, yet still
    To fill
The platter high with Fish?

Is it to faste an houre
    Or rag'd to go,
    Or show
A downcast look, and sour?

No; 'tis a Fast, to dole
    Thy sheaf of wheat
    And meat
Unto the hungry soule.

It is to fast from strife,
    From old debate
    And hate;
To circumcise thy life.

To shew a heart grief-rent;
    To starve thy sin,
    Not Bin;
and that's to keep thy Lent.

ROBERT HERRICK

Joyful Sorrow

Those who have tasted the gift of the Spirit are conscious of two things at the same time: on the one hand, of joy and consolation; on the other, of trembling and fear and mourning. They mourn for themselves and for the whole race of Adam, because the nature of all human beings is one. To such people tears are daily bread, and in mourning they find sweetness and refreshment.

THE HOMILIES OF ST MACARIUS

Small sins, if neglected . . .

He that walks in his love and mercy, and being free from great and deadly sins, such crimes as murder, theft, adultery, is also sorry for those that seem to be small, sins of thought or of tongue, or of want of moderation in things permitted, does the truth of confession and comes to the light in good works, seeing that many small sins, if neglected, are fatal. Small are the drops that swell the river, tiny the grains of sand, but if such sand is heaped up, it presses and crushes. Bilge-water, allowed to accumulate in a ship's hold, does the same thing as a rushing wave. Little by little it leaks through the hold; and by long leaking and no pumping, sinks the ship. What is this pumping, but that by good works, by sighing, fasting, giving, forgiving, we take care that sins do not overwhelm us.

ST AUGUSTINE

A Prayer of Repentance

Lord Jesus Christ our God, who hast lamented for Lazarus and wept tears of grief and compassion for his sake, accept the tears I shed in my bitterness.

By thy Passion heal my passions.

By thy wounds cure my wounds.

By thy blood purify my blood, and mingle with my body the fragrance of thy lifegiving Body.

May the gall, which enemies gave thee to drink, sweeten my soul from the bitterness that I have drunk at the hands of the adversary.

May thy Body, outstretched upon the wood of the cross, give wings to my intellect which is dragged down by the demons, and make it ascend to thee.

May thy head, which thou hast bowed on the cross, lift up my head which the enemies buffet.

May thy most holy hands, nailed by unbelievers to the cross, lift me out of the abyss of destruction and raise me up to thee, as thou thyself hast promised.

May thy face, struck and spat upon by accursed men, illumine my face, disfigured by transgressions.

May thy soul, which on the cross thou hast rendered up to thy Father, guide me to thee by thy grace.

I have no heart full of anguish with which to search thee out. I have no repentance, no contrition, which bring back children to their own inheritance. O Master, I have no tears to intercede on my behalf.

May the Father, who brings thee forth from himself timelessly and eternally, renew in me the marks of thine image.

I have forsaken thee: do not thou forsake me.

I have departed from thee. But come out to seek me: lead me into thy fold and number me among the sheep of thy chosen flock. Make me feed with them on the green pasture of thy divine mysteries, for their pure heart is thy resting-place.

PRAYER ATTRIBUTED TO ST ISAAC THE SYRIAN

Words to God from the depths of my heart

There was a time when I did not exist,
And thou hast created me;
I did not beseech thee for a wish,
And thou hast fulfilled it;
I had not come into the light,
And thou hast seen me;
I had not yet appeared,
And thou hast taken pity on me;
I had not invoked thee,
And thou hast taken care of me;
I did not raise my hand,
And thou hast looked at me;
I had not entreated thee,
And thou wast merciful to me;
I had not uttered a sound,
And thou hast heard me;
I had not groaned,
And thou hast lent an ear;
With prescient eyes thou sawest
The crimes of my guilty self,
And yet thou hast fashioned me.
And now, I who have been created by thee,
And saved by thee,
And have been tended with such care,
Let me not wholly perish by the blow of sin
That is but the slanderer's invention;
Let not the fog of my stubbornness
Triumph over the light of thy forgiveness;
Nor the hardness of my heart
Over thy forbearing goodness;
Nor my mortal carnal-being
Over thy most perfect plenitude;
Nor my material weakness
Over thine unconquerable grandeur.

ST GREGORY OF NAREK

Self-knowledge

The best trained dogs are liable to be at fault and to lose the track of the stag; whose cunning teaches it a thousand stratagems and subtleties, whereby it gives the hounds a wrong scent, and so escapes their pursuit. In the same way we often lose sight of our own heart and are totally incapable of understanding its operations; it has many different movements, and these succeed each other so rapidly, that its ways become indiscernible.

God, whose knowledge is infinite, can alone read clearly into its recesses, and fathom its most secret foldings. He sees our thoughts even before we have formed them; he discovers our most hidden paths, he views all our stratagems and evasions. This is what made the royal prophet say, 'Your knowledge is too wonderful for me; it is high, and I cannot reach it' (Ps. 138.6). To reflect on all our ordinary actions by a continual self-examination would be to entangle ourselves in a labyrinth from which we could never be extricated. Besides this, the continual attention and restraint would be insupportable, if it were necessary by incessant reflection to enter into ourselves, and to remember that we are thinking, to observe what we are considering, to see that we are seeing, to discern that we are discerning, to reflect that we are meditating. In this confusion and variety of thoughts, the mind would engage itself in a labyrinth from whose mazes it would vainly seek to disengage itself. We may infer from this, that only persons endowed with the spirit of prayer can clearly explain this subject.

ST FRANCIS DE SALES

Confession

In the practice of the Russian Church, the priest brings the penitent before a desk on which rest the Book of the Gospels and the cross, and he says to him:

Behold, my child, Christ stands here invisibly and receives your confession. Therefore do not be ashamed, do not be afraid, hide nothing from me; but tell me without hesitation all the things that you have done, and so you shall have pardon from our Lord Jesus Christ. See, his holy icon is before us; and I am only a witness, bearing testimony before him about all the things that you have to say to me. But if you hide anything from me, you shall have greater sin. Take care, then, lest having come to the Physician's you depart unhealed.

Who can refuse?

Christ became our brother in order to help us. Through him our brother has become Christ for us in the power and authority of the commission Christ has given to him. Our brother stands before us as the sign of the truth and the grace of God. He has been given to us to help us. He hears the confession of our sins in Christ's stead and he forgives our sins in Christ's name. He keeps the secret of our confession as God keeps it. When I go to my brother to confess, I am going to God.

Confession is within the liberty of the Christian. Who can refuse, without suffering loss, a help that God has deemed it necessary to offer?

DIETRICH BONHOEFFER

March

LENT

The Renewal of Baptism

In the early Church, the main purpose of Lent was to prepare the 'catechumen', that is to say, the newly converted Christian, for baptism which at that time was performed during the paschal liturgy. But even when the Church no longer baptized adults and the institution of the catechumenate disappeared, the basic meaning of Lent remained the same. For even though we are baptized, what we constantly lose and betray is precisely that which we received at baptism. Therefore, Easter is our return every year to our own baptism, whereas Lent is our preparation for that return – the slow and sustained effort to perform, at the end, our own 'passage' or 'pascha' into the new life in Christ. Each year Lent and Easter are, once again, the rediscovery and the recovery by us of what we were made through our own baptismal death and resurrection.

FATHER ALEXANDER SCHMEMANN

Spiritual Springtime

The springtime of the Fast has dawned,
The flower of repentance has begun to open.
O brethren, let us cleanse ourselves from all impurity
And sing to the Giver of Light:
Glory be to thee, who alone lovest mankind.

ORTHODOX HYMN IN THE WEEK BEFORE LENT

Flying Kites

Clean Monday, the first day of Lent, is an open-air holiday and symbolizes the first meeting with spring and the dismissal of winter. In all the villages and towns of Greece, it is celebrated by a general exodus to the country. Each family sets out for the fields or the woods. The grown-ups carry large hampers of food and demijohns of wine, and the children hold coloured kites – kite-flying being one of the main features of Clean Monday.

GEORGE MEGAS

The wilderness within

Most people's wilderness is inside them, not outside. Thinking of it as outside is generally a trick we play upon ourselves – a trick to hide from us what we really are, not comfortingly wicked, but incapable, for the time being, of establishing communion. Our wilderness, then, is an inner isolation. It's an absence of contact. It's a sense of being alone – boringly alone, or saddeningly alone, or terrifyingly alone.

Our isolation is really us – inwardly without sight or hearing or taste or touch. But it doesn't seem like that. Oh no. I ask myself what I am isolated from, and the answer looks agonizingly easy enough. I feel isolated from Betty whom I love desperately and who is just the sort of woman who never could love me. And so to feel love, I think, must be at the same time to feel rejection. Or I feel isolated from the social people who, if noise is the index of happiness, must be very happy indeed on Saturday evenings. Or I feel isolated from the competent people, the success-boys who manage to get themselves into print without getting themselves into court. Or I feel isolated, in some curious way, from my work. I find it dull and uninviting. It's meant – it used – to enliven me and wake me up. Now it deadens me and sends me to sleep.

Is it to go on always like now, just – tomorrow and tomorrow and tomorrow – a slow procession of dusty greyish events with a lot of forced laughter, committee laughter, cocktail laughter, and streaks of downright pain?

This then is our Lent, our going with Jesus into the wilderness to be tempted. And we might apply to it some words from the First Epistle of St Peter: 'Beloved, do not be surprised at the fiery ordeal which comes upon you to prove you, as though something strange were happening to you. But rejoice, in so far as you share Christ's sufferings, that you may also rejoice and be glad when his glory is revealed.'

H. A. WILLIAMS

A time for suffering and ascetic effort

However just and pure a man may be, there is always an element of sin in him which cannot enter the Kingdom of God and which must be burned up. Our sins are burned up by our sufferings.

Our love of God is measured by our willingness to accept sufferings and misfortunes and to see in them the hand of God. We can find support in the fact that these sufferings are also the measure of the love that God bears us.

Sweat, tears, blood . . . If sweat is accompanied by inner rebellion, anger, murmuring; if tears are caused by pain, offence, rage; if blood is shed without faith – the soul will not obtain any benefit. But if all this is accomplished in a spirit of obedience, contrition and faith, it purifies and elevates us.

The world is crooked and God straightens it. That is why Christ suffered (and still suffers), as well as all the martyrs, confessors and saints – and we who love Christ cannot but suffer as well.

Illness has taught me a great deal. It has confirmed me even more deeply in the conviction that if a man is with Christ, then he is with suffering, and that there is no other way for the Christian than the way of pain, inward and outward. And as I thought of the innocent suffering in the world, I said to myself that through such undeserved, innocent suffering the invisible Kingdom of God is built up, his suffering Body – the Church of God – is created and gathered together into unity.

FATHER ALEXANDER ELCHANINOV

The Holy Icons

On the first Sunday in Lent, the Orthodox Church celebrates 'the Triumph of Orthodoxy', which is more particularly a feast in honour of the holy icons. The icon, as the following passages indicate, is to an Orthodox Christian much more than a piece of religious decoration. It has a liturgical and theological significance, safeguarding the true fullness of Christ's incarnation, emphasizing the spiritual value of material things and man's power, as priest of the creation, to transfigure the cosmos.

We preserve unchanged all the traditions of the Church, whether handed down to us in written or unwritten form. Of these traditions, one is the painting of icons. The pictorial image in iconography and the verbal narrative in the Gospels are in agreement with one another, and both alike emphasize that the incarnation of God the Word is genuine and not illusory.

THE SEVENTH ECUMENICAL COUNCIL

Of old the incorporeal and invisible God was not depicted at all; but now, since God has appeared in flesh and dwelt among men, I make an icon of God in so far as he has become visible. I do not venerate matter but I venerate the Creator of matter, who for my sake has become material, who has been pleased to dwell in matter and has through matter effected my salvation. I shall not cease to venerate matter, for it was through matter that my salvation came to pass. Do not insult matter, for it is not without honour; nothing is without honour that God has made.

ST JOHN OF DAMASCUS

Through man alone the material becomes articulate in praise of God. Because man is body he shares in the material world around him, which passes within him through his sense perceptions. Because man is mind he belongs to the world of higher reality and pure spirit. Because he is both, he is, in Cyril of Alexandria's phrase, 'God's crowned image'; he can mould and manipulate the material and render it articulate. The sound in a Byzantine hymn, the gestures in a liturgy, the bricks in a church, the cubes in a mosaic are matter made articulate in the divine praise.

FATHER GERVASE MATHEW

The artistic perfection of an icon is not only a reflection of the celestial glory – it is a concrete example of matter restored to its original harmony and beauty, and serving as a vehicle of the Spirit. The icons are part of the transfigured cosmos.

NICOLAS ZERNOV

Because man is made in the image and likeness of God, there is something divine about the act of painting an icon.

ST THEODORE THE STUDITE

The Second Sunday ST GREGORY PALAMAS *1296–1359*

On the second Sunday in Lent, the Orthodox Church commemorates St Gregory Palamas, monk of Mount Athos and subsequently archbishop of Thessalonica, the leading exponent of Hesychast theology. St Gregory based his spirituality upon Christ's transfiguration: he believed that through ascetic effort, love and prayer – especially the Jesus Prayer – the Christian is granted a vision of the divine light of Tabor, which is not a physical, created light, but the uncreated energies of God. Palamas maintains that this divine light may equally be designated by the symbol of darkness:

The divine darkness, says Dionysius, *is* the unapproachable light – unapproachable because of the superabundance of the outpouring of supra-essential radiance. Thus he identifies darkness and light, seeing and not seeing, knowing and unknowing. In the strict sense it is light, but by virtue of its transcendence it is described as darkness, because it is invisible to those who strive to approach or to see it through the activity of sense or intellect.

There is an unknowing that is higher than all knowledge, a darkness that is supremely bright; and in this dazzling darkness divine things are given to the saints.

March 1 ST DAVID *d. 602*

His dates are uncertain, but he certainly founded a monastery in the place now called after him, Menevia in Pembrokeshire. The writer of his life thus describes his death:

He preached a most noble sermon and consecrated the Lord's Body with pure hands. Having partaken of the Body and Blood of the Lord he was immediately seized with pain and became unwell. When he had finished the office and blessed the people, he addressed them all, saying: 'My brethren, persevere in what you have learnt from me and seen with me. On the third day of the week on the first of March I shall go the way of my fathers. Farewell in the Lord. I shall depart. Never shall we be seen on the earth again.'

Then the voice of the faithful was lifted in lamentation and in wailings, saying: 'O that the earth would swallow us, the fire consume us, the sea cover us! O that death by a sudden irruption would overtake us! Would that the mountains would fall on us!' From Sunday night till the fourth day of the week when he was dead, all who came remained weeping, fasting and watching.

And when the third day of the week was come, at the crowing of the cock, the monastery was filled with angelic choirs and became melodious with heavenly songs and full of the sweetest fragrance. At the hour of Matins, when the clerks were replying to the songs with psalms and hymns, the Lord Jesus vouchsafed his presence for the consolation of the father, as he had promised by the angel. When he saw him, he altogether rejoiced in spirit. 'Take me', he said, 'after you.' With these words he gave back his life to God, Christ being his companion, and with the angelic host went up to the abodes of heaven.

RHYGYVARCH

> Bishop of Lincoln. A man of great holiness; once described by Professor Owen Chadwick as 'the fragrant flower of the Oxford Movement'.

I will thank him for the pleasures given me through my senses, for the glory of the thunder, for the mystery of music, the singing of the birds and the laughter of children. I will thank him for the pleasures of seeing, for the delights through colour, for the awe of the sunset, the beauty of flowers, the smile of friendship and the look of love; for the changing beauty of the clouds, for the wild roses in the hedges, for the form and the beauty of birds, for the leaves on the trees in spring and autumn, for the witness of the leafless trees through the winter, teaching us that death is sleep and not destruction, for the sweetness of flowers and the scent of hay. Truly, O Lord, the earth is full of thy riches!

And yet, how much more I will thank and praise God for the strength of my body enabling me to work, for the refreshment of sleep, for my daily bread, for the days of painless health, for the gift of my mind and the gift of my conscience, for his loving guidance of my mind ever since it first began to think, and of my heart ever since it first began to love. Oh, from what unknown errors has he guarded me, from what beginnings of sins has he kept me back. I will praise him for my family, my father and my mother, my brothers and sisters, my home, for my husband, for my wife, for the kindness of servants and the love of children.

These are but a few things we can call to mind instantly when we think attentively and reverently of our creation and preservation and of the blessings of this life. Let us resolve each of us to make the text our own today. 'I will extol thee, my God, O King, and I will bless thy name for ever and ever. Every day will I bless thee; and I will praise thy name for ever and ever.' Today will I praise thee, O Lord, both today and all the days of my life.

March 12   ST SYMEON THE NEW THEOLOGIAN   *949–1022*

Abbot of the monastery of St Mamas in Constantinople, mystical theologian
and poet, in common with St Gregory Palamas three centuries later he
assigns central place to the vision of divine light.

O Light in three persons, Father, Son and Spirit,
O dominion and power of the unoriginate Principle,
O Light that none can name, for it is altogether nameless,
O Light with many names, for it is at work in all things,
O single glory and authority, rule and kingdom,
O Light that is one in will and thought, in counsel and strength,
Have mercy, take pity on me in my affliction.
O power of the divine Fire, O strange energy!
You who dissolve the rocks and hills by your fear alone,
By the very sight of your face, O Christ my God,
You who dwell in Light wholly unapproachable,
How in your essence totally divine do you mingle yourself with grass?
How, while continuing unchanged, altogether inaccessible,
Do you preserve the nature of the grass unconsumed?
How, while keeping it unaltered, do you yet transform it entirely?
Remaining grass it is light, and yet the Light is not grass;
But you, the Light, are joined to the grass in a union without confusion,
And the grass becomes light; it is transfigured yet unchanged.

March 14 ST BENEDICT *480–547*

The influence of his Rule on Western monasticism was immense. He spoke of the condition of those who became monks to remain civilized in a society where law and order was breaking down. He wrote in the prologue to the Rule:

Therefore we must establish a school of the Lord's service; in the foundation of this we hope to ordain nothing harsh or burdensome. If, for a good reason, for the amendment of evil habits or for the preservation of charity, there is some strictness of discipline, do not be immediately dismayed and run from the way of salvation, to which the entry must needs be narrow. But, as we progress in our monastic life and in faith, our hearts will be enlarged, and we shall run with unspeakable sweetness of love in the way of God's commandments; so that by never abandoning the rule but persevering in Christ's teaching in the monastery until death, we shall by patience share in his sufferings, that we may be partakers of his Kingdom.

Evidently there are four kinds of monks. The first are the Cenobites, who live in monasteries under a rule and an abbot. The second are the Anchorites or Hermits, who, not in the first fervour of their conversion, but after long probation, go out well armed from the ranks of their community to the solitary combat of the desert.

The third kind of monks is that detestable one of the Sarabites, who have never been tested, like gold in the furnace, by any rule or by lessons of experience, are soft and yielding as lead. What they think or choose to do, they call holy; what they dislike, they regard as unlawful. The fourth kind of monks are called Gyrovagues. They spend their whole lives wandering from province to province, ever roaming and never stable, given up to their own wills and to the allurements of gluttony.

March 17 ST PATRICK *389–461*

The first of these dates is open to doubt, with much in the saint's biography before and after his return to Ireland as a missionary. He writes in his *Confession*:

I blush and fear exceedingly to reveal my lack of education. This indeed I know most certainly that before I was humiliated I was like a stone lying in the deep mire; and he that is mighty came and in his mercy lifted me and raised me aloft, and placed me on the top of the wall.

Among the Irish poems attributed to him, the most famous is *The Deer's Cry* or *St Patrick's Breastplate*:

I bind myself today to a strong strength, to a calling on the Trinity. I believe in a Threeness with confession of a Oneness in the Creator of the World.

I bind myself today to the strength of Christ's birth and his baptism; to the strength of his crucifixion with his burial; to the strength of his resurrection with his ascension;

In stability of earth, in steadfastness of rock, I bind to myself today God's strength to pilot me;

God's power to uphold me; God's wisdom to guide me; God's eye to look before me; God's ear to hear me;

God's word to speak for me; God's hand to guard me; God's path to lie before me; God's shield to protect me; God's host to save me;

Against snares of demons; against the begging of sins; against the asking of nature; against all my ill-wishers near me and far from me; alone and in a crowd.

So I have called on all these strengths, to come between me and every fierce and merciless strength that may come between my body and my soul;

Against incantations of false prophets; against black laws of heathens; against false laws of heretics; against craft of idolatry; against spells of women and smiths and druids; against every knowledge forbidden to the souls of men;

Christ with me, Christ before me; Christ behind me, Christ in me; Christ under me, Christ over me; Christ to the right of me, Christ to the left of me; Christ in lying down, Christ in sitting, Christ in rising up; Christ in the heart of everyone that thinks of me; Christ in the mouth of everyone that speaks to me; Christ in every eye that sees me; Christ in every ear that hears me.

March 18 ST CYRIL OF JERUSALEM *c. 304–386*

He was bishop of Jerusalem from 349. His *Catechetical Lectures* were probably first given before this, in the years when pilgrimages began to multiply after the consecration in 335 of the Martyrium, the great church next to the Holy Sepulchre. In this passage he speaks of the place:

Whence did the Saviour rise? He says in the Song of Songs (2.10): 'Rise up, my fair one, and come away', and afterwards (14) 'in the cleft of the rock', for 'the cleft of the rock' is what he calls the cleft that used to be at the door of the saving sepulchre, and was hewn of the rock itself, as is the custom here in front of tombs. But now it does not appear, since the outer cave has been hewn away for the sake of present adornment; for before the sepulchre was decorated by imperial zeal, there was a cave in the face of the rock.

March 19 ST JOSEPH

He appears in the Gospels as a descendant of the house of David, 'espoused' to the Virgin Mary before the conception of our Lord. In other early accounts he is a mature man with sons and daughters of his own, who has taken charge of her after the death of her father and mother. In the *Protevangelion of James* the family belong to Bethlehem.

An order came from Augustus for the enrolment of all the inhabitants of Bethlehem in Judaea. Joseph said: 'I will enrol my sons, but what shall I do with this girl? How shall I put her down? As my wife? I am ashamed to do that. As my daughter? But all the children of Israel know that she is not my daughter. The day of the Lord will bring it about as the Lord wills.'

He saddled an ass and put Mary upon it. His son led the beast and Joseph followed. When they had gone less than three miles, Joseph turned to Mary and saw her sad. He said to himself: 'Perhaps what is in her is giving her distress.' He looked at her again and saw her laughing. He said to her, 'Mary, why are you like this, that I see your face laughing one minute and sad at another?'

And Mary said to Joseph: 'Because I see with my eyes two peoples, one weeping and sorrowing and the other rejoicing and exulting.'

They were in the middle of the road when Mary said to him: 'Take me down from the ass, for what is in me presses to come forth.' He took her down from the ass and said to her: 'Where shall I take you and hide your shame, here where we are in the wilderness?'

They found a cave and he made Mary go in. He left his sons with her and went to look for a midwife in the country of Bethlehem.

And I, Joseph, was walking and stopped walking. I looked up into the sky and found the sky itself full of fear; I looked to the pole of heaven and saw that it stood still and the birds of the heaven were stayed in their flight . . . I saw the current of the river and young goats with their mouths open to take the water; they did not drink; and then all things in one moment were set in motion again.

March 20 ST CUTHBERT *630–688*

Bede describes his missionary activity in Northumberland.

It was then the custom of the English people, that when a cleric or priest came into a town they all, at his command, flocked to hear the word, willingly heard what was said, and more willingly practised what they could hear and understand. But Cuthbert was so skilful a speaker, so fond of making his point, and had so much brightness showing in his angelic face, that no one present tried to conceal from him the most hidden secrets of his heart, but all openly confessed what they had done; because they thought the guilt of this could not be hidden from him. They wiped away the guilt that they had confessed with worthy fruits of penance, as he commanded.

He was accustomed especially to reach those places, and preach in those villages, as are high up among crags and wild moorland, inaccessible because of their poverty and wildness, which nevertheless he, in his entire devotion to duty, would seek industriously to polish with his teaching. When he left the monastery he would often stay a week, sometimes two or three, and sometimes a whole month, before he returned home, continuing in the mountains to allure the rustics to heavenly employments by preaching and example.

March 20 THOMAS KEN *1637–1711*

Bishop of Bath and Wells and the author of two famous morning and evening hymns. He refused to take the oath of allegiance to King William and was deposed from his see. He lived an ascetic life as a celibate.

For what is Lent, in its original institution, but a spiritual conflict to subdue the flesh to the spirit, to beat down our bodies, and to bring them into subjection? A devout soul, that is able duly to observe it, fastens himself to the cross on Ash Wednesday, and hangs crucified by contrition all the Lent long; that, having felt in his closet the burthen and the anguish, the nails and the thorns, and tasted the gall of his own sins, he may by his own crucifixion be better disposed to be crucified with Christ on Good Friday, and most tenderly sympathize with all the dolors and pressures and anguish and torments and desertion, infinite, unknown, and unspeakable, which God incarnate endured when he bled upon the cross for the sins of the world; that being purified by repentance and made conformable to Christ crucified, he may offer up a pure oblation at Easter and feel the power and the joys and the triumph of his Saviour's resurrection.

March 21 THOMAS CRANMER *1489–1556*

Archbishop of Canterbury who served Henry VIII and was burnt at the stake in the reign of Mary Tudor. He was largely responsible for the Prayer Book of 1549 and his English style in that and elsewhere has been much admired.

Wherefore I would advise you all, that cometh to the reading or hearing of this book, which is the word of God, the most precious jewel, and most holy relic that remaineth upon earth, that ye bring with you the fear of God, and that ye do it with all due reverence, and use your knowledge thereof, not to vainglory of frivolous disputation, but to the honour of God, increase of virtue, and edification both of yourselves and other.

And to the intent that my words may be the more regarded, I will use in this part the authority of St Gregory Nazianzene. It appeareth that in his time there were some (as I fear me, there been also now at these days a great number) which were idle babblers and talkers of the Scripture out of season and all good order, and without any increase of virtue or example of good living.

Therefore, every man that cometh to the reading of this holy book ought to bring with him first and foremost this fear of Almighty God, and then next a firm and stable purpose to reform his own self according thereunto.

March 25 ANNUNCIATION

After an Ethiopian Liturgy

In fear of God let us stand to praise
The grace and glory of our Lady,
The channel of joy, of more beauty
Than the thousand eyes of the Cherubim
Or the multiple wings of the Seraphim.
    The Father looked down from heaven
    East and west, north and south,
    Into every end of the earth.
Smelling the savour of every scent
He found nothing like you where He went;
    And of your prepared singularity
    He made His beloved the baby.
You are the loom from which Emmanuel took
His robe of flesh; the warp and the woof
Are yours and Adam's; the Word Himself,
Jesus Christ is the shuttle; the long thread
In the warp is the shadow of high Godhead.
    The Spirit wove this wonderful web,
    Seven curtains of fiery red,
    Round the throne and Cherubim,
    Pitched this in the narrow room
    Of a young bride, not burning
    Your virgin womb, nor turning
    Your milk in the same flame.

GEORGE EVERY

Today is revealed the mystery that is from all eternity.
The Son of God becomes the Son of Man;
Sharing in what is lower,
He makes me share in what is higher.
Once Adam was deceived:
He sought to become God, but failed.
Now God becomes man,
So as to make Adam God.
Let creation rejoice and nature exult:
For the Archangel stands in fear before the Virgin,
And with his salutation 'Hail!' he brings
The joyful greeting whereby our sorrow is healed.
O God, made man in merciful compassion:
Glory to thee!

FROM ORTHODOX MATINS FOR THE FEAST

The incarnation of the Word was not only the work of Father, Son and Spirit – the first consenting, the second descending, the third overshadowing – but it was also the work of the will and the faith of the Virgin. Without the three divine persons this design could not have been set in motion; but likewise the plan could not have been carried into effect without the consent and faith of the all-pure Virgin. Only after teaching and persuading her does God make her his Mother and receive from her the flesh which she consciously wills to offer him. Just as he was conceived by his own free choice, so in the same way she became his Mother voluntarily and with her free consent.

ST NICOLAS CABASILAS

March 29   JOHN KEBLE   *1792–1866*

> Together with John Newman and E. B. Pusey one of the three key figures in
> the Oxford Movement. A man of great beauty of character who was widely
> influential in his time through his book of poems, *The Christian Year*.
>   This sermon contains a characteristic theme shared by the movement as a
> whole, the renewal of the present in the light of the past.

Let us be only true to our sacred trust: let us put everything else by for the
sake of handing down the whole counsel of God, our good deposit, entire as
we received it: and who knows but we may by God's mercy be made
instrumental in saving the English Church from ruin not unlike that which
has fallen on Ephesus, Smyrna, or Sardis? At any rate, the Church
Catholic, in one country or another, we are sure, will survive and triumph.
As of old she has stood before kings and governors, and it turned to her for
a testimony, so now blessed are they whom divine providence shall choose
and enable worthily to support her cause against popular delusion and
tyranny. We, indeed, as priests of the second order, are but under-
labourers in that most holy cause. Yet the least and lowest among us may
look for his share of the blessing, as he has undoubtedly his share of the
burthen and of the peril. Is there not a hope, that by resolute self-denial
and strict and calm fidelity to our ordination vows, we may not only aid in
preserving that which remains, but also may help to revive in some
measure, in this or some other portion of the Christian world, more of the
system and spirit of the apostolical age? New truths, in the proper sense of
the word, we neither can nor wish to arrive at. But the monuments of
antiquity may disclose to our devout perusal much that will be to this age
new, because it has been mislaid or forgotten; and we may attain to a light
and clearness, which we now dream not of, in our comprehension of the
faith and discipline of Christ. We may succeed beyond what humanly
appears possible in rekindling a primitive zeal among those who shall be
committed to our charge.

30 March ST JOHN CLIMACUS *seventh century*

A monk of Mount Sinai, he wrote *The Ladder of Divine Ascent*, an ascetic treatise in thirty chapters or 'steps', which has proved remarkably popular among Orthodox Christians, both monastic and lay. In monasteries it is read in Lent every year. Here, from Step 7, is his description of the gift of tears. In his view tears are not merely penitential but the expression of what he terms 'joy-creating sorrow'.

The tears that come after baptism are greater than baptism itself, though it may seem rash to say so. Baptism washes off those evils that were previously within us, whereas the sins committed after baptism are washed away by tears. The baptism received by us as children we have all defiled, but we cleanse it anew with our tears. If God in his love for the human race had not given us tears, those being saved would be few indeed and hard to find.

31 March ST INNOCENT OF ALASKA *1797–1879*

The most outstanding Orthodox missionary of modern times, he worked for forty-five years in Alaska and Eastern Siberia, becoming Metropolitan of Moscow at the end of his life. He showed a warm compassion towards the native Aleuts, preaching and writing in their language and making a close and sympathetic study of their customs and beliefs: his writings remain an important primary source for ethnography. A man of great physical strength, he undertook year-long journeys of extreme hardship to the more remote islands, often travelling through heavy seas in the frail native kayak, 'with not a single board to save you from death – just skins', as he put it. The following anecdote illustrates his practical approach, which proved so effective in missionary teaching:

'Vladikha,' a deacon asked him, 'if God is infinitely merciful, how can he deprive anyone of his heavenly Kingdom?'

'And why do you keep twisting your head about from side to side?' Innocent countered. 'Why don't you sit still?'

'Because the sun keeps hitting me right in the eye and just won't leave me in peace,' the deacon replied.

'There. You've answered your own question,' the bishop laughed. 'God doesn't deprive of his heavenly Kingdom sinners who don't repent. They themselves simply can't bear its light – any more than you can bear the light of the sun.'

April

THE RAISING OF LAZARUS

O Lord, thou hast shed tears for Lazarus,
Showing that thou art man;
And then hast raised him from the dead,
Showing to the peoples that thou art the Son of God.

There is none like thee, forbearing Lord.
Thou doest all things for our sake as God,
and thou sufferest as man.
Make us all partakers of thy Kingdom, at the prayers of Lazarus.

ORTHODOX HYMNS FOR THE SATURDAY OF LAZARUS

> That imperious summons! Spring's
> restlessness among dry
> leaves. He stands at the grave's
> entrance and rubs death from his eyes,
>
> while thought's fountain recommences
> its play, watering the waste ground
> over again for the germination
> of the blood's seed, where roses should blow.

R. S. THOMAS

It was the amazing white, it was the way he simply
Refused to answer our questions, it was the cold pale glance
Of death upon him, the smell of death that truly
Declared his rising to us. It was no chance
Happening, as a man may fill a silence
Between two heart-beats, seem to be dead and then
Astonish us with the closeness of his presence;
This man was dead, I say it again and again.
All of our sweating bodies moved towards him
And our minds moved too, hungry for finished faith.
He would not enter our world at once with words
That we might be tempted to twist or argue with:
Cold like a white root pressed in the bowels of earth
He looked, but also vulnerable – like birth.

ELIZABETH JENNINGS

PALM SUNDAY

Let the mountains and all the hills
Break out into great rejoicing at the mercy of God,
And let the trees of the forest clap their hands.
Give praise to Christ, all nations,
Magnify him, all peoples, crying:
Glory to thy power, O Lord.

Seated in heaven upon thy throne
And on earth upon a foal, O Christ our God,
Thou hast accepted the praise of the angels
And the songs of the children who cried out to thee:
Blessed art thou that comest to call back Adam.

ORTHODOX HYMNS FOR PALM SUNDAY

MAUNDY THURSDAY

The mystery of Jesus

Jesus suffered in his Passion the torments which men inflicted on him, but in his agony he suffered torments which he inflicted on himself: *turbare semetipsum*. This is suffering from no human, but an almighty hand, and he who bears it must also be almighty.

Jesus sought some comfort at least in his three dearest friends, and they were asleep. He prayed them to watch with him a while, and they left him with utter carelessness, having so little compassion that it could not hinder their sleeping even for a moment. And thus Jesus was left alone to the wrath of God.

Jesus was without one on earth not merely to feel and share his suffering, but even to know of it; he and heaven were alone in that knowledge.

Jesus was in a garden, not of delight as the first Adam, in which he destroyed himself and the whole human race, but in one of agony, in which he saved himself and the whole human race.

He suffered this sorrow and this desertion in the horror of night.

I believe that Jesus never complained but on this single occasion, but then he complained as if he could no longer restrain his extreme sorrow: 'My soul is sorrowful, even to death.'

Jesus sought companionship and consolation from men. This was the only time in his life, as it seems to me; but he received it not, for his disciples were asleep.

Jesus will be in agony even to the end of the world. We must not sleep during that time.

BLAISE PASCAL

Lachrymae

Slow are the years of light:
and more immense
Than the imagination. And the years return
Until the Unity is filled. And heavy are
The lengths of Time with the slow weight of tears.
Since thou didst weep, on a remote hillside
Beneath the olive-trees, fires of unnumbered stars
Have burnt the years away, until we see them now:
Since thou didst weep, as many tears
Have flowed like hourglass sand.
Thy tears were all.
And when our secret face
Is blind because of the mysterious
Surging of tears wrung by our most profound
Presentiment of evil in man's fate, our cruellest wounds
Become thy stigmata. They are thy tears which fall.

DAVID GASCOYNE

So to fatness come

Poor human race that must
Feed on pain, or choose another dish
And hunger worse.

There is also a cup of pain, for
You to drink all up, or,
Setting it aside for sweeter drink,
Thirst evermore.

I am thy friend. I wish
You to sup full of the dish
I give you and the drink,
And so to fatness come more than you think
In health of opened heart, and know peace.

Grief spake these words to me in a dream. I thought
He spoke no more than grace allowed
And no less than truth.

STEVIE SMITH

GOOD FRIDAY

Thou hast given thyself for redemption:
Soul for soul,
Body for body,
And blood for blood,
Man for man,
And death for death.

O strange and unspeakable mystery:
The Judge was judged,
He who loosed the bound was bound,
He who created the world was fixed with nails,
He who measures heaven and earth was measured,
He who gives creatures life died,
He who raises the dead was buried.

What is this new creation?
The Judge is judged and is silent;
The Invisible is seen on the cross and is not ashamed;
The Infinite is contained and does not complain;
The Impassible suffers and does not seek vengeance,
The Immortal dies and says nothing,
The King of heaven is buried and endures it.
What is this strange mystery?

ST MELITO OF SARDIS

'God so loved the world' (John 3.16). See! There is nothing except the holy and blessed love of the Father, the Son and the Holy Spirit towards a sinful and despairing mankind:

The love of the Father crucifying;
The love of the Son crucified;
The love of the Spirit triumphing by the power of the cross.

METROPOLITAN PHILARET OF MOSCOW

I am the great sun

From a Normandy crucifix of 1632

I am the great sun, but you do not see me,
  I am your husband, but you turn away.
I am the captive, but you do not free me,
  I am the captain you will not obey.

I am the truth, but you will not believe me,
  I am the city where you will not stay,
I am your wife, your child, but you will leave me,
  I am that God to whom you will not pray.

I am your counsel, but you do not hear me,
  I am the lover whom you will betray,
I am the victor, but you do not cheer me,
  I am the holy dove whom you will slay.

I am your life, but if you will not name me,
Seal up your soul with tears, and never blame me.

CHARLES CAUSLEY

The Penitent Thief

You did not see him on the mountain of Transfiguration
Nor walking the sea at night;
You never saw corpses blushing when a bier or sepulchre
Was struck by his cry.

It was in the rawness of his flesh and his dirt that you saw him,
Whipped and under thorns,
And in his nailing like a sack of bones outside the town
On a pole, like a scarecrow.

You never heard the making of the parables like a Parthenon of words,
Nor his tone when he talked of his Father,
Neither did you hear the secrets of the room above,
Nor the prayer before Cedron and the treachery.

It was in the racket of a crowd of sadists revelling in pain
And their screeches, howls, curses and shouts
That you heard the profound cry of the breaking heart of their prey:
'Why hast thou forsaken me?'

You, hanging on his right; on his left, your brother;
Writhing like skinned frogs,
Flea-bitten petty thieves thrown in as a retinue to his shame,
Courtiers to a mock king in his pain.

O master of courtesy and manners, who enlightened you
About your part in this harsh parody?
'Lord, when you come into your kingdom, remember me,'
The kingdom that was conquered through death.

Rex Judaeorum; it was you who saw first the vain
Blasphemy as a living oracle,
You who first believed in the Latin, Hebrew and Greek,
That the gallows was the throne of God.

O thief who took Paradise from the nails of a gibbet,
Foremost of the *nobilitas* of heaven,
Before the hour of death pray that it may be given to us
To perceive him and to taste him.

SAUNDERS LEWIS

DESCENT INTO HELL

Thou who art the Life wast laid in a tomb, O Christ,
And the hosts of angels were amazed
And glorified thy self-abasement.

O Life, how canst thou die?
How canst thou dwell in a tomb?
Yet thou dost destroy death's kingdom and raise the dead from hell.

The whole creation was altered by thy Passion:
For all things suffered with thee,
Knowing, O Word, that thou holdest all in unity.

To earth hast thou come down, O Master, to save Adam,
And not finding him on earth
Thou hast descended into hell, seeking him there.

Of old the lamb was sacrificed in secret;
But thou, longsuffering Lord, wast sacrificed beneath the open sky
And hast cleansed the whole creation.

Adam was afraid when God walked in paradise,
But now he rejoices when God descends to hell.
Then he fell, but now he is raised up.

FROM THE LAMENTATION AT THE TOMB

While Hades so debated with Satan, the King of glory held out his right hand, and took hold of our father Adam and raised him. He turned to the rest and said: 'All of you come with me, as many as have died through the touch of his hand on the tree; for behold, I raise you all up through the tree of the cross.' He brought them all out and our ancestor Adam seemed full of joy, for he cried: 'I thank your majesty that you, O Lord, have brought me up from the abyss of Hades.'

Then likewise all the prophets and saints said: 'We thank you, O Christ, the Saviour of the world, for bringing us up alive out of doom.'

After they had spoken, the Saviour blessed Adam with the sign of the cross on his forehead, and did the same to the patriarchs, prophets and martyrs and all the ancestors. He took them up and jumped out of Hades. As he went the holy fathers with him sang praises saying: 'Blessed is he who comes in the name of the Lord, Alleluia: to him be the glory of all the saints.'

GOSPEL OF NICODEMUS

Then I shall come as a king, crowned with angels,
And have all men's souls out of hell.
Demons great and small shall stand before me
And be at my bidding where I will.
My kinship demands that I have mercy
On man, for we all be brethren
In blood, if not in baptism.

My righteousness and right shall rule
In hell, and mercy over all mankind before me
In heaven. I were an unkind king
If I did not help my kin.

WILLIAM LANGLAND

Speaking of the ceremony of immersion at baptism, St John Chrysostom
remarks: 'The action of descending into the water and then rising out of it
again symbolizes the descent of Christ into hell and his return from hell
once more.' To undergo baptism, then, means not only to die and to rise
with Christ: it means also that we descend into hell, that we bear the
stigmata of Christ the Priest, his sacerdotal care, his apostolic anguish for
the destiny of those who choose hell.

PAUL EVDOKIMOV

We must make a hell for ourselves, if we cannot find a heaven. Yes, a hell!
the simple language is the best. What glimpse of daylight can we discern in
the trackless abyss?

'He descended into Hell.' Mighty words! which I do not pretend that I
can penetrate, or reduce under any forms of the intellect. If I could, I think
they would be of little worth to me. But I accept them as news that there is
no corner of God's universe over which his love has not brooded – none
over which the Son of God and the Son of Man has not asserted his
dominion. I claim a right to tell this news to every peasant and beggar of
the land. I may bid him rejoice, and give thanks, and sing merry songs to
the God who made him, because there is nothing created which his Lord
and Master has not redeemed, of which he is not the King; I may bid him
fear nothing around him or beneath him where he trusts in him.

F. D. MAURICE

RESURRECTION

Homily read at Easter Midnight in the Orthodox Church

If any be a devout lover of God, let him partake with gladness from this fair and radiant feast.

If any be a faithful servant, let him enter rejoicing into the joy of his Lord.

If any have wearied himself with fasting, let him now enjoy his reward.

If any have laboured from the first hour, let him receive today his rightful due. If any have come after the third, let him celebrate the feast with thankfulness. If any have arrived after the sixth, let him not be in doubt, for he will suffer no loss. If any have delayed until the ninth, let him not hesitate but draw near. If any have arrived only at the eleventh, let him not be afraid because he comes so late. For the Master is generous and accepts the last even as the first. He gives rest to him who comes at the eleventh hour in the same way as to him who has laboured from the first. He accepts the deed, and commends the intention.

Enter then, all of you, into the joy of our Lord. First and last, receive alike your reward. Rich and poor, dance together. You who have fasted and you who have not fasted, rejoice today. The table is fully laden: let all enjoy it. The calf is fatted: let none go away hungry.

Let none lament his poverty; for the universal Kingdom is revealed. Let none bewail his transgressions; for the light of forgiveness has risen from the tomb. Let none fear death; for the death of the Saviour has set us free.

He has destroyed death by undergoing death.

He has despoiled hell by descending into hell.

Hell was filled with bitterness when it met thee face to face below:

    filled with bitterness, for it was brought to nothing;

    filled with bitterness, for it was mocked;

    filled with bitterness, for it was overthrown;

    filled with bitterness, for it was put in chains.

It received a body, and encountered God. It received earth, and confronted heaven.

O death, where is thy sting? O hell, where is thy victory?

    Christ is risen, and thou art cast down.

    Christ is risen, and the demons are fallen.

Christ is risen, and the angels rejoice.
Christ is risen, and life reigns in freedom.
Christ is risen, and there is none left dead in the tomb.
For Christ, being raised from the dead, has become the first-fruits of
those that slept. To him be glory and dominion to the ages of ages. Amen.

ATTRIBUTED TO ST JOHN CHRYSOSTOM

A country curate writes about Easter

I rose early and went out into the fresh, brilliant morning, between six and
seven o'clock. The sun had already risen some time, but the grass was still
white with the hoar frost. I walked across the common in the bright sunny
quiet empty morning, listening to the rising of the lark as he went up in an
ecstasy of song into the blue unclouded sky and gave in his Easter
morning hymn at Heaven's Gate. Then came the echo and answer of
earth as the Easter bells rang out their joy peals from the church towers all
round. It was very sweet and lovely, the bright silent sunny morning, and
the lark rising and singing alone in the blue sky, and then suddenly the
morning air all alive with music of sweet bells ringing for the joy of the
resurrection. 'The Lord is risen' smiled the sun, 'The Lord is risen' sang
the lark. And the church bells in their joyous pealing answered from
tower to tower, 'He is risen indeed'.

FRANCIS KILVERT

Canticle of the Sun

Dancing on Easter Morning

I am the great Sun. This hour begins
My dancing day – pirouetting in a whirl of white light
In my wide orchestral sky, a red ball bouncing
Across the eternal hills;
For now my Lord is restored: with the rising dew
He carries his own up to his glittering kingdom –
Benedicite, benedicite, benedicite omnia opera.

Look, I am one of the morning stars, shouting for joy –
And not the least honoured among those shining brothers,
O my planetary children – now that my dark daughter,
The prodigal Earth, is made an honest woman of;
Out of her gapped womb, her black and grimy tomb,
Breaks forth the Crowned, victory in his pierced hands –
Benedicite, benedicite, benedicite omnia opera.

You too, my lovers – little lark with trembling feathers,
Sing your small heart out in my streaming rays;
And you, grave narrow-browed eagle, straining your eyes
Against my wound – foretell
These fiery dales and flame-anemoned meadows
Shall be a haunt for shy contemplative spirits –
Benedicite, benedicite, benedicite omnia opera.

And now with joy I run my recurring race;
And though again I shall have to hide my face
With a hand of cloud out of the heart of schism,
Yet the time is sure when I once more shall be
A burning giant in his marriage-chamber,
A bright gold cherub, as I came from my Father's halls –
Benedicite, benedicite, benedicite omnia opera.

JOHN HEATH-STUBBS

The Sun Dances

The people say that the sun dances on this day in joy for a risen Saviour.

Old Barbara Macphie at Dreimsdale saw this once, but only once, during her long life. And the good woman, of high natural intelligence, described in poetic language and with religious fervour what she saw or believed she saw from the summit of Benmore:

'The glorious gold-bright sun was after rising on the crests of the great hills, and it was changing colour – green, purple, red, blood-red, white, intense-white, and gold-white, like the glory of the God of the elements to the children of men. It was dancing up and down in exultation at the joyous resurrection of the beloved Saviour of victory.

'To be thus privileged, a person must ascend to the top of the highest hill before sunrise, and believe that the God who makes the small blade of grass to grow is the same God who makes the large, massive sun to move.'

ALEXANDER CARMICHAEL

Easter

Rise, heart; thy Lord is risen. Sing his praise
    Without delays,
Who takes thee by the hand, that thou likewise
    With him mayst rise:
That, as his death calcined thee to dust,
His life may make thee gold, and much more just.

Awake, my lute, and struggle for thy part
    With all thy art.
The crosse taught all wood to resound his name,
    Who bore the same.
His streched sinews taught all strings, what key
Is best to celebrate this most high day.

Consort both heart and lute, and twist a song
    Pleasant and long:
Or since all musick is but three parts vied
    And multiplied;
O let thy blessed Spirit bear a part,
And make up our defects with his sweet art.

GEORGE HERBERT

April 3 ST RICHARD OF WYCH *1197–1253*

He became bishop of Chichester, and died on a preaching tour.

One of his attendants said to him: 'My Lord, your supper is but scanty today; it consists of one dish, of which I hope you will eat heartily.' Richard said: 'It is enough; one dish only is wanted at that supper.' He added: 'Do you know what I mean? This is that of which St Philip said to our Lord: "Show us the Father, and it is enough for us." May the Lord give me that dish for my supper.'

Shortly before he died, he asked for a crucifix, and receiving it with joy, kissed the marks of the five wounds, saying:

'Thanks be to thee, my Lord Jesus Christ, for all the benefits which thou hast given me, for the pains and insults which thou hast suffered for me; so great were they, that that mournful cry suited thee right well, "There is no grief like my grief".'

His voice grew weaker, but his faculties were unimpaired and he still managed to speak in broken accents to those about him. When his end was drawing near, he said: 'Lay this putrid carcass on the ground.' So when they had laid his suffering frame on the floor, he repeated over and over again: 'Lord, into thy hands I commend my spirit.'

April 7 ST NILUS OF SORA *c. 1433–1508*

Russian by birth, in his youth he visited Athos and was much influenced by Greek Hesychasts. He later became a leading member of the monastic movement known in fifteenth-century Russia as the 'Non-possessors', who preferred to live in remote hermitages rather than in large communities, and stressed the need for strict poverty, silence and inner prayer. Here are a few of his monastic precepts:

Above all, pray for the gift of tears.

We should strive to maintain our intellect in silence, free even from thoughts that seem to be good.

Listen to your heart.

Wear the poorest clothes and prefer the most menial tasks.

Regard each of the brethren as a saint.

Never leave your cell, but sit in it as in your coffin.

April 9   WILLIAM LAW   *1686–1761*

He was ordained deacon in the Church of England, but could not take the oath of allegiance to the Hanoverian dynasty and of abjuration of the Stuarts in 1714. He did not go into schism, but continued to communicate at the parish church. His writings influenced the Methodists and Evangelicals as well as the Tractarians. In a tract of 1742 he wrote:

The whole system of Christianity has generally been looked upon as a mystery of salvation solely founded on the divine pleasure; and to be such a scheme of redemption as is wholly to be resolved into the contriving of the will and wisdom of God; and therefore men can think as differently of it, can fall into as many opinions of it, as they can of the will and wisdom of God. Hence has arisen all the speculative opposition to the Gospel; it is because reason, human speculation, and conjecture, is always imagining it can form a religion more worthy of the wisdom and designs of the Supreme Being than the Christian is; and would be thought to oppose the Gospel only for the honour of God, and the divine attributes . . . Hence also has arisen another species of idolatry, even among Christians of all denominations; who, though receiving and professing the religion of the Gospel, yet worship God not in spirit and truth, but either in the deadness of an outer form, or in a pharisaical, carnal trust in their own opinions and doctrines. This body of people, whether they be clergy or laity, are but nominal Christians, because they have little more than the name of every mystery of the Gospel; historical Christians, because satisfied with the history of Gospel-salvation, literal Christians, because only looking to, and contending for, the letter of the institutions and mysteries of Jesus Christ.

April 10   ST JOHN BAPTIST DE LA SALLE   *1651–1719*

He began his work for schools in 1679, and later founded the order of Christian brothers to teach in them. His first biographer says of him:

Blessed De La Salle was rather above the middle height, and well proportioned. His constitution, weak in childhood, had grown strong from exercise and work, until mortification and excessive fatigue weakened his health. His forehead was broad, his nose straight, his eyes large and of a bluish grey, his skin was tanned by exposure and travelling, his hair, which curled and had been chestnut in his youth, was grey and white in his declining years. His countenance bore the stamp of great sweetness and dignity. His air was modest and serene, his manners were simple and gracious. An atmosphere of holiness breathed from his whole person.

April 21   ST ANSELM   *c. 1033–1109*

A native of the north of Italy, be became abbot of Bec in Normandy and then archbishop of Canterbury. His meditations and dialogues became starting points for scholastic argument on the existence of God and the work of Christ.

My flesh, what do you love? My soul, what is your desire? There it is, it is there; whatever you love, whatever you want. If beauty delights you, 'the just shall shine as the sun'. If melody is your pleasure, there the choirs of angels sing without ending to God. If any pleasure that is pure and not impure pleases you, 'God shall make them drink of the torrent of his pleasure'.

If wisdom delights you, 'the very wisdom of God will show herself to them'. If friendship, they shall love God more than themselves, and each other as themselves; and God will love them more than they love themselves, for they love him and themselves and each other through him, while he loves himself and through himself them.

What joy must there be, how great a joy, where there is such a good and such a great one. O human heart, heart full of need, heart experienced in hardships – indeed overcome by hardships – how much you would rejoice if you were to abound in all these things.

April 23   ST GEORGE   *d. 304*

He came from Lydda in Palestine and was martyred, probably at
Nicomedia, in the persecution under Diocletian. He became the patron
saint of England through pilgrimages to Jerusalem.

The Secret People

Smile at us, pay us, pass us; but do not quite forget.
For we are the people of England, that never have spoken yet.
There is many a fat farmer that drinks less cheerfully,
There is many a rich French peasant who is richer and sadder than we.
There is no folk in the world so helpless and so wise.
There is hunger in our bellies, there is laughter in our eyes;
You laugh at us and love us, both mugs and eyes are wet:
Only you do not know us, for we have not spoken yet.

We only know the last sad squires ride slowly to the sea,
And a new people takes the land; and still it is not we.
They have given us into the hand of new unhappy lords,
Lords without anger or honour, who dare not carry their swords.
They fight by shuffling papers; they have bright dead alien eyes;
They look at our labours and laughter as a tired man looks at flies.
But we are the people of England; and we have not spoken yet.
Smile at us, pay us, pass us. But do not quite forget.

G. K. CHESTERTON

Nationhood as a gift from God

In recent times it has been fashionable to talk of the levelling out of nations,
of the disappearance of different races in the melting-pot of contemporary
civilization. I do not agree with this opinion . . . The disappearance of
nations would have impoverished us no less than if all men had become
alike, with one personality and one face. Nations are the wealth of
mankind, its collective personalities; the very least of them wears its own
special colours and bears within itself a special facet of divine intention.

ALEXANDER SOLZHENITSYN

In Dostoevsky's words: 'A nation is not a collection of different beings, it is an organized being and moreover a *moral personality*.'

Personalities are not just *individual*, but also *national*. This concept in particular is symbolized in the events of Pentecost, when the Holy Ghost descended on the apostles and they were endowed with the gift of speaking in *different tongues*. The Christian Church was not born in a single world language but in the *different tongues* of the apostles, reaffirming the plurality of national paths to a single goal.

If the *nation* is a corporate personality endowed with its being by God, then it cannot be defined as a 'historical community of people' or a 'force of nature and history' (Vladimir Soloviev). The nation is a level in the hierarchy of the Christian cosmos, a part of God's immutable purpose. Nations are not created by a people's history. Rather, the nation's personality realizes itself through that history or, to put it another way, the people in their history fulfil God's design for them.

VADIM BORISOV

The paradox in patriotism

There is an ethical paradox in patriotism which defies every but the most astute and sophisticated analysis. The paradox is that patriotism transmutes individual unselfishness into national egoism. Loyalty to the nation is a high form of altruism when compared with lesser loyalties and more parochial interests. It therefore becomes the vehicle of all the altruistic impulses and expresses itself, on occasion, with such fervour that the critical attitude of the individual towards the nation and its enterprises is almost completely destroyed.

Unquestionably there is an alloy of projected self-interest in patriotic altruism. The man in the street, with his lust for power and prestige thwarted by his own limitations and the necessities of social life, projects his ego upon his nation and indulges his anarchic lusts vicariously. So the nation is at one and the same time a check upon, and a final vent for, the expression of individual egoism.

REINHOLD NIEBUHR

April 25 ST MARK

Eutychius of Alexandria gives this account of the foundation of his church:

In the ninth year of Claudius Caesar, Mark the Evangelist was in the city of Alexandria, inviting people to believe in Christ. As he walked about the streets the strap of his sandal broke, and he took it for repair to a cobbler called Hanania, who pierced his finger with his needle as he held it to run it into the sandal. The blood flowed copiously, and in severe pain he began to curse under his breath in front of Mark, who said to him: 'If you believe in Jesus Christ the Son of God, your finger will be healed.'

He took hold of it and said: 'In the name of Jesus Christ let this finger be healed.'

Immediately the flow of blood stopped and the finger was healed. From that moment Hanania believed in Christ. He was the first of the patriarchs who presided over the church of Alexandria.

April 29 ST CATHERINE OF SIENA *c. 1347–1380*

She belonged to an influential family in the city. As a Dominican of the third order, living in the world, she came to exercise a spiritual ministry with political implications. She wrote in her revelations on *The Three Heights of Perfection*:

There yet remains the third, where you shall use your utmost endeavour to attain such a disposition of spirit that you may become one with Me, and that your will may become so utterly assimilated and conformed to my all-perfect will, that not only shall you never desire what is evil, but you shall not even desire what is good, if it be not according to my will; so that whatever befall you in the miseries of this life, from whatever direction it may come, whether in temporal or in spiritual matters, nothing shall ever disturb your peace or trouble your quietness of spirit; but you shall be established in a firm belief that I, your Almighty God, love you with a dearer love and take more watchful care of you than you can for yourself.

And the more perfectly you abandon and resign yourself to me, the more I will console you with my grace and make you feel my presence. But you will never reach this measure of perfection except by a firm, constant and absolute denial of self-will.

May

The Woodland Mass

A pleasant place I was at today,
under mantles of the worthy green hazel,
listening at day's beginning
to the skilful cock thrush
singing a splendid stanza
of fluent signs and symbols;
a stranger here, wisdom his nature,
a brown messenger who had journeyed far,
coming from rich Carmarthenshire
at my golden girl's command.
About him was a setting
of flowers of the sweet boughs of May,
like green mantles, his chasuble
was of the wings of the wind.
There was here, by the great God,
nothing but gold in the altar's canopy.
I heard, in polished language,
a long and faultless chanting,
an unhesitant reading to the people
of a gospel without mumbling;
the elevation, on the hill for us there,
of a good leaf for a holy wafer.
Then the slim eloquent nightingale
from the corner of a grove nearby,
poetess of the valley, sings to the many
the Sanctus bell in lively whistling.
The sacrifice is raised
up to the sky above the bush,
devotion to God the Father,
the chalice of ecstasy and love.
The psalmody contents me;
it was bred of a birch-grove in the sweet woods.

DAFYDD AP GWILYM

THE ASCENSION

The ascension of Christ is his liberation from all restrictions of time and space. It does not represent his removal from the earth, but his constant presence everywhere on earth.

During his earthly ministry he could only be in one place at a time. If he was in Jerusalem he was not in Capernaum; if he was in Capernaum he was not in Jerusalem. But now he is united with God, he is present wherever God is present; and that is everywhere. Because he is in heaven, he is everywhere on earth; because he is ascended, he is here now. In the person of the Holy Spirit he dwells in his Church, and issues forth from the deepest depths of the souls of his disciples, to bear witness to his sovereignty.

WILLIAM TEMPLE

Jesus does not return to his Father in isolation. It was the incorporeal Logos that descended among men. But today it is the Word made flesh, at the same time true God and true man, that enters the Kingdom of heaven. Jesus takes there with him the human nature in which he is clothed. He opens the gates of the Kingdom to humanity. We take possession, in some way by anticipation, of the blessings which are offered to us and possible for us. Places are reserved for us in the Kingdom provided we continue faithful. Our presence is desired and awaited there.

So the ascension renders the thought of heaven more present and more alive for us. Do we think enough of our permanent dwelling-place? For most Christians heaven is envisaged as a kind of postscript, an appendix to a book of which life on earth constitutes the actual text. But the contrary is true. Our earthly life is merely the preface to the book. Life in heaven will be the text – a text without end.

A MONK OF THE EASTERN CHURCH

PENTECOST

The gift of the Spirit as an eschatological reality

People hardly know the Holy Spirit as a person, and then only in an incomplete, dim and confused fashion. It cannot be otherwise. For a full knowledge of the Holy Spirit would make all created being entirely spirit-bearing, entirely deified, and would confer a completely realized illumination. Then history would be ended; then the fullness of time would be at hand, and all waiting would be over; then there would indeed be no more time.

But as long as history continues, only instants of illumination by the Spirit are possible; only certain individuals at certain moments know the Paraclete, when they are raised above time into eternity.

Certainly, the Holy Spirit is indeed at work in the Church. But knowledge of the Spirit has always been a pledge or reward – at special moments and with exceptional people; and this is how it will be until 'all is fulfilled'. That is why, when reading the Church's writings, we cannot fail to be struck by something that seems strange at first but that later, in the light of what precedes, manifests its inner necessity. It is this: that all the holy fathers and mystical philosophers speak of the importance of the idea of the Spirit in the Christian world-view, but hardly any of them explains himself precisely and exactly. It is evident that the holy fathers know *something*; but what is even clearer is that this knowledge is so intimate, so hidden, without echo, ineffable, that they lack the power to express it in precise language.

Even Athanasius does not make clear the meaning of the 'procession' (*ekporevsis*) of the Spirit, as distinct from the 'begottenness' (*gennesis*) of the Son. Of the three personal characteristics of the divine hypostases, 'unbegottenness', 'begottenness', 'procession', the first two are spiritually understandable, whereas the third represents only the sign of a certain spiritual experience that is still to come.

But the closer we draw to the End of History, the more do new, hitherto invisible roseate rays of the coming Day without evening appear on the domes of the holy Church.

Our characteristic attitude towards the Holy Spirit, it seems to me, is precisely one of expectation, of hope; a gentle and reconciling hope.

FATHER PAUL FLORENSKY

Veni, Creator Spiritus

Creator spirit, by whose aid
The world's foundations first were laid,
Come visit every pious mind;
Come pour thy joys on human kind;
From sin and sorrow set us free,
And make thy temples worthy thee.

O source of uncreated light,
The Father's promised Paraclete!
Thrice holy fount, thrice holy fire,
Our hearts with heavenly love inspire;
Come, and thy sacred unction bring
To sanctify us, while we sing.

Plenteous of grace, descend from high,
Rich in thy sevenfold energy!
Thou strength of his Almighty hand,
Whose power does heaven and earth command.
Proceeding spirit, our defence,
Who do'st the gift of tongues dispense,
And crown'st thy gift with eloquence.

Refine and purge our earthly parts;
But, O, inflame and fire our hearts!
Our frailties help, our vice controul,
Submit the senses to the soul;
And, when rebellious they are grown,
Then lay thy hand, and hold them down.

Chace from our minds the infernal foe;
And peace, the fruit of love, bestow;
And, lest our feet should step astray,
Protect and guide us in the way.

Make us eternal truths receive,
And practise all that we believe;
Give us thyself, that we may see
The Father, and the Son, by thee.

Immortal honour, endless fame,
Attend the Almighty Father's name;
The Saviour Son be glorified,
Who for lost man's redemption died;
And equal adoration be,
Eternal Paraclete, to thee.

JOHN DRYDEN

Consider secondly, that the Holy Ghost came down upon the Apostles, in the shape of *tongues*, to signify that he came to make them fit preachers of his word; and to endow them with the gift of *tongues*, accompanied with heavenly wisdom, and understanding, of the mysteries of God, and all the gospel truths; to the end that they might be enabled to teach and publish, throughout the whole world, the faith and law of Christ. And these *tongues* were *of fire*, to signify how this divine Spirit sets those souls on fire, in which he abides; enflaming them with divine love; consuming the dross of their earthly affections; putting them in a continual motion of earnest desires and endeavours, to go forward from virtue to virtue, as fire is always in motion; and carrying them upwards towards the God of gods in his heavenly Son; as the flame is always ascending upwards towards its element. O blessed fire, when shall I partake of thy sacred flames? O come and take possession of my heart; consume all these bonds that tie it to the earth; and carry it up with thee, towards the heavenly furnace, from whence thou comest. Sweet Jesus, thou hast said (Luke 12.49): *I am come to cast fire on the earth; and what will I but that it be kindled?* O cast this fire into my soul, that it may be kindled there!

RICHARD CHALLONER

Prayer to the Holy Ghost

O holy God behind the silent stone
Beneath the under and the elder fire,
Beyond the Milky Way, within the bone,
The grace desired and grace of our desire.

The night is spent; the day is near at hand.
We who have wrestled lonely with the flesh
Listen in solitude for your command,
Our fingers on the curtains, in the mesh

Of cords and concepts which your glory hide.
Come whom no word of ours can symbolize.
Let wiring of your word in us abide.
Light us in every dark and make us wise,

Wise that through all the night our souls may see
The Father and the Son alive in thee.

GEORGE EVERY

We find in the Spirit unity and plurality at the same time. There is plurality in that unity and unity in that plurality. There is no uniformity. It is the fullness of the Father, of the Son and of the Spirit. Let us look at that image, that oneness in plurality. In a way we could say about God that he has to be three to be God. This image of the Trinity can be a sort of guideline in our ecumenical striving to obtain, by the grace of God, but also by working and praying together, that visible unity of love shining forth among us. 'Oh Lord, pray for us, because we so strongly need someone to be our go-between, to bring us from this level of coexistence to a new stage of communion.'

LEON-JOSEPH, CARDINAL SUENENS

A Prayer for those in Hell

On this final and saving festival thou art pleased to accept propitiatory prayers for those imprisoned in hell, granting us great hopes that thou wilt send down relaxation and refreshment to all held fast in bitter bondage. Hear us who humbly and piteously beseech thee: and to the souls of thy servants who have fallen asleep before us, grant rest in a place of light, a place of green pasture, a place of refreshment, whence all pain, sorrow and sighing have fled away; make their spirits to dwell where the righteous rest, and grant them peace and pardon.

For thine in very truth, O Master and Maker of all, is the great mystery both of the temporary dissolution of thy creatures, and of their subsequent restoration and repose unto all ages. We thank thee for thy grace in all things: for our entry into this world and our departure from it, and for the hopes that we enjoy of resurrection and eternal life, pledged to us by thine own infallible promise, which shall be our portion at thy second coming. For thou art the precursor of our resurrection, the impartial and compassionate judge of all who have lived, the Master and Lord who gives us our reward.

VESPERS OF PENTECOST IN THE ORTHODOX CHURCH

THE HOLY TRINITY

Progressive revelation

The Old Testament preached the Father clearly, but the Son only in an obscure manner. The New Testament revealed the Son, but did no more than hint at the godhead of the Holy Spirit. Today the Spirit dwells among us, manifesting himself to us more and more clearly. For it was not safe, when the divinity of the Father had not yet been acknowledged, plainly to proclaim the Son; nor, when that of the Son had not yet been accepted, to burden us further – if I may use a somewhat bold expression – with the Holy Spirit.

So, by gradual additions and ascents, advancing from glory to glory, the splendour of the Holy Trinity shines upon the more enlightened. You see illuminations breaking upon us gradually; while the order of theology, which it is better for us to observe, prevents us both from proclaiming everything at once and from keeping it all hidden to the end.

ST GREGORY OF NAZIANZUS

Sun, light and heat

One of the comparisons or likenesses I am speaking of is taken from the most glorious object which our eyes see, the sun. That ball of light and heat, which we call most properly the Sun, may be compared to the Father, from whom both the Word and the Spirit come. From this sun the light issues, and is as it were a part of it, and yet comes down to our earth and gives light to us. This we may compare to the Word, who came forth from the Father, and came down on earth, and was made man, and who, as St John tells us, is 'the true light, which lighteth every man that cometh into the world'. But beside this there is the heat, which is a different thing from the light: for we all know, there may be heat without light: and so may there be light – moonlight for example, and starlight – without any perceivable heat. Yet the two are blended and united in the sun; so that the same rays, which bring us light to enlighten us, bring us heat also to warm us, and to ripen the fruits and herbs of all kinds which the earth bears. This heat of the sun may not unfitly be compared to the Holy Spirit, the Lord and Giver of life, as the Creed calls him, for heat is the great fosterer of life: as we see, for example, in an egg. As that is hatched by the warmth of the parent bird, sitting on it lovingly, and brooding over it, until it is quickened into life; just so does the Holy Spirit of God brood with more than dove-like patience over the heart of the believer, giving it life and warmth; and though he be driven away again and again by our backslidings, he still hovers round our hearts, desiring to return to them, and to dwell in them, and cherish them for ever. Moreover, if any seed of the Word has begun to spring up in any heart, the Spirit descends like a sunbeam upon it, and ripens the ear, and brings the fruit to perfection. Thus have we first the sun in the sky, secondly, the light, which issues from the sun, and thirdly, the heat, which accompanies the light – three separate and distinguishable things; yet distinct as they are, what can be more united than the sun and its rays, or than the light and heat which those rays shed abroad?

AUGUSTUS WILLIAM HARE

Mutual relationship

First of all let me state what we all instinctively recognize as established in practice by day-to-day experience. It is plain that in a plurality of persons the nearer is their relationship, the closer is their union with one another, and the more intimate their unity, the greater is their joy. Who then would dare to contend or to take for granted that in the fullness of supreme felicity there is absent what is known to be a great source of joy, and something else is there that works the other way?

What, I ask, seems to you the more beautiful, the more suitable sort of plurality? One where distinction comes through an ordered variety of properties, and is drawn into one by some delicate pattern of proportions in a marvellous way, or another where there is no reconciliation of differences and the connection is between a series of concords in succession, not brought into order by any arrangement of their distinctions? No one, I think, could suppose that the fairer could be lacking to the supreme beauty, while the less fair is in it. And so it is needful to believe that neither is the most joyous relationship of the persons lacking in the supreme felicity, nor can the most ordered variety of properties be lacking in the supreme beauty.

RICHARD OF ST VICTOR

Diversity in unity

Paradoxically, the One moves from itself into the Three and yet remains One, while the Three return to the One and yet remain Three.

The single divinity of the Trinity is undivided and the three Persons of the one divinity are unconfused.

We confess Unity in Trinity and Trinity in Unity, divided yet without division and united yet with distinctions.

ST THALASSIUS THE LIBYAN

Wholly one and wholly three

God is one because there is one divinity: unoriginate, simple, beyond being, without parts, indivisible. The divinity is both Unity and Trinity—wholly one and wholly three. It is wholly one in respect of the essence, wholly three in respect of the hypostases or persons. For the divinity is Father, Son and Holy Spirit, and is in Father, Son and Holy Spirit. The whole divinity is in the whole Father, and the whole Father is in the whole divinity. The whole divinity is in the whole Son, and the whole Son is in the whole divinity. The whole divinity is in the whole Holy Spirit, and the whole Holy Spirit is in the whole divinity. For the divinity is not partially in the Father, nor is the Father part of God; and so likewise with the other two persons. For the divinity is not divisible; nor is the Father, or the Son, or the Holy Spirit incomplete God. On the contrary, the whole and complete divinity is completely in the complete Father; and so likewise with the other two persons. The whole Father dwells completely in the whole Son and Spirit; and they in their turn dwell completely in the Father and in each other. In this way Father, Son and Holy Spirit are one God. The essence, power and energy of Father, Son and Spirit are one, for none of the three persons either exists or is intelligible without the other two.

ST MAXIMUS THE CONFESSOR

Truths which ought to be hidden

The errors of heretics and blasphemers force us to deal with unlawful matters, to scale perilous heights, to speak unutterable words, to trespass on forbidden ground. Faith ought in silence to fulfil the commandments, worshipping the Father, reverencing with him the Son, abounding in the Holy Spirit. The error of others compels us to err in daring to embody in human terms truths which ought to be hidden in the silent veneration of the heart.

ST HILARY OF POITIERS

I glorify the Holy Father,
I honour the Holy Son,
I sing the praises of the Holy Spirit:
Simple Trinity, one in essence.
Each person is God: three lights,
Yet one light coming from a single sun.

The Trinity supreme in Godhead
Is by essence an undivided unity:
　　single in nature, yet distinguished in persons;
　　indivisible, yet divided;
　　one, yet three:
Father, Son and Spirit of life,
Together guarding all things.

O simple and undivided Trinity, one consubstantial nature:
Thou art praised as light and lights, one holy and three holies.
Sing, O my soul, and glorify
Life and lives, the God of all.

ORTHODOX HYMNS TO THE TRINITY

THE MAY MAGNIFICAT

May is Mary's month, and I
Muse at that and wonder why:
　　Her feasts follow reason,
　　Dated due to season –

Candlemas, Lady Day;
But the Lady Month, May,
　　Why fasten that upon her,
　　With a feasting in her honour?

Is it only its being brighter
Than the most are must delight her?
　　Is it opportunest
　　And flowers finds soonest?

Ask of her, the mighty mother:
Her reply puts this other
    Question: What is Spring? –
    Growth in everything –

Flesh and fleece, fur and feather,
Grass and greenworld all together;
    Star-eyed strawberry-breasted
    Throstle above her nested

Cluster of bugle blue eggs thin
Forms and warms the life within;
    And bird and blossom swell
    In sod or sheath or shell.

All things rising, all things sizing
Mary sees, sympathizing
    With that world of good,
    Nature's motherhood.

Their magnifying of each its kind
With delight calls to mind
    How she did in her stored
    Magnify the Lord.

Well but there was more than this:
Spring's universal bliss
    Much, had much to say
    To offering Mary May.

When drop-of-blood-and-foam-dapple
Bloom lights the orchard-apple
    And thicket and thorp are merry
    With silver-surfèd cherry.

GERARD MANLEY HOPKINS

May 1 ST PHILIP AND ST JAMES

'Jesus said to him, "Have I been with you so long, and yet you do not know me, Philip? He who has seen me has seen the Father"' (John 14.9).

When Plato says that it is 'difficult to see the Maker and Father of the universe', we Christians agree with him. And yet he can be seen; for it is written, 'Blessed are the pure in heart, for they shall see God' (Matt. 5.8). Moreover, he who is the image of the invisible God has said, 'He who has seen me has seen the Father.'

No one of intelligence would claim that Jesus was here referring merely to his physical body which was visible to everyone. No: he meant that he is the only-begotten divine Son of God, the 'first-born of all creation' (Col. 1.15), the Word made flesh; and so anyone who sees the image of the invisible God will in this way come to know the Maker and Father of the universe.

ORIGEN

The life of God, the ultimate Word of Love in which all things cohere, is bodied forth completely, unconditionally and without reserve in the life of a man – the man for others and the man for God. He is perfect man and perfect God – not as a mixture of oil and water, of natural and supernatural – but as the embodiment through obedience of 'the beyond in our midst', of the transcendence of love.

J. A. T. ROBINSON

May 1   ST JOSEPH THE WORKER

Since the care of Jesus was, by the eternal wisdom, left to a humble tradesman, have not all here of that degree a great instruction that sanctity and perfection is not to be thought the property of ecclesiasticks and Religious, but that their condition also is capable of it, and that in the New Law, it is expected of them. In this they see, the daily toil of a laborious life is no exclusion to Jesus, but that he may dwell in the midst of them, while with the sweat of their brows they are working for bread and the provision of their families.

'Tis true, they have not that opportunity for frequent prayer; but they may pray still. They ought to begin the day with prayers; so to consecrate their labours and themselves to God. Other prayers they may say, even at their work, by raising up their hands to God in short ejaculations, asking for mercy, grace and protection from sin. This may be done in shops, in the field, in the kitchen, with the needle, broom or hammer in the hand; there being scarce any exercise of corporal labour but where the mind has liberty of raising itself above the employment of the hands.

JOHN GOTER

May 2   ST ATHANASIUS THE GREAT   *c. 296–373*

Archbishop of Alexandria for forty-five years, he defended the full divinity of Christ against the Arians, who regarded our Lord as less than true and perfect God. He also played a decisive part in the growth of Egyptian monasticism (see January 17: St Antony of Egypt). The following extract is taken from his best-known work, *On the Incarnation of the Word*.

Through death immortality has come to all, and through the incarnation of the Word God's universal providence has been made known, together with him who is the giver and artificer of this providence, God the Word himself. For he became man that we might be made god; and he revealed himself through a body that we might receive an idea of the unseen Father; and he endured humiliation at men's hands that we might inherit incorruption. In himself he was in no way injured, for he is impassible and incorruptible, the very Word and God; but he endured these things for the sake of suffering men, and through his own impassibility he preserved and saved them. In short, the victories achieved by the Saviour through his incarnation are so great and so many that, if one wished to describe them, it would be like gazing across the open sea and trying to count the waves.

May 8 ST ARSENIUS THE GREAT *c. 354–449*

Born in Rome, well-educated and of senatorial rank, he was at first tutor to the children of the Emperor Theodosius I. In 394 he left the palace secretly, to become a monk in Egypt, where he was renowned for his austerity, silence and intense prayer. The following stories come from the *Sayings of the Desert Fathers*.

While still living in the palace, Abba Arsenius prayed to God: 'Lord, lead me in the way of salvation.' And a voice came to him, saying: 'Arsenius, flee from men, and you will be saved.' After withdrawing into the solitary life he made the same prayer again, and he heard a voice saying to him: 'Arsenius, flee, keep silent, be still; for these are the roots of sinlessness.'

Abba Mark said to Abba Arsenius, 'Why do you flee from us?' The old man said to him, 'God knows that I love you; but I cannot be both with God and with men. The thousands and ten thousands of the heavenly hosts have one single will, but men have many. So I cannot leave God to be with men.'

Abba Arsenius used to say that one hour's sleep is enough for a monk if he is a fighter.

A brother came to the cell of Abba Arsenius at Scetis. Looking through the window he saw the old man entirely as a flame; for the brother was worthy to see this. When he knocked, the old man came out and saw the brother standing bewildered. 'Have you been knocking for long?' Arsenius asked him. 'You didn't see anything here, did you?' 'No,' said the brother. And, after talking to him, Arsenius sent him away.

They also said of him that on Saturday evening, preparing for the start of Sunday, he turned his back on the setting sun and lifted his hands to heaven in prayer; and so he remained until the rising sun shone in his face. Then he sat down.

Once a senator's will was brought to Abba Arsenius, leaving him a great inheritance. But he refused to accept it, saying, 'I died before he did.'

May 8 DAME JULIAN *1342–1418*

> She lived for more than forty years in a cell attached to the church of St Julian and St Edward at Conisford in Norwich.

And thus I saw full surely that it is ready to us, and more easy to come to the knowing of God than to know our own soul. For our soul is so deep-grounded in God, and so endlessly treasured, that we may not come to the knowing thereof, till we have first knowing of God; who is the maker to whom it is owed. But notwithstanding, I saw that we have of our natural fullness, the desire wisely and truly to know our own soul, whereby we be learned to seek it where it is, and that is into God. And thus by the gracious leading of the Holy Ghost we shall know them both in one. Whether we be stirred to know God or our soul, both stirrings are good and true. God is more near to us than our own soul; for he is ground in whom our soul standeth, and he is the mean that keepeth the substance and sensuality together, so that it never shall depart: for our soul sitteth in God in very rest, and our soul standeth in God in sure strength: and our soul is kindly rooted in God in endless love. And therefore if we will have knowing of our soul, and communing and dalliance therewith, it behoveth us to seek into our Lord God, in whom it is inclosed.

May 14 ST MATTHIAS THE APOSTLE

Of the divine lot that fell miraculously on Matthias some say one thing and some another, not very well in my judgement. Let me have my say. The words seem to me to mean that the divine lot is a gift, showing to the choir of hierarchs who it was who had been chosen by divine election. So indeed a good bishop should never confer holy orders on his own motion.

THE ECCLESIASTICAL HIERARCHY OF DIONYSIUS

May 20 ST BERNARDINE OF SIENA *1380–1444*

> He was a leader in the Observantine reform of the Franciscan Order and at
> one time Provincial of the Observantines in his part of Italy. Preaching on St
> John 11.41, 'Jesus raised his eyes to heaven', he said:

By this action Christ our Master teaches us how in prayer we ought to use
gestures by which the mind may be moved and uplifted, as we raise our
eyes above, and join our hands, and bend our knees, using outward actions.
Not that these outward signs make our prayer more effectual with God, for
God is a searcher of hearts and he is not moved by outward signs. But these
actions are done, or ought to be done, so that you may know that body and
soul are united in prayer: for through the outer outward actions the body is
conformed to the soul; and also that you, on your side, ought to help
yourself to the utmost of your power; and then God will help you too. For
he inspires you, and you ought to recognize his inspirations, and help
yourself by following them; and you ought not to pray for yourself only,
but for others also.

May 21 ST HELENA *c. 255–c. 330*

> The mother of Constantine, the first Roman emperor to be a Christian. In
> great old age she visited the Holy Land and founded basilicas; and,
> according to later tradition, discovered the cross on which our Lord was
> crucified. According to medieval belief Helen was an English girl. This
> extract comes from a novel by Evelyn Waugh, based on these traditions. She
> has discovered the cross and now reflects on her destiny:

Meanwhile the beacons blazed news of the discovery to the capital and
post-horsemen carried it throughout Christendom. Te Deums were sung
in the imperial basilicas. No one who watched that day, while the Empress
calmly divided her treasure, could have discerned her joy. Her work was
finished. She had done what only the saints succeed in doing; what indeed
constitutes their patent of sanctity. She had completely conformed to the
will of God. Others a few years back had done their duty gloriously in the
arena. Hers was a gentler task, merely to gather wood. That was the
particular, humble purpose for which she had been created. And now it
was done. So with her precious cargo she sailed joyfully away.

John Wesley travelled over 8,000 miles a year on horseback, preaching innumerable sermons. His brother Charles wrote over 5,500 hymns and is the most gifted and indefatigable hymn-writer that England has known.

Wrestling Jacob

Come, O thou Traveler unknown
   Whom still I hold, but cannot see!
My company before is gone,
   And I am left alone with thee;
With thee all night I mean to stay,
And wrestle till the break of day.

I need not tell thee who I am,
   My misery or sin declare,
Thyself hast called me by my name,
   Look on thy hands, and read it there.
But who, I ask thee, who art thou?
Tell me thy name, and tell me now.

In vain thou strugglest to get free,
   I never will unloose my hold:
Art thou the Man that died for me?
   The secret of thy love unfold.
Wrestling I will not let thee go,
Till I thy name, thy nature know.

Yield to me now – for I am weak,
   But confident in self-despair!
Speak to my heart, in blessings speak,
   Be conquered by my instant prayer,
Speak, or thou never hence shalt move,
And tell me if the name is *Love*.

'Tis Love, 'tis Love! Thou died'st for me,
   I hear thy whisper in my heart.
The morning breaks, the shadows flee,
   Pure Universal Love thou art:
To me, to all, thy bowels move –
Thy nature, and thy name, is Love.

CHARLES WESLEY

May 25 THE VENERABLE BEDE *673–735*

The death of the great theologian and historian of the English people is thus described in a letter from Cuthbert to Cuthwin:

In those days he had two other works in hand, besides his lectures to us and the chanting of the psalms. He turned into English, for the use of the Church, the Gospel of St John, up to the place where it is written: '*sed haec quid inter tantos?*' ('what are they among so many?'), and some extracts from Isidore's notes, saying: 'I would not have it that my disciples read what is false, or go on with this unprofitably after my death.'

On the Tuesday before the Ascension he began to be more seriously short of breath, and a small abscess developed on his foot. All that day he cheerfully went on dictating, and among other remarks he said: 'Hurry up, for I don't know how long I shall be here, and whether my Maker will soon take me away.' It seemed to us that he knew well when his end would be. He passed the night watching in thanksgiving, and when the morning came on Wednesday, he told us to write diligently, and so we did until nine.

At nine we went in procession with the relics of the saints, as the custom of that day is. One of us stayed with him and said to him: 'Dear master, there is one chapter left to be done; is it too much trouble if I ask you questions again?' He said: 'It is no trouble. Take your reed and write quickly.' He did it. At the ninth hour he said to me: 'I have some valuables in my chest, some pepper, and boats of incense. Run quickly and get the priests of our monastery here, that I may give out to them the little gifts that God has given to me.' He passed the rest of the day joyfully until evening, when the boy beside him said: 'There is still one more sentence, beloved master, to be written.' 'Write,' he said, 'quickly.' After a little while the boy said: 'Now the sentence is written.' 'Good,' said Bede, 'you have spoken truth. It is finished. Take my head in your hands. It would please me much to sit opposite the place where I used to pray, so that I can speak to my Father sitting up.' And so, chanting 'Glory be to the Father . . .', as he reached the name of the Holy Spirit, he let the last of his spirit out of his body.

May 26 ST PHILIP NERI *1515–1595*

He founded the Oratory, a congregation of priests with a mission to the cultivated classes. His first foundation was in Rome, but others were made in France in the seventeenth century and in the nineteenth century by Newman in Birmingham and Faber in London.

He wrote to Monsignor Mercati on 3 May 1591:

Your letter gave me more than one cause to rejoice. I was so glad to hear that you not only arrived there safely, but that the journey, instead of fatiguing you, has brought on an improvement in your health, thus fulfilling one of my most ardent desires at the present moment. The other cause for rejoicing is that there is not only a beginning of improvement, according to what you say, but that your health is daily progressing, for which I thank the Lord, hoping that you may regain your former health, thanks to the delightful air, and the satisfaction that will help you to consolidate the whole. Moreover, the rock from which you enjoy the view of gardens, forests, apple orchards, and other beauties, is to be also a source of happiness, as I rejoice and share your contentment in the present moment, whatever it may be.

May 30 VISITATION OF THE BLESSED VIRGIN

In this account from the *Protevangelion of James* Elizabeth and Mary are both living near the temple in Jerusalem. The blessed Virgin is spinning purple and scarlet thread for the veil of the temple when she is interrupted for the annunciation. She continues, and brings the thread to the priest.

He blessed her and said: 'Mary, the Lord God has magnified your name, and you will be blessed in all generations on earth.'

Full of joy, Mary went to Elizabeth her kinswoman, and knocked at the door. Elizabeth heard her and dropped her sieve as she ran to open the door. When she saw Mary she blessed her, saying: 'Whence is this for me, that the mother of my Lord should come to me; for behold what is in me leaped and blessed you.'

June

THE CHURCH

What the soul is in a body . . .

Christians are not distinguished from the rest of mankind in locality or in speech or customs. But while they dwell in the cities of Greeks and barbarians, and follow the native customs in dress and food, yet the constitution of their own citizenship is marvellous, and contradicts expectation. They dwell in their countries, but only as sojourners; they bear their share as citizens, and they endure all hardships as strangers. Every foreign country is their fatherland, and every fatherland foreign. They marry like other men and beget children; but they do not expose their offspring. They have their meals, but not their wives in common. They are in the flesh, but do not live after the flesh. Their existence is on earth, their citizenship in heaven. They obey the laws and surpass them in their lives. They love all men and are persecuted by all. They are ignored and condemned, put to death and endowed with life. They are beggars, who make many rich, in want of everything and abounding in everything. They are dishonoured and in their dishonour glorified. They are abused and vindicated. Reviled, they bless; insulted, they pay their respects. They are punished for doing good, and rejoice in this, as thereby quickened to life. The Jews wage war with them as aliens, while the Greeks persecute them, and yet those who hate them cannot tell the reason of their hostility to them.

In a word, what the soul is in a body, this the Christians are in the world. The invisible soul is guarded in the visible body: so Christians are recognized in the world, and yet their religion remains invisible. The flesh hates the soul and goes to war with it, although it receives no wrong, because it is forbidden to indulge in pleasures; so the world hates Christians, although it receives no wrong from them, because they set themselves against its pleasures.

The soul is enclosed in the body, and yet holds the body together; so Christians are in the world as in a prison, and yet they themselves hold the world together.

EPISTLE TO DIOGNETUS

181

Members one of another

'And when one member suffers, all the members suffer with it' (1 Cor. 12.26): this is said of the Church. If we do not feel this, we are not within the Church.

Holiness and knowledge are given by the spirit of *sobornost*.[1] Ignorance and sin are the characteristics of isolated individuals. Only in the unity of the Church do we find these defects overcome. Man finds his true self in the Church alone: not in the helplessness of spiritual isolation but in the strength of his communion with his brothers and with his Saviour. The Church is a living organism, integrated by common love, forming an absolute unity in Christ of the living and the dead.

FATHER ALEXANDER ELCHANINOV

[1] The Russian term for 'catholicity', signifying above all the unity of many persons in the one Body of Christ, harmony without loss of individual freedom, the attainment of a 'common mind'.

The meaning of 'Catholic'

Now we may form a clearer notion than is commonly taken of the one Church Catholic which is in all lands. Properly it is not on earth, except so far as heaven can be said to be on earth, or as the dead are still with us. It is not on earth, except in such sense as Christ or his Spirit are on the earth. I mean it is not locally or visibly on earth. The Church is not in time or place, but in the region of spirits; it is in the Holy Ghost; and as the soul of man is in every part of his body, yet in no part, not here nor there, yet everywhere; not in any one part, head or heart, hands or feet, so as not to be in every other; so also the heavenly Jerusalem, the mother of our new birth, is in all lands at once, fully and entirely, as a spirit; in the East and in the West, in the North and in the South – that is, wherever her outward instruments are to be found. The ministry and sacraments, the bodily presence of bishop and people, are given us as keys and spells, by which we bring ourselves into the presence of the great company of saints; they are but the outskirts of it; they are but porches to the pool of Bethesda, entrances into that which is indivisible and one. Baptism admits, not into a mere visible society, varying with the country in which it is administered, Roman here, and Greek there, and English there, but through the English or the Greek or the Roman porch into the one invisible company of elect souls, which is independent of time and place, and untinctured with the imperfections or errors of that visible porch by which entrance is made.

JOHN HENRY NEWMAN

Although the Church is diverse in the multiplicity of her members, she is nevertheless welded into one by the fire of the Holy Spirit. If she seems divided into parts across bodily space the sacrament of her interior unity is none the less too strong for her own integrity to be disrupted, for 'the love of God is spread abroad in our hearts by the Holy Spirit given to us'. This Holy Spirit is indubitably one and multiple, one in the essence of his majesty, multiple in the diversity of his gifts of grace, given by him to fill the holy Church, that she may be one in her universality, and whole in all her members. This secret of indivisible unity the Word of Truth commended, when he said to his Father about his disciples: 'I do not pray for these alone, but for all who shall believe in me through their word, that they all may be one, as you, Father, are in me and I in you, that they also may be one in us, that the world may believe that you sent me.'

If believers in Christ are one, wherever one member seems to be to the natural eye, there indeed is the whole body by the sacramental mystery. Whatever belongs to the whole in some way seems to fit in with any part. Therefore what the Church sings together, her members say for themselves, and this is in no way absurd, and what properly belongs to one man's part is recited by many without giving offence. So when we are in chapel we all say, 'Incline your ear, Lord, and hear me, for I am poor and in misery'; and when we are on our own we properly sing, 'Exult in the Lord our helper; rejoice for the God of Jacob.'

ST PETER DAMIANI

I knew a man who longed so intensely for the salvation of his brethren, that with scalding tears and with his whole heart he often implored God, who is full of love for mankind, that either they might be saved with him or he might be condemned with them, for he refused absolutely to be saved alone. He was so bound to them spiritually by a holy love in the Holy Spirit that he would have preferred not to enter the Kingdom of heaven itself if it meant being separated from them.

ST SYMEON THE NEW THEOLOGIAN

Responsible for everyone and everything

There is only one way of salvation, and that is to make yourself responsible for all men's sins. As soon as you make yourself responsible in all sincerity for everyone and everything, you will see at once that it is really so, and that you are in fact to blame for everyone and for all things.

Remember especially that you cannot be a judge of anyone. For no one can judge a criminal, until he recognizes that he himself is just such a criminal as the man standing before him, and that perhaps he is more to blame than anyone else for the crime which the man on trial has committed. When he understands that, he will be able to act as a judge. That may sound absurd, but is in fact true. For if I had been righteous myself, perhaps there would have been no criminal standing before me.

FYODOR DOSTOEVSKY
'The Discourses of Father Zossima'

Tradition

One day the abbot took me to see the monastery library. It was not a very large collection of books. There were a lot of elderly, well-used volumes of the Fathers. 'Here', said the abbot, 'is a book which you give to beginners.' 'This is a work which is useful for someone who is depressed.' 'Here is a book which will give very clear instructions about the Jesus Prayer.' Any Westerner showing you round this collection of books, even someone to whom they were of practical use, would have said: 'Here is an interesting sixth-century text.' 'This writer shows influences from the Syrian tradition.' 'Here is a work important in the later development of Hesychasm.' We look at books chronologically and classify them in terms of influences and development. To the abbot they all had a simultaneous existence and composed a simultaneous order. They were all books which were useful for life in the Spirit. Their authors were fathers and teachers who had become friends, to whom one spoke in church and at other times; it was of little importance whether they had lived six hundred, twelve hundred or fifty years ago. He showed me the library rather in the way in which an expert gardener might show you his collection of books on gardening, or a cook a collection of cookery books. These help you on your way. They are not an end in themselves.

A. M. ALLCHIN

EUCHARIST

Thou art thyself both he who offers and he who is offered, he who receives and he who is distributed.

LITURGY OF ST JOHN CHRYSOSTOM

Christ is present and active, in various ways, in the entire eucharistic celebration. It is the same Lord who through the proclaimed word invites his people to his table, who through his minister presides at that table, and who gives himself sacramentally in the Body and Blood of his paschal sacrifice. It is the Lord present at the right hand of the Father, and therefore transcending the sacramental order, who thus offers to his Church, in the eucharistic signs, the special gift of himself.

The sacramental Body and Blood of the Saviour are present as an offering to the believer awaiting his welcome. When this offering is met by faith, a lifegiving encounter results. Through faith Christ's presence – which does not depend on the individual's faith in order to be the Lord's real gift of himself to his Church – becomes no longer just a presence *for* the believer, but also a presence *with* him. Thus, in considering the mystery of the eucharistic presence, we must recognize both the sacramental sign of Christ's presence and the personal relationship between Christ and the faithful which arises from that presence.

ANGLICAN-ROMAN CATHOLIC INTERNATIONAL COMMISSION (ARCIC)

> The Lamb of God is broken and distributed,
> Which being broken yet is not divided,
> Being ever eaten never is consumed,
> But sanctifies those that partake.

LITURGY OF ST JOHN CHRYSOSTOM

Let all mortal flesh be silent, and stand with fear and trembling, and think
on nothing earthly:
For the King of Kings, Christ our God, comes forth to be sacrificed and
given as food to the faithful.
Before him go the choirs of angels with every principality and power, the
cherubim with many eyes and the six-winged seraphim,
Veiling their faces and crying aloud:
Alleluia, alleluia, alleluia.

LITURGY OF ST JAMES

In the words *Take, eat . . . drink* there is contained the abyss of God's love
for mankind.
O perfect love, O all-embracing love, O irresistible love! What shall we
give to God in gratitude for this love?

FR JOHN OF KRONSTADT

We offer ourselves . . .

In the very thing that the Church offers, she herself is offered.
If you wish to understand what is meant by 'the Body of Christ', listen to
the apostle saying to the faithful, 'You are the Body of Christ and his
members' (1 Cor. 12.27). It is the mystery of yourselves that is laid on the
Lord's table; it is the mystery of yourselves that you receive. To that which
you are you answer 'Amen', and in answering you assent. For you hear the
words 'the Body of Christ', and you reply 'Amen'. Be a member of the
Body of Christ, that the *Amen* may be true. If you have received well, you
are that which you have received.
There you are on the table, there you are in the chalice.

ST AUGUSTINE

O Christ who holds the open gate,
O Christ who drives the furrow straight,
O Christ, the plough, O Christ, the laughter
Of holy white birds flying after,
Lo, all my heart's field red and torn,
And Thou wilt bring the young green corn
The young green corn divinely springing,
The young green corn for ever singing;
And when the field is fresh and fair
Thy blessèd feet shall glitter there.
And we will walk the weeded field,
And tell the golden harvest's yield,
The corn that makes the holy bread
By which the soul of man is fed,
The holy bread, the food unpriced,
Thy everlasting mercy, Christ.

JOHN MASEFIELD

At thy mystical supper, Son of God, today accept me as a communicant:
For I will not speak of the mystery to thine enemies,
I will not betray thee with a kiss like Judas,
But as the thief I confess to thee:
Lord, remember me in thy Kingdom.

ORTHODOX PRAYER BEFORE HOLY COMMUNION

May all of us, who share in the one loaf and the one cup, be united with each other in the fellowship of the one Holy Spirit. May communion in the holy Body and Blood of thy Christ bring judgement and condemnation upon none of us: but may we find grace and mercy with all the saints, who have been well-pleasing to thee from all ages.

LITURGY OF ST BASIL THE GREAT

Hoping all

Not, alas, that in the face of all this beauty I was worshipping. Love it as I might, I was still an outsider and as I knelt or stood I was only watching and thinking. All through the service I was only thinking.

Now it was the Communion of the Faithful, and as I watched the people going up to the altar rails I was only thinking dreamily. My mind wandered away to many other things than the wish that I could, once again, go up with them.

Then all of a sudden, I was aware of a steady direction in my thoughts. It was as if I were being impelled along this straight path from behind or perhaps drawn along it from in front because there was a light in the distance.

'Surely,' I decided, 'the only thing to do is to give oneself to a love one feels, and leave all else with the God unknown.' Next time, then – or perhaps one day – I would go up with the people and share with them in their communion. I would go in a kind of blind love and trust, asking pardon all the way for any unworthiness in a faith so unsure.

If I was such a Quaker I was also one who, untypically, loved and needed services like these in St Justin Martyr's: majestic parables of God's love given to men, and their love returned to him with every beauty they could offer. An Anglo-Catholic Quaker, let us say. Believing much, if less than all. While hoping all.

Such was my decision that Sunday morning in the old church of Prenders, my teacher.

Am I then home again at last? I do not know. Perhaps I shall never know. I hope and trust and do not know.

ERNEST RAYMOND

Almighty and everlasting God,
behold we approach the sacrament
of thy only-begotten Son, our Lord Jesus Christ.
As sick, we come to the Physician of life:
As unclean, to the Fountain of mercy:
As blind, to the Light of eternal splendour:
As needy, to the Lord of heaven and earth:
As naked, to the King of glory.

ST THOMAS AQUINAS

When Jesus Christ leads us to the holy table and gives us his own Body to eat, he transforms us completely and changes us into what he is himself. Marked now with the impress of the royal seal, our clay is clay no longer, but itself becomes the very Body of the King; and it is not possible to imagine any state more blessed than this. This is the final mystery, and beyond this it is not possible to go, nor can anything be added to it.

'This is a great mystery', says St Paul (Eph. 5.32), referring to our union with Christ in the Eucharist. The Eucharist is that mystical marriage, praised throughout all the world, in which the divine Bridegroom espouses the Church as his virgin bride. By this sacrament we are made 'flesh of his flesh, and bone of his bone' (Gen. 2.23).

Under normal circumstances food is changed into the person who consumes it: fish, bread, and the like become human flesh and blood. But in holy communion the exact opposite happens. The Bread of Life himself changes the person who eats, assimilating and transforming him into himself.

See in what sense the Kingdom of heaven is within us.

ST NICOLAS CABASILAS

We give thanks to thee, our Father, for the life and the knowledge which thou hast made known to us through Jesus thy Child: to thee be glory unto the ages. As this broken bread was once scattered upon the mountains, and was then gathered together and became one, so may thy Church be gathered together from the ends of the earth into thy Kingdom: for thine is the glory and the power through Jesus Christ unto the ages.

THE TEACHING OF THE APOSTLES

Finished and perfected, so far as we are able, is the mystery of thine
  incarnate work, O Christ our God.
For we have kept the memorial of thy death,
We have seen the figure of thy resurrection,
We have been filled with thine unending life,
We have rejoiced in thine unfailing joy.
Grant that we may all be counted worthy of that same joy also in the age
  to come.

LITURGY OF ST BASIL THE GREAT

June 1   JUSTIN MARTYR   *c.100 – c.165*

A native of Samaria who was a philosopher before he was a Christian, he taught afterwards in Rome, and gives this account of the Eucharist:

On the day called Sunday all who live in the city or in the country gather in one place, and the memoirs of the apostles or the writings of the prophets are read as long as time permits; then when the reading is finished, the president in his own words exhorts and invites us to imitate the good things that we have heard. Then we all rise to pray and, as I said before, when the prayer ends, bread, wine and water are brought, and the president in like manner prays and thanks God to the best of his ability. The people assent, saying Amen, and a distribution is made for participation of those things over which thanksgiving has been pronounced. To those who are absent the deacons take a portion. Those who are prosperous and willing give as much as each one thinks fit; and this collection is deposited with the president, who takes care of the widows and orphans, and of those who are in want through sickness or any other cause, of those who are in prison and of strangers who sojourn among us. In short, he is the protector of all who are in need. We all hold this gathering on Sunday, since this is the first day on which God, by making a transformation of darkness and chaos, made the universe, and on the same day Jesus Christ our Saviour rose from the dead.

June 3   ST CHARLES LWANGA AND OTHER MARTYRS OF UGANDA

In October 1884 King Mwanga of Uganda succeeded his father, Mutesa. In May 1886 he came into conflict with most of his pages, who refused to submit themselves to be partners in his sexual vices. Many of these had been enrolled as learners by Anglican and Roman Catholic missionaries.

He asked all those of his pages who had accepted this Christian status to confess themselves. Immediately thirty youths came forward, both Anglican and Roman Catholic. Mwanga gave them the choice between submission to his will and being burnt alive. All chose martyrdom. They were trussed and thrown into a slow fire; yet not one saved himself by submission.

June 5 ST BONIFACE *675–754*

He was born in Devon and educated at Crediton. Not long before 718 he went overseas and became a missionary bishop in parts of Germany outside any diocese. He became the organizing genius of the German Church. In a letter of 746–7 to Archbishop Egbert of York he writes:

When I received your gifts and books I lifted up my hands and gave thanks to Almighty God who has given me such a friend in my long wanderings, to help me in my worldly affairs and comfort me with his prayers and with the divine solace of spiritual communion.

Meanwhile, as a token of fraternal love, I am sending you a copy of some letters of St Gregory which I have received from the archives of the Roman Church, and which, so far as I know, have not reached Britain. If you so order, I will send more, and I have received many of them. I am sending also a cloak and a towel for drying the feet of the servants of God. We pray that your Holiness may keep your health and go onward in virtue.

June 6 ST CYRIL OF ALEXANDRIA *d. 444*

He was patriarch of Alexandria from 412 to 444. In November 430 he wrote in his third letter to Nestorius of Constantinople:

We do not distribute the words of our Saviour in the Gospels between two several subsistences or persons. For the one and only Christ is not twofold, although we do think of him as including two distinct substances inseparably united, as a man consists of body and soul, and yet is not twofold but single out of both. If we believe the right faith we shall believe that the human language and the divine have both been used by a single person.

June 9 ST COLUMBA *521–597*

He left Ireland for Iona in the western islands of Scotland, where he built up a community that became a centre of Christian influence not only in Scotland and the islands around the Scottish coast, but in the north and centre of England. His biographer, Adamnan, gives this vivid account of his dealings with a famous monster:

At another time when the blessed man was staying for some days in the land of the Picts, he had to cross Loch Ness. As he came to the bank, he saw some of those who dwelt by it burying a poor little chap. They told him that he had only just now been swimming when a water-beast put its head out and gave him a most savage bite. They had picked up his body too late by putting out hooks. When the holy man heard this, he told one of his companions to swim over and get a boat that was on the other bank. Hearing this order from the saint, Lugne Mocumin obeyed without delay. He took off everything except his vest and dived into the water. The monster, not satisfied but eager for more, lay at the bottom, but sensing that the water above was disturbed by swimming, emerged suddenly and with a great roar from an open mouth, went for the man as he swam in the middle of the stream. The blessed man saw it, and while everyone around, whether brethren or strangers, were smitten with excessive terror, he put up his holy hand in the empty air and made the saving sign of the cross. Invoking the name of God, he commanded the fierce beast, saying, 'Go no further, don't touch the man, but go back at once.'

Then the beast, hearing the saint's voice, turned right over, and went back as though drawn with cords more quickly than he came, although he had just been so near to Lugne as he swam, that there was no more than the length of a punt-pole between them.

June 9 ST EPHREM THE SYRIAN *c. 306–373*

> One of the greatest of Christian poets, he was born in Nisibis, on the easternmost edge of the Roman Empire, and died at Edessa, in what is now south-east Turkey. The poem that follows reflects his keen sense of the natural order. Man, in his view, is a denizen of two worlds, and must labour for both: his worldly labour is rewarded in October, with its harvests and the rains after the long hot summer months of drought, while his spiritual toil is rewarded in April, the month of Easter, when it is the custom for baptisms to take place after the spiritual labour of the Lenten fast.

October gives rest to the weary after the dust and dirt of the summer,
Its rain washes, its dew anoints the trees and their fruit.
April gives rest to the fasters, it anoints, baptizes and clothes in white;
It cleanses off the dirt of sin from our souls.
October presses out the oil for us, April multiplies mercies for us;
In October fruit is gathered, in April sins are forgiven.

The poet as theologian

All theology starts with the human mind reaching out to evoke some echo or reflection of the ineffable by means of poetic imagery, knowing that the ineffable cannot be pinned down; there follows a period of rising confidence in the intellect's power, then of declining vision and confidence; finally, in decadence, an abject literalism which can no longer distinguish the levels of discourse and discern what was poetic imagery, what was philosophical symbolism and what was matter-of-fact language. The peaks of theological poetry remain to inspire us again – Ephrem, Dante, Milton, Blake, T. S. Eliot. It would be good for the Church if they were put more in the forefront of theological study.

ROBERT MURRAY

June 11   ST BARNABAS

Barnabas was a good man, full of the Holy Spirit (Acts 11.24). Two things
are necessary for man, interior perfection and exterior conversation, the
first for himself, the second for his neighbour. Interior perfection is in two
parts, knowledge of truth and love of goodness. The first is perfection of
the intellect, the second the fullness of all the affections. Exterior
conversation consists in two things, acts of usefulness and gravity of
manners. These four are indicated in these words of commendation of
Barnabas, illumination of mind, inflammation of love, utility in action, and
a serious way of life.

ST THOMAS AQUINAS

June 22   ST THOMAS MORE   *1478–1535*

He was the first layman to be Lord Chancellor, and wrote his *Dialogue of
Comfort in Tribulation* while he was in prison in the Tower of London in
1534, before his execution for resistance to the demands of Henry VIII.

Finally let us consider that if we would not suffer the strength and fervour
of our faith to wax lukewarm, or rather key-cold, and in manner lose his
vigour by scattering our minds abroad about so many trifling things, that
of the matters of our faith we very seldom think, but that we would
withdraw our thought from the respect and regard of all worldly fantasies,
and so gather our faith together into a little narrow room, and like the little
grain of a mustard seed, which is of nature hot, set it in the garden of our
soul; all weeds pulled out for the better feeding of our faith; then shall it
grow, and so spread up in height, that the birds, that is, the holy angels of
heaven, shall breed in our soul and bring forth virtues in the branches of
our faith. And then with the faithful trust, that through the true belief of
God's word we shall put in his promises, we shall be able to command a
great mountain of tribulation to void from the place where it stood in our
heart; whereas, with a very feeble faith and a faint, we shall be scant able to
remove a little hillock. And therefore, for the first conclusion, as we must of
necessity before any spiritual comfort presuppose the foundation of faith;
so sith no man can give us faith, but only God, let us never cease to call
upon God therefore.

June 22 ST JOHN FISHER *1469–1535*

He was the bishop of Rochester who, with the Carthusians and Sir Thomas More, was executed for refusing the oaths of supremacy and succession imposed by King Henry VIII at the time of his breach with Rome. He was already known as the author of perceptive theological and spiritual works, among them this *Treatise on the Seven Penitential Psalms*, where his comments range outside the Scriptures:

Socrates was asked a question (as it appears in the Georgick of Plato) by one named Polus; whether Archelaus, who then had in governance the kingdom of Macedonia, in great glory, were happy and blessed, or no. Socrates answer'd and said, he could not tell: 'It is to me uncertain.' Then said Polus, 'He is a king.' Socrates said, 'Altho' he be so, yet he may be a wretch.' Polus added more, and said, 'He hath a glorious kingdom, a great household, and great riches.' Socrates answered, 'What of all this? These commodities make not a man blessed; for under them there may be privately hidden a wretched soul.' 'If thou wilt', said Socrates, 'that I tell you whether this man be blessed or wretched, show me his soul, and I will presently resolve thy question; for the demonstration of the matter dependeth on the soul.'

Truly a soul subject to sin is wretched; which our prophet David witnesseth, saying, *Miser factus sum*; by reason of my sin.

June 22 ST ALBAN *d. ?305*

According to Bede, he suffered in the persecution under Diocletian.

The reverend confessor ascended a hill, about 500 paces from the place, adorned or rather clothed with all kinds of flowers, having its sides neither perpendicular nor even craggy, but sloping down into a most beautiful plain, worthy from its lovely appearance to be the scene of a martyr's sufferings. On the top of the hill St Alban prayed that God would give him water, and immediately a living spring broke out before his feet. Here the head of our most courageous martyr was struck off, and here he received the crown of life which God promised to those who love him.

BEDE

June 24 NATIVITY OF ST JOHN THE BAPTIST

The doubt of Zacharias is, like the doubt of St Thomas the apostle, an indirect testimony: it brings out a supernatural fact. In this case the supernatural fact is the miraculous character of John's birth. With Elizabeth we are not, of course, in the presence of a miraculous phenomenon of transcendent glory as in the case of Mary's motherhood: Zacharias is truly the father of John the Baptist. Yet it was at the same time so evident a sign of God's favour to Elizabeth that Mary no longer hesitated in her mind as to the possibility of her own motherhood, the moment she heard the news from the angel that Elizabeth was with child.

Elizabeth's motherhood may be considered as a term of comparison, to enable us the better to understand and measure the excellence of Mary's motherhood. With Elizabeth's motherhood God's action and grace surround, as with an odour of heavenly life, the laws of created life. With Mary it will be all heavenly life. God's action is not merely the companion of created causality; it is supreme, exclusive, absolutely unconditioned by the created laws of life.

ANSCAR VONIER

June 28 ST IRENAEUS OF LYONS *c.130 – c.200*

Born in Asia Minor, as a boy he listened to St Polycarp of Smyrna (see February 23). Moving to the West he became priest and then bishop at Lyons, possibly dying as a martyr. In his theology of the atonement he sees Christ as the second Adam, summing up or recapitulating the whole human race in himself, and by his obedience to the Father undoing the effects of the first Adam's disobedience. He also sees Mary as the second Eve, reversing the disobedience of the virgin Eve in paradise.

Just as through a disobedient virgin man was struck down and fell into death, so through the Virgin who was obedient to the Word of God man was reanimated and received life. For it was necessary that Adam should be summed up in Christ, so that mortality might be swallowed up and overwhelmed by immortality; and Eve summed up in Mary, so that a virgin should be a virgin's intercessor, and by a virgin's obedience undo and put away the disobedience of a virgin.

He passed through every stage of life, restoring to all communion with God. As our race went down to death through a vanquished man, so we ascend to life through a victorious man.

June 29   ST PETER AND ST PAUL, APOSTLES

Christ gave to Peter, not only a primacy of order, but built his Church upon him, committed the charge of the whole flock to him, gave him power answerable to this charge, for the preservation of unity in the whole body.

Now this is not so to be understood, as to exclude Christ from being the rock and foundation on which the Church is built; for as he is the head and corner stone, so he is the foundation too; but only that he appointed Peter the ministerial head, and left him the commission of superintendency over the Church, for the prevention of schisms, and preservation of unity, without which the Church could not subsist. As therefore in the civil government, Christ's being supreme governor, does not exclude a supreme visible head, so neither in the Church.

Neither does it exclude the other apostles from being the foundations of the Church, in as much as they received power from Christ of preaching the gospel, and founding churches throughout the world; and had the power of the keys given them, in which St Cyprian, and other fathers say, they were all equal; but only, that, as the Church was, by Christ's appointment, to be one, so the origin of unity should be in one, and a power left with that one; to answer the end of the institution in the preservation of unity.

JOHN GOTER

THE GIFTS OF THE SPIRIT

A royal priesthood, a holy nation

Do you not realize or understand your own nobility? Each of those who have been anointed with the heavenly chrism becomes a Christ by grace, so that all are kings and prophets of the heavenly mysteries.

THE HOMILIES OF ST MACARIUS

In Old Testament times only kings and priests received a mystical anointing. But after our Lord, the true king and eternal priest, had been anointed by God the heavenly Father with this mystical unction, it was no longer only kings and priests but the whole Church that was consecrated with the anointing of chrism,[1] because every person in the Church is a member of the eternal King and Priest.

Because we are a royal and priestly nation, we are anointed after the washing of baptism, that we may be bearers of the name of Christ.

ALCUIN

[1] Chrism or chrismation, more commonly known in the West as confirmation: the second sacrament of Christian initiation, conferring on each of the baptized the gifts of the Holy Spirit.

Let us hang upon the lips of all the faithful, for the Spirit of God breathes upon every one of them.

ST PAULINUS OF NOLA

Expectant faith

In this renewal in the Church today we have a new awareness of the full spectrum of the gifts of the Holy Spirit. We must not be afraid to accept the Spirit with all its manifestations, just as we find them in the Gospels and in the writings of St Paul. We must not be afraid of accepting that the Holy Spirit is manifesting himself in the same ways today. We must open our faith to that. What is needed from each of us today is what I should call an 'expectant faith'. In order to receive the gifts of God, we must expect them, be open to them. And in the measure that we are 'expectantly' open to him, the Holy Spirit can accomplish all those wonders that we read about at the beginning of the Church. Each one of us needs that expectant faith. Come, Holy Spirit! I do not ask of you any special gift but neither do I refuse any gift either, because we receive those manifestations not for ourselves but for the Kingdom of God, for the building up of his Church. One person will receive a certain manifestation of the Spirit, another a different one, but all will use their particular gifts to share in the upbuilding of the Church. This is charismatic reality and at the same time visible and sacramental reality.

LEON-JOSEPH, CARDINAL SUENENS

Professional life and personal discipleship

And, behold, a certain lawyer stood up, and tempted him, saying, 'Master, what shall I do to inherit eternal life?' (Luke 10.25).

It falls to the lot of those who are engaged in the active and arduous profession of the law to pass their lives in great cities, amidst severe and incessant occupation, requiring all the faculties, and calling forth, from time to time, many of the strongest passions of our nature. In the midst of all this, rivals are to be watched, superiors are to be cultivated, connections cherished; some portion of life must be given to society, and some little to relaxation and amusement. When, then, is the question to be asked, 'What shall I do to inherit eternal life?', what leisure for the altar, what time for God? I appeal to the experience of men engaged in this profession, whether religious feelings and religious practices are not, without any speculative disbelief, perpetually sacrificed to the business of the world? Are not the habits of solicitude, hurry, and care, totally incompatible with habits of devotion? Is not the taste for devotion lessened? Is not the time for devotion abridged? Are you not more and more conquered against your warnings and against your will; not, perhaps, without pain and compunction, by the Mammon of life? And what is the cure for this great evil to which your profession exposes you? The cure is, to keep a sacred place in your heart, where Almighty God is enshrined, and where nothing human can enter; to say to the world, 'Thus far shalt thou go, and no further'; to remember you are a lawyer, without forgetting you are a Christian; to wish for no more wealth than ought to be possessed by an inheritor of the Kingdom of heaven; to covet no more honour than is suitable to a child of God; boldly and bravely to set yourself limits, and to show to others you have limits, and that no professional eagerness, and no professional activity, shall ever induce you to infringe upon the rules and practices of religion: remember the text; put the great question really, which the tempter of Christ only pretended to put. In the midst of your highest success, in the most perfect gratification of your vanity, in the most ample increase of your wealth, fall down at the feet of Jesus, and say, 'Master, what shall I do to inherit eternal life?'

SYDNEY SMITH

Facing despair

I can picture one teacher there – I can't recall her name. She was short and spare, and I remember her eager jutting chin. Quite unexpectedly one day (in the middle, I think, of an arithmetic lesson) she suddenly launched forth on a speech on life and religion. 'All of you,' she said, 'every *one* of you – will pass through a time when you will face despair. If you never face despair, you will never have faced, or become, a Christian, or known a Christian life. To be a Christian you must face and accept the life that Christ faced and lived; you must enjoy things as he enjoyed things; be as happy as he was at the marriage at Cana, know the peace and happiness that it means to be in harmony with God and with God's will. But you must also know, as he did, what it means to be alone in the Garden of Gethsemane, to feel that all your friends have forsaken you, that those you love and trust have turned away from you, and that *God himself* has forsaken you. Hold on then to the belief that that is *not* the end. If you love, you will suffer, and if you do not love, you do not know the meaning of a Christian life.'

She then returned to the problems of compound interest with her usual vigour, but it is odd that those few words, more than any sermon I have ever heard, remained with me, and years later they were to come back to me and give me hope at a time when despair had me in its grip. She was a dynamic figure, and also, I think, a *fine* teacher; I wish I could have been taught by her longer.

AGATHA CHRISTIE

The precept of courtesy

Finally be ye all of one mind, having compassion one of another, love as brethren, be pitiful, be courteous (1 Peter 3.8)

For courteous some substitute the word humble; the difference may not be considered as great, for pride is a quality that obstructs courtesy.

That a precept of courtesy is by no means unworthy of the gravity and dignity of an apostolical mandate, may be gathered from the pernicious effects which all must have observed to have arisen from harsh strictness and sour virtue: such as refuses to mingle in harmless gaiety, or give countenance to innocent amusements, or which transacts the petty business of the day with a gloomy ferociousness that clouds existence. Goodness of this character, is more formidable than lovely; it may drive away vice from its presence, but will never persuade it to stay to be amended; it may teach, it may remonstrate, but the hearer will seek for more mild instruction. To those, therefore, by whose conversation the heathens were to be drawn away from error and wickedness; it is the Apostle's precept, that they be courteous, that they accommodate themselves, as far as innocence allows, to the will of others; that they should practise all the established modes of civility, seize all occasions of cultivating kindness, and live with the rest of the world in an amicable reciprocation of cursory civility, that Christianity might not be accused of making men less chearful as companions, less sociable as neighbours, or less useful as friends.

SAMUEL JOHNSON

The Singer and the Priest

Whenever I look at an audience – and, among musicians, only we singers have this privilege – I recall that I am not there to express myself or to impress others by making noises. On behalf of everyone present I have to render articulate things that are stirring in every heart, but which without me would have no point of focus. Without the aspirations of the listeners I am as powerless to kindle a flame as a burning glass on a sunless day. Yet, were it not for a mediator, the poem would remain so much print, the melody a crazy string of dots – mere ink. The dormant cyphers can be brought to life only by the exercise of a sacramental gift, and God has generously given this gift to people like me who have done nothing whatever to deserve it.

It is therefore my duty to stand in all weathers at the cross-roads of human experience, assimilating all that I may observe, so that the quintessence of any given emotion may irradiate my voice as I sing of it and my listeners thrill to this as being the articulation of something within themselves.

What Wilfred Brown wrote of the singer, we see as true also of the priest. His pastoral ministry, out among people, takes him to 'the cross-roads of human experience'. His theology, in Scripture and in liturgy, is to him what the score, a contrived pattern of dots and lines, is to the singer: it embodies that experience, the common property of all mankind, in a pattern of words and actions which he is educated, or ought to be, to interpret, to articulate, with the musician's fidelity. The experience includes, of course, the human experience of God, the Christian experience of God in Christ, sealed upon men by the Holy Ghost – wider than the experience of his own local cross-roads, whether it be a village, or suburban, or industrial, or academic, community. So Christian liturgy must articulate this wider experience: it speaks for all mankind.

It is the priest's office so to read the words before him that they awaken in those for whom he ministers an awareness of those theological truths which are the substance of the Christian faith; that they evoke a response to those truths of a sort which might, perhaps would, lie dormant, were it not for his ministry. Good liturgy, like the Bible itself, cannot be read without effort, without a determined study to find the meaning of the words, to make that meaning one's own, and then to convey it so that others are seized of it; the priest's task is no less demanding than the singer's.

G. R. DUNSTAN

Speaking with a full voice

Before I became a priest there was so much I had to be silent about, holding myself back. Priesthood, for me, means the possibility of speaking with a full voice.

Every sermon, every lesson, has meaning and value only when it is the result of personal spiritual experience and knowledge. Every sermon pronounced only with our lips is dead and false, and those who listen always unmistakably feel it.

During confession what many people, if not all, need most is that the priest should pray with them. This joint prayer softens the heart, sharpens repentance, refines the spiritual sight.

You cannot cure the soul of others or 'help people' without having changed yourself. You cannot put in order the spiritual economy of others so long as there is chaos in your own soul. You cannot bring peace to others if you do not have it yourself.

Hear each person's confession as if it were his last confession before death.

In preaching, the creative process should be performed aloud, in front of the people. But there are two conditions: a full heart and complete simplicity. One must keep in mind a precise theme, divided according to the essential ideas. But the real creation must take place during the actual sermon; otherwise one is burnt out during the preparation, and offers one's listeners only cold ashes.

FATHER ALEXANDER ELCHANINOV

Advice to a preacher

I take it for granted, that you intend to pursue the beaten Track, and are already desirous to be seen in a Pulpit; only I hope you will think it proper to pass your Quarantine among some of the desolate Churches five Miles round this Town, where you may at least learn to Read and to Speak before you venture to expose your Parts in a City-Congregation; not that these are better Judges, but because, if a Man must needs expose his Folly, it is more safe and discreet to do so, before few Witnesses, and in a scattered Neighbourhood. And you will do well, if you can prevail upon some intimate and judicious Friend to be your constant Hearer, and allow him with the utmost Freedom to give you notice of whatever he shall find amiss, either in your Voice or Gesture; for want of which early Warning, many Clergymen continue defective, and sometimes ridiculous, to the End of their Lives; neither is it rare to observe among excellent and learned Divines, a certain ungracious Manner, or an unhappy Tone of Voice, which they never have been able to shake off.

I could likewise have been glad if you had applied yourself a little more to the Study of the English Language, than I fear you have done; the neglect whereof is one of the most general Defects among the Scholars of this Kingdom, who seem to have not the least conception of a Style, but run on in a flat kind of Phraseology, often mingled with barbarous Terms and Expressions and the frequent Use of obscure Terms.

I am the more earnest in this Matter, because it is a general Complaint, and the justest in the World. For a Divine has nothing to say to the wisest Congregation of any Parish in this Kingdom, which he may not express in a manner to be understood by the meanest among them.

JONATHAN SWIFT

The importance of preaching

Pray, are you ignorant that that Body is subject to more diseases and attacks than this flesh of ours, and is marred more quickly and cured more slowly? Those who treat the human body have devised manifold medicines, and divers kinds of instruments, and forms of diet suited to the needs of the sufferer; and the character of the climate has often been sufficient by itself to restore the patient's health. There are occasions also when seasonable sleep has relieved the physician of all trouble. But in the present case none of these devices is of avail; but one only means and one way of cure has been given us after any trouble, and that is teaching of the Word. This is the best instrument, this the best diet and climate; this serves instead of medicine, this serves instead of cautery and cutting; whether it be needful to burn or to amputate, this one method must be used; and without it nothing else will avail. By it we rouse the lethargy, we allay the swelling, we remove the growths and make good the defects of the soul, and in short we do everything which tends to promote its health. To help a man to order his life aright it is true that the life of another may excite him to emulation; but when the soul is suffering under spurious doctrines then there is great need of the Word not only for the safety of those within the fold, but also to meet the attacks of foes without.

ST JOHN CHRYSOSTOM

The eternal dilemma

Someone once said that hell would be, and now is, living without God and with evil, and being unable to get used to it. Having to do without God, without love, in utter loneliness and fear, knowing that God is leaving us alone for ever; we have driven ourselves out, we have lost God and gained hell. I live now in two hells, for I have lost God and live also without love, or without the love I want, and I cannot get used to that either. Though people say that in the end one does. To the other, perhaps never.

However this may be, I have now to make myself a life in which neither has a place. I shall go about, do my work, seek amusements, meet my friends, life will amble on, and no doubt in time I shall find it agreeable again. One is, after all, very adaptable; one has to be. One finds diversions; these, indeed, confront one at every turn, the world being so full of natural beauties and enchanting artefacts, of adventures and jokes and excitements and romance and remedies for grief. And, when the years have all passed, there will gape the uncomfortable and unpredictable dark void of death, and into this I shall at last fall headlong, down and down and down, and the prospect of that fall, that uprooting, that rending apart of body and spirit, that taking off into so blank an unknown, drowns me in mortal fear and mortal grief. After all, life, for all its agonies of despair and loss and guilt, is exciting and beautiful, amusing and artful and endearing, full of liking and of love, at times a poem and a high adventure, at times noble and at times very gay; and whatever (if anything) is to come after it, we shall not have this life again.

Still the towers of Trebizond, the fabled city, shimmer on a far horizon, gated and walled and held in a luminous enchantment. It seems that for me, and however much I must stand outside them, this must for ever be. But at the city's heart lie the pattern and the hard core, and these I can never make my own: they are too far outside my range. The pattern should perhaps be easier, the core less hard.

This, indeed, seems the eternal dilemma.

ROSE MACAULAY

July 3   ST THOMAS THE APOSTLE

Faith and doubt

We too often forget that Christian faith is a principle of questioning and struggle before it becomes a principle of certitude and of peace. One has to doubt and reject everything else in order to believe firmly in Christ, and after one has begun to believe, one's faith itself must be tested and purified. Christianity is not merely a set of foregone conclusions. The Christian mind is a mind that risks intolerable purifications, and sometimes, indeed very often, the risk turns out to be too great to be tolerated. Faith tends to be defeated by the burning presence of God in mystery, and seeks refuge from him, flying to comfortable social forms and safe conventions in which purification is no longer an inner battle but a matter of outward gesture.

THOMAS MERTON

It is scarcely necessary to observe, that what our Saviour says to Thomas so clearly and impressively, he has implied, in one way or other, all through his ministry; the blessedness of a mind that believes readily. His demand and trial of faith in the case of those who came for his miraculous aid, his praise of it where found, his sorrow where it was wanting, his warnings against hardness of heart – all are evidence of this.

JOHN HENRY NEWMAN

July 4 ST ANDREW OF CRETE *c. 660–740*

Born in Damascus and subsequently archbishop of Gortyna in Crete, he is
one of the most celebrated hymn-writers of the Orthodox Church. He is
remembered in particular for his 'Great Canon' of repentance, running to
more than 250 stanzas and sung during Lent. Here are three typical verses:

Like the thief I cry to thee, 'Remember me';
Like Peter I weep bitterly;
Like the publican I call out, 'Forgive me, Saviour';
Like the harlot I shed tears.
Accept my lamentation, as once thou hast accepted
The entreaties of the woman of Canaan.
Have mercy upon me, O God, have mercy upon me.

Christ became man, calling to repentance
Thieves and harlots. Repent, my soul:
The door of the Kingdom is already open,
And Pharisees and publicans and adulterers
Pass through it before you, changing their life.
Have mercy upon me, O God, have mercy upon me.

Christ saved the wise men and called the shepherds;
He revealed as martyrs a multitude of young children;
He glorified the elder and the aged widow.
But you, my soul, have not followed their lives and actions.
Woe to you when you are judged!
Have mercy upon me, O God, have mercy upon me.

July 5   ST ATHANASIUS OF ATHOS   *c. 920–1003*

In 963 he founded the Great Lavra, the first fully-organized monastery on the Holy Mountain of Athos. Until the present day the Athonite peninsula remains the chief centre of Orthodox monasticism. The following account, written by an English Orthodox layman, stresses one of the most precious features of the Mountain: the quality of its silence.

It was mid-day on 6 August 1968. The motorboat from Daphni stopped at the harbour of Simonopetra. No one else had landed, so after a friendly greeting from a monk on the jetty, I started climbing alone up the steep path as the motorboat went on down the coast. I sat down in the shade and looked out across the sea, listening to the silence.

All was still.

This stillness, this silence, is everywhere, pervades all, is the very essence of the Holy Mountain. The distant sound of a motorboat serves only to punctuate the intensity of the quietness; a lizard's sudden rustling among dry leaves, a frog plopping into a fountain, are loud and startling sounds, but merely emphasize the immense stillness. Often as one walks over the great stretches of wild country which form much of this sacred ground, following paths where every stone breathes prayers, it is impossible to hear a sound of any kind. Even in the monastery churches, where the silence is, as it were, made more profound by the darkness, by the beauty and by the sacred quality of the place, it seems that the reading and chanting of priests and monks in the endless rhythm of their daily and nightly ritual is no more than a thin fringe of a limitless ocean of silence.

But this stillness, this silence, is far more than a mere absence of sound. It has a positive quality, a quality of fullness, of plenitude, of the eternal Peace which is there reflected in the Veil of the Mother of God, enshrouding and protecting her Holy Mountain, offering inner silence, peace of heart, to those who dwell there and to those who come with openness of heart to seek this blessing.

July 15 ST SWITHUN *802–862*

He was bishop of Winchester. His story is told in William of Malmesbury's *Gesta Pontificum*:

There was in him a store of all virtues, but he excelled especially in two, humility and clemency. Let my pen provide instances of both. Once upon a time he was standing where workmen were making a bridge on the east side of the city, so that the sight of his presence might keep up the energies of those who were disposed to slack. And, as it happened, a woman came walking over the bridge into the city, carrying a basket of eggs for sale. They jostled her on both sides in the manner of that sort of men, and in their petulant rudeness broke all the eggs at once. This seemed no light matter for men of gravity, and was reported to the lord bishop. He listened to her complaint as she was brought before him, elderly and slovenly in dress, and deplored the damage. The compassion of his mind overcame his hesitation to work a miracle, and making the sign of the cross he consolidated the fractures of all the eggs.

In the sickness at the end of his life he commanded that his body should be buried outside the church, where it would be trodden by the feet of passers-by and made wet by the rain that falls from heaven.

July 15 ST BONAVENTURA *1217–1274*

He was an early Franciscan, Minister-General of the Franciscan Order, a professor in Paris and eventually a cardinal. His spiritual writings were and are greatly admired. This is from *The Goad of Divine Love*:

If therefore a man would get up as high as he can, and there rest, and not go back at all, and the next day go up higher, and there set the foot of his heart, and after that ascend still higher and higher, and thus do always, I say to you that such a one would profit more in one month than another that goes back to take his rest, and returns from whence he first came, would do in forty years. And I do believe that in a short time he would be perfect in his state, and would become glorious before God, and beloved of all the court of heaven. And if there be anything in the mountain that shall make you afraid, have recourse to the holes in the side of Christ.

July 15 ST VLADIMIR *956–1015*

'Equal of the apostles', 'enlightener of the Russian land', as he is known in
the Orthodox Church, Vladimir was brought up a pagan, although his
grandmother St Olga had been a Christian. Around 988, some ten years
after becoming Prince of Kiev, he accepted baptism, marrying Anna, sister
of the Byzantine Emperor Basil II. His own conversion was followed by the
mass baptism of his subjects, described as follows in the *Russian Primary
Chronicle*:

Then Vladimir sent heralds throughout the whole city, saying: 'If anyone,
rich or poor, does not come down tomorrow to the river bank, he will be my
enemy.' When the people heard these words, they wept for joy and
exclaimed in their enthusiasm: 'If this were not good, the Prince and his
boyars would not have accepted it.'

On the morrow the Prince went down to the Dnieper with the priests of
the Princess Anna and those from Kherson, and a countless multitude
assembled. They all went into the water: some stood in it up to their necks,
others to their chests, the younger near the bank, some of them holding
their children in their arms, while the adults waded farther out. The priests
stood on the bank and said the prayers. There was joy in heaven and on
earth to see so many souls saved. But the devil groaned, lamenting, 'Woe is
me! How am I driven out from here! I am vanquished, not by apostles and
martyrs, but by the ignorant; and my reign in these regions is at an end.'

When the people had been baptized, they returned each to his own
home. Vladimir, rejoicing that he and his subjects now knew God, looked
up to heaven and said, 'O God, who hast created heaven and earth, look
down, I beseech thee, on this thy new people, and grant them, O Lord, to
know thee as true God, just as the other Christian nations have come to
know thee.'

And he began to build churches in all the towns and to send priests
there.

July 22 ST MARY MAGDALENE

'Touch me not'

See the dust on the path lamely dragging:
No, let her be, Mary moves towards her peace,
Deep calls unto deep, a grave for a grave,
A carcass drawing towards a carcass in that unhappy morning;
Three days was this one in a grave, in a world that died
In the cry in the afternoon. It is finished,
The cry that drew blood from her like the barb of a sword.

See her, Christ's Niobe, drawing with her towards the hill
The rock of her pain from the leaden Easter
Through the dark dawn, through the cold dew, through the heavy dust,
To the place where there is a stone that is heavier than her torn heart;
Uneasily the awkward feet find their way over thorns
With the annoyance of tears doubling the mist before her,
And her hands reaching out to him in barren grief.

Her moan is as monotonous as a dove's,
Like Orpheus mourning Eurydice
She stands amongst the roses and cries without mourning
'They have taken away my Lord, taken him away,'
To disciple and angel the same cry
'And I know not where they have laid him.'
And to the gardener the same frenzy.

Made wild. Broken. She sank within herself in her grief.
The understanding reels and reason's out of joint, until
He comes and snatches her out of the body to crown her –
Quickly like an Alpine eagle falling on its prey –
With the love that moves the stars, the power that is a Word
To raise up and make alive: 'and he said unto her, Mary,
She turned herself and said unto him, Rabboni.'

SAUNDERS LEWIS

July 24 ST BORIS AND ST GLEB

Children of St Vladimir (see July 15), after their father's death they were murdered by emissaries of their elder brother Svyatopolk. Although they could easily have offered resistance, they refused to take up arms in self-defence, preferring to avoid bloodshed. As St Gleb says in the ancient *Life* of the two saints, 'It is better that I alone should die rather than such a multitude of souls'; in Mahatma Gandhi's words, 'If blood be shed, let it be our blood.' Although they were victims in a political struggle, not martyrs for the faith – and although, according to the *Life*, they met death with fear, bitterly lamenting their tragic fate – the Russian Church proclaimed them as saints only five years after their death, giving them the special title 'Passion-bearers'. They were the first Russian saints to be canonized.

Boris and Gleb could not be fitted into any of the traditional classes of Christian saints known to the Byzantine Church. Their sacrifice might appear unreasonable, even foolish, but it reveals such an integral acceptance of Christianity, such a determination to reject violence, such a deep penetration into the redeeming mystery of innocent suffering, that these two princes have rightly become the first saints of Russia, the very incarnation of its peculiar interpretation of Christianity. To become a 'Passion-bearer', to be an innocent victim, slain for Christ's sake, to refuse the use of violence even in the face of death, these were the implications of Christianity which produced the deepest impression upon the newly converted Russians.

NICOLAS ZERNOV

July 25 ST JAMES THE GREAT

From a sermon of St Leo:

This advice was given by Jesus to all his disciples: 'If any man will come after me, let him deny himself, and take up his cross, and follow me.' He added: 'He that will save his life shall lose it, and he that shall lose his life for my sake, shall find it.' And the more to strengthen them in his unmovable firmness, by which they were prompted to embrace without fear even the sharpest crosses; to prevent them from being ashamed of the capital sentence he was to undergo, and lastly to instruct them not to be scandalized at the patience he was going to show at his Passion, when the brilliant signs of his almighty power would be hidden, he took Peter and James, and John his brother, and brought them up into an exceeding high mountain apart, and there made manifest the brightness of his glory.

July 26 ST ANNE, MOTHER OF THE BLESSED VIRGIN

From a Coptic Apocryphal Gospel:

Joachim saw a vision in the night, forty days before Anna conceived the Virgin. It was as if he were by a spring of water, and a white dove was there, drinking. It flew up and landed on the head of Joachim, and kept on flying around him. And Joachim rose and told the vision to Anna his wife, and she wondered greatly. When she herself fell asleep on the same night, she too was shown a vision. It was as if a tree was planted by the banks of a spring of water, and a white dove sat in the midst of the tree. It flew from the tree and perched on the hands of Anna and then in her bosom, and kept kissing her mouth for a long time. She got up and told her vision to Joachim.

July 29   WILLIAM WILBERFORCE   *1759–1833*

He was a member of Parliament for Yorkshire from 1796 to 1825 and played a prominent part in agitation against the slave trade. In 1797, when he had been a converted Evangelical for twelve years, he wrote his Practical View of the prevailing religious system of professed Christians in the higher and middle classes in the country, contrasted with real Christianity.

Take the case of young men of condition, brought up by what we have termed nominal Christians. When children, they are carried to church, and thence they become acquainted with such parts of Scriptures as are contained in the Public Services. If their parents preserve still more of the customs of better times, they are taught their catechism, and furnished with a little further religious knowledge. After a while, they go from under the eye of their parents; they enter the world, and move forward on the path of life, wherever it may be, which has been assigned to them. They yield to the temptations which assail them, and become, more or less, dissipated and licentious. At last they neglect to look into their Bible, they do not enlarge the sphere of their religious acquisitions; they do not even endeavour, by reflection or study, to mature their knowledge, or to turn into rational conviction the opinions which in their childhood they had taken on trust.

They travel perhaps into foreign countries; a proceeding which naturally tends to weaken their nursery prejudice in favour of the religion in which they were bred, and by removing them from all means of public worship, to relax their practical habits of religion. They return home, and commonly are either hurried round in the vortex of dissipation, or engage with the ardour of youthful minds in some public or professional pursuit.

July 31 ST IGNATIUS LOYOLA *1491–1556*

He came from the Basque country in the north of Spain. Crippled by a wound in 1521 he had no romances of chivalry to read and turned to a life of Christ and lives of the saints instead. His change of direction took shape in *Spiritual Exercises* based on his experiences in retreat at Manresa, near Montserrat. These he gave to the companions who joined him while he was a mature student at Paris in 1530–4, and came to be founder members of the Society of Jesus when this developed later, in Rome between 1539 and 1541.

The *Exercises* contain:

Rules for the discernment of spirits; for in some degree perceiving and knowing the various motions excited in the soul; the good, that they may be admitted; the bad, that they may be rejected.

In the case of those who are making progress from good to better, the good angel touches the soul gently, lightly, sweetly, as a drop of water entering into a sponge; and the evil spirit touches it sharply, and with noise and disturbance, like a drop of water falling on a rock. In the case of those who go from bad to worse, the contrary happens; and the reason for this difference is the disposition of the soul, according as it is contrary or similar to these spirits; for when it is contrary they enter in with perceptible commotion; but when it is similar to them, they enter in silence, as into their own house, through the open doors.

Rules for thinking with the Church include:

Although it is very true that no one can be saved without being predestined, we must speak with great circumspection on this matter, for fear that, giving too much to grace, we should appear to destroy man's free will and the merit of good works; or that giving too much to free will, we should weaken the power and efficacy of grace.

The final prayer at the end is:

Take, Lord, and receive my entire liberty, my memory, my understanding and my whole will. All that I am, all that I have, you have given me, and I give it back again to be at your disposal, according to your good pleasure. Give me only your love and your grace; with them I am rich enough.

August

August 2 ST BASIL THE BLESSED *1469–1552*

A native of Moscow, he was a *iurodivyi*, a 'fool in Christ' or 'holy fool'. Such 'fools' were familiar figures in sixteenth-century Russia, as the Elizabethan traveller Giles Fletcher testifies: 'They use to go stark naked save a clout about their middle, with their hair hanging long and wildly about their shoulders, and many of them with an iron collar or chain about their necks or middle, even in the very extremity of winter. These the people take as prophets and men of great holiness, giving them a liberty to speak what they list without any controlment, though it be of the very highest himself.' Basil conformed closely to this picture. Destitute and homeless, he wandered naked through the streets; folly gave him freedom, and through his words and symbolic actions – seemingly eccentric but with a sharp, hidden point – he acted as the living conscience of society.

'If any man thinketh that he is wise among you in this world, *let him become a fool*, that he may become wise' (1 Cor. 3.18); 'We are *fools* for Christ's sake' (1 Cor. 4.10). What Paul means, in the first place, is the paradox of faith in the crucified Messiah. Foolish, in the eyes of the world, is our faith. Yet were the Orthodox holy fools really fools to accept literally the invitation of Paul, 'Let him become a fool'? We are so accustomed to the paradox of Christianity that we hardly see in the tremendous words of Paul anything but a rhetorical exaggeration. But Paul insists here upon the radical irreconcilability of two orders – that of the world and that of God. In the Kingdom of God reigns a complete inversion of our earthly values. Folly for Christ's sake expresses essentially the need to lay bare the radical contradiction between the Christian truth and both the common sense and the moral sense of the world.

G. P. FEDOTOV

August 4 ST JEAN VIANNEY *1786–1859*

He was *curé* of Ars, near Lyons, for forty years from 1818. His insight was exercised with an accuracy that was uncanny without being spectacular. A lady who intended to make her own escape from an insoluble dilemma found herself in the small space between his church and his house. He did not know her but spoke to her quietly: 'What are you going to do with what you have in your pocket? Give it to me.' She was sure that he knew all about her and gave him her phial of poison without protest. Next day she came to him for advice.

Another instance is taken from a parish magazine. Mlle Thérèse-Apollonie Servonat, whose home was in Tourdan, had been in service in Lyons for some years. Every year her employers went into the country for a few weeks' holiday. She took advantage of their absence to set out at her own convenience, and when she reached Ars thought of staying for a few days. She visited the church and found it full. She had barely time for a prayer before she saw the *curé* come out of the choir and make straight for her.

'My child, so you have just come here to stay for a while. Well, you must go home quickly, for the owners of the house that you are looking after in Lyons are coming back.' He named the day, and she followed his advice, fulfilled her spiritual requirements with all speed and left for Villefranche, where she took the boat down the Saône to Lyons. Two hours after her return her master and mistress came back.

August 6   TRANSFIGURATION OF CHRIST

Two Icons

There are two icons of the transfiguration which struck me very deeply when I saw them in the original in the Tretiakov Gallery in Moscow. One is by Rublev and the other by his master, Theophan the Greek. In both there are three mountain peaks, the Lord Jesus in the centre, with Moses and Elijah on the right and left-hand sides, and the three disciples on the slopes of the mountain. The difference between the two icons lies in the way in which the things are seen. The Rublev icon shows Christ in the brilliancy of his dazzling white robes which cast light on everything around. This light falls on the disciples, on the mountain and the stones, on every blade of grass. Within this light, which is the divine splendour – the divine glory, the divine light itself inseparable from God – all things acquire an intensity of being which they could not have otherwise; in it they attain to a fullness of reality which they can have only in God. The other icon is more difficult to perceive in a reproduction. The background is silvery and appears grey. The robes of Christ are silvery, with blue shades, and the rays of light falling around are also white, silvery and blue. Everything gives an impression of much less intensity. Then we discover that all these rays of light falling from the divine presence and touching the things which surround the transfigured Christ do not give relief but give transparency to things. One has the impression that these rays of divine light touch things and sink into them, penetrate them, touch something within them so that from the core of these things, of all things created, the same light reflects and shines back, as though the divine life quickens the capabilities, the potentialities of all things, and makes all reach out towards itself. At that moment the eschatological situation is realized, and in the words of St Paul, 'God is all and in all'.

METROPOLITAN ANTHONY OF SOUROZH

A revelation of our true humanity

He who once spoke through symbols to Moses on Mount Sinai,
Saying, 'I am he who is',
Was transfigured today upon Mount Tabor before the disciples;
And in his own person he showed them the nature of man,
Arrayed in the original beauty of the image.

Having gone up the mountain, O Christ, with thy disciples,
Transfigured thou hast made our human nature,
Grown dark in Adam, to shine again as lightning,
Transforming it into the glory and splendour of thine own divinity.

The light of the Holy Trinity

Today on Tabor in the revelation of thy light, O Word,
Thou unaltered light from the light of the unbegotten Father,
We have seen the Father as light
And the Spirit as light,
Guiding with light the whole creation.

ORTHODOX HYMNS FOR THE FEAST

All light, all glory, all spirit

When the soul is counted worthy to enjoy communion with the Spirit of the light of God, and when God shines upon her with the beauty of his ineffable glory, preparing her as a throne and dwelling for himself, she becomes all light, all face, all eye: and there is no part of her that is not full of the spiritual eyes of light. There is no part of her that is in darkness, but she is made wholly and in every part light and spirit.

As the sun is the same all over, not having any back part nor any part that falls short, but is wholly glorified with light all over and is all light, being alike in every part; or as fire – the very light of fire – is all alike in every part, and does not contain in itself first or last, greater or less: so also when the soul is perfectly illumined in ineffable beauty and glory by the light of Christ's countenance, and when she is granted perfect communion with the Holy Spirit and is counted worthy to become the dwelling-place and throne of God, she becomes all eye, all light, all face, all glory, all spirit.

THE HOMILIES OF ST MACARIUS

August 8   ST DOMINIC   *1170–1221*

He was a Guzman, born in Old Castille, who became a canon of the cathedral at Osma, where the rule of St Augustine was observed. He became involved with his bishop, Diego, in missionary enterprises, first around the Baltic and then in the south of France, where the Albigensians were preaching a different religion and the Waldensians a reformation of the Church. The Order of Preachers came into being to deal with this situation as it developed after the death of Diego. This left Dominic in charge of a group who made their base at Prouille, where a group of their converts, women of intelligence, established a religious community.

These were the first Dominican Sisters. The Order of Preachers developed their own characteristics later. First they were a company at work in the diocese of Toulouse, but they were soon encouraged to extend themselves across diocesan boundaries and to make their own adaptation of the rule of St Augustine to practical needs. St Dominic, unlike St Francis, was a capable organizer. By the time of his death in 1221 there were twenty-five houses of his order in France, Italy and Spain, including one at the University of Paris, where they came to be called Jacobins. He was regarded by those who knew him as an affectionate, outgoing person. A tale is told of how he came to a house of Dominican Sisters after they had all gone to bed. They got up and heard a long address from him in the church. But he then said: 'It would be good, my daughters, to have a little something to drink.' Wine was brought, and according to one of them, who clearly remembered the occasion, St Dominic kept on encouraging the nuns to drink more. '*Bibite satis*', he said to them, 'drink your fill'; and they did. He had familiarity in the sense behind 'Familiarity breeds contempt'. He opened himself up to people, and that is why they loved him, but they had no great store of wonder stories to tell about him. They remembered him as a very nice man, who drew followers to him by understanding what their problems were.

August 11 ST CLARE *1193–1253*

She was born into a knightly family at Assisi who had planned a distinguished marriage for her when, at the age of eighteen, she was moved by the preaching of St Francis to be with the Lord alone in poverty. According to the bull for her canonization, published in 1255 by Pope Alexander IV, who knew her well and had been much involved in her history:

She collected all that she had and devoted it to the service of the Christ in alms, changing everything into what might serve as gifts for the poor. In her flight from the world's clamour she went first to a church in the fields, and there received the holy tonsure from the blessed Francis himself. She then went on to another church, from whence her family tried to drag her away, but she took hold of the altarcloth and held on to it, in such a way that her relatives could see the cut made in her hair, and offered a determined and continued resistance, on the ground that in the integrity of her mind she was joined to God already, and could not be drawn away from his service. In the end, after she had been taken by the same blessed Francis to the church of St Damiano, outside the city of Assisi, the place from which she came, the Lord added many companions to her in the love and service of his name.

August 13   JEREMY TAYLOR   *1613–1667*

Anglican bishop and writer; best known for his devotional writings, he has also come to be appreciated for his moral theology..

O Holy and eternal Jesus, who wert pleased to lay aside the glories and incomprehensible Majesty, which clothed thy infinity from before the beginning of creatures, and didst put on a cloud upon thy brightness, and wert invested with the impure and imperfect broken robe of human nature, and didst abate those splendours which broke through the veil, commanding devils not to publish thee, and men not to proclaim thy excellencies, and the apostles not to reveal those glories of thine, which they discovered encircling thee upon Mount Tabor in thy transfiguration . . . teach us to approach near to these glories, which thou hast so covered with a cloud, that we might without amazement behold thy excellencies.

August 13   ST TIKHON OF ZADONSK   *1724–1783*

After only seven years as a bishop (1761–8), he retired to spend the rest of his life in solitude. Despite its relatively short length, his episcopal ministry made a profound impression on the Russian people. He was a true pastor in the tradition of St John Chrysostom – indefatigable in teaching his flock, and outspoken on questions of social righteousness. Coming from an extremely poor family, he always remained close in spirit to the people: we find in him, as one author puts it, 'the smell of freshly planed wood'. His many writings are direct and practical, an attempt to formulate a living theology founded on experience, in contrast to the academic scholasticism prevalent in eighteenth-century Russian seminaries. He had a warm, truly evangelical devotion to the person of Jesus Christ, and a particular love for the Bible.

Blessed are those who saw Christ in the flesh. But still more blessed are we who see his image portrayed in the Gospels, and hear his voice speaking from them.

If an earthly king – our tsar – wrote you a letter, would you not read it with joy? Certainly, with great rejoicing and careful attention. The King of heaven has sent a letter to you, an earthly and mortal man: yet you almost despise such a gift, so priceless a treasure. Whenever you read the Gospel, Christ himself is speaking to you. And while you read, you are praying and talking with him.

August 15   THE CORONATION OF THE BLESSED VIRGIN MARY

The End of the Age

Written on or about 15 August 1945.

The woman went up in a whirlwind into heaven,
Caught by the Son of God and to his throne
Whither the saints wheel, each in his order,
While we in this world watch and wonder
Seeing the present age, and the age to come
Under the wings of archangels in wisdom;

While Japan is lifted high into heaven
Light on the burning air of an explosion:
An emperor in compassion for his people
Slips to the microphone, and ends the struggle.
After an instant, the dust settles again.
Will the world forget the horrible pain?

Everything we know by a single example,
A beautiful image, a bitter taste, a sample
Of silk from a weaver's loom, far in the past.
So small men come to understand at last
How all the science that has gone before
Has led them, step by step, to modern war.

Only Omnipotence has infinite power.
Teach us, dear Lady, even in this hour
When we are afraid of the small
Electron that no engine can control.
Planets and atoms the same law obey,
And when they swerve, explode, and die away.

GEORGE EVERY

Beyond death and judgement

The destiny of the Church and world has already been fulfilled, not only in the uncreated person of the Son of God, but also in the created person of his Mother. That is why St Gregory Palamas calls the Mother of God 'the boundary between the created and the uncreated'. Beside the incarnate divine hypostasis there is a deified human hypostasis.

We have said above that in the person of the Mother of God it is possible to see the transition from the holiness of the Old Testament to the holiness of the Church. But if the all-holy Mother of God has reached and consummated the holiness of the Church, and all holiness which is possible for a created being, we are now concerned with yet another transition: the transition from the world of becoming to the eternity of the Eighth Day, the passage from the Church to the Kingdom of God. This last glory of the Mother of God, the *eschaton* realized in a created person before the end of the world, henceforth places the Mother of God beyond death, beyond the resurrection, and beyond the Last Judgement. She participates in the glory of her Son, reigns with him, presides at his side over the destinies of the Church in time, and intercedes on behalf of all before him who will come again to judge the living and the dead.

VLADIMIR LOSSKY

O full of grace, thou art the joy of all creation,
Of the hierarchy of angels and the race of men.
      Hallowed temple,
      Paradise of the Word,
      The glory of virginity,
From thee God took flesh and became a little child,
He who is from all eternity our God.
Thy womb he took as throne,
Thy body he made wider than the heavens.
O full of grace, thou art the joy of all creation:
      Glory to thee!

LITURGY OF ST BASIL THE GREAT

August 18 ST FLORUS AND ST LAURUS

Twin brothers from Constantinople, stoneworkers by profession, they suffered martyrdom in the early fourth century. More particularly in the Russian Church, they are regarded as the patron saints of animals.

Abba Paul said, 'If a man acquires purity, all things are subject to him, as they were to Adam in paradise, before he transgressed the commandment.'

THE SAYINGS OF THE DESERT FATHERS

The humble man approaches the beasts of prey, and as soon as they see him their wildness is tamed. They come up to him and follow him as their master, wagging their tails and licking his hands and feet. For they smell on him the smell that Adam had before the Fall, when the animals gathered before him in paradise and he gave them their names.

ST ISAAC THE SYRIAN

It is also worth considering whether man, at his first coming into the world, had not already a redemptive function to perform. Man, even now, can do wonders to animals: my cat and dog live together in my house and seem to like it. It may have been one of man's functions to restore peace to the animal world, and if he had not joined the enemy he might have succeeded in doing so to an extent now hardly imaginable.

Man is to be understood only in his relation to God. The beasts are to be understood only in their relation to man and, through man, to God. The tame animal is therefore, in the deepest sense, the only 'natural' animal.

C. S. LEWIS

A place for animals in the age to come?

There will be little dogs, with golden hair, shining like precious stones.

MARTIN LUTHER

August 20 ST BERNARD *1090–1153*

He came to Cîteaux in 1112 to join the Cistercians, who lived by a new and rigorous revision of the Benedictine Rule. In 1115 he became abbot of a second foundation at Clairvaux, from which he exercised a magnetic spiritual influence. This is from his last work, on the love of God:

It is this conformity which makes a marriage between the soul and the Word, when, being like him by nature, she endeavours to resemble him in will, loving him as he loves her. If she loves perfectly, she becomes his spouse. What can there be more delightful than this conformity, what more desirable than this love, which, not content with the instructions which she receives from men, boldly approaches the Word in her own person, attaches herself firmly to him, interrogates and consults him familiarly about all things, the capacity of her understanding being the only measure of the hardihood of her desires? This is a true marriage-contract: nay, more, it is a real embrace; for the complete conjunction of their wills makes one spirit of them.

August 24 ST BARTHOLOMEW

It is generally agreed that Bartholomew is a Syrian, not a Hebrew name, and means 'the son of a water-carrier'. Perhaps then, Nathanael, who was of Cana of Galilee, is Bartholomew, the son of the water-carrier; for on the third day, when there was a marriage in the village, it may be that through him the Lord was invited to the wedding, where, to the general wonder, he turned the water that he carried into wine. To this his confession we hear the Son of God and King of Israel replying: 'Because I say to you, I saw you under the fig tree, do you believe? You shall see greater things than these.' Any faithful Christian can hope this for himself.

RUPERT OF DEUTZ

August 24 ST COSMAS THE AETOLIAN *1714–1779*

A monk of Mount Athos, he travelled throughout Greece as a missionary to the oppressed Christian population, preaching to vast crowds and founding several hundred schools where education was given free. After more than three centuries of Turkish rule, the life of the Greek people, both spiritual and cultural, was at a very low ebb; and St Cosmas therefore believed that religious renewal should go hand in hand with the revival of education. Known as 'the equal of the apostles' and 'the apostle of the poor', he died as a martyr at the hands of the Turks. Here is a description of his preaching journeys, by one of his disciples:

Because of the large crowds, when there was not enough room in the church he was forced to preach out of doors in the fields. He asked the people to set up a large wooden cross for him, and then he put his portable pulpit against it, climbed up and preached. After the sermon he had the pulpit taken apart and took it with him, but the cross remained there as a permanent reminder of his preaching.

He had about forty or fifty priests who accompanied him, and when he was about to go from one place to another he sent word ahead to the Christians to make their confession, to fast, and to celebrate a vigil service, lighting many candles. He distributed candles free of charge to all, and then had the priests hold a service of Holy Unction; and all the Christians were anointed. After this he preached. Because of the large numbers that accompanied him as he went from place to place – two or three thousand – he used to tell them the night before to prepare many sacks of bread and cauldrons of boiled wheat, and to have them ready at the roadside.

August 25 ST LOUIS *1215–1270*

He succeeded to the throne of France in 1226 at the age of eleven, and died in Tunis on a Crusade. This illustration of his·wisdom is given by his biographer; it points to a problem that vexed succeeding centuries:

There was no one in his council so wise as himself, and it appeared in this, that of himself, without consulting anyone, and offhand, as I have heard, he replied to all the prelates of France.

Bishop Guy of Auxerre spoke to him in the name of all, saying: 'Christianity is decaying and perishing in your lands, and it will decay still further, if you do not see to it, because no one nowadays has any fear of excommunication. We require of you therefore, sire, that you command your bailiffs and sergeants to constrain those who have been excommunicated for a year and a day to render satisfaction to the Church.'

The King replied to them, without consultation, that he would be quite willing to command his bailiffs and sergeants to constrain the excommunicated, as he requested of them, provided that they would give him cognizance of the sentence, to decide whether it was just or not. Then they consulted together, and answered the King that they would not give him cognizance of what belonged to the ecclesiastical court. The King thereupon replied that he would not give them cognizance of what belonged to himself, nor would he command his sergeants to constrain the excommunicated to seek absolution, whether they were in the right or in the wrong.

August 25 ST MONICA *c. 331–387*

The mother of St Augustine. In this passage in his *Confessions* St Augustine describes their last conversation:

When the day of her death was coming – a day you, Lord, knew but we did not – she and I were alone, leaning out of a window that overlooked the garden in the courtyard of the house where we were staying, there at Ostia on the Tiber, where we waited, away from crowds, after our long journey by land, and prepared for our sea voyage.

Our conversation led us to conclude that no bodily pleasure, however great and whatever earthly light might shed lustre upon it, could be compared, or even noticed, by contrast with the happiness of the life of the saints. And so we went on by interior thinking, and speaking to one another with wonder at your works, O Lord, and finally came to our own minds and passed beyond them to reach the land of unfailing plenty where you feed Israel eternally with the fodder of truth, where life is wisdom through whom all things were made, all that have been and ever will be; but she herself is not made but only is, since she is eternal: for to have been and to be in the future, are not to be in eternity. And while we spoke of her, and strained after her with the whole of our heart-beat, we touched her for a moment.

That was the burden of our talk, although we did not speak in these precise words or exactly as I have set them down. Yet you know, Lord, that as we talked that day the world, with all its pleasures, seemed a paltry place compared to the life of which we spoke. And then my mother said, 'My son, for my part I find no further point in being in this life. What I am still to do and why I am here in this world I do not know, for I have no more to hope for on this earth. I had one reason alone for wishing to remain a little longer in this life, and that was the wish to see you a Catholic Christian before I died. God has granted me this and more beside, for I now see you as his servant, despising any happiness that the world can give. What is left for me to do in this world?'

August 28 ST AUGUSTINE OF HIPPO *353-430*

The son of a pagan father and a Christian mother, he became an orthodox Christian only after a long intellectual pilgrimage, recorded in the first of all autobiographies, the *Confessions*, from which our first extract is taken. The second is from *The City of God*, a series of reflections on the role of the Church in the declining Western Empire. This had an immense influence on Western theology in the Middle Ages, as other works of his, interpreting St Paul, dominated the Reformation.

I have learnt to love you too late, Beauty so old and so new! I have learnt to love you too late! You were within me, and I looked out into the world, where I sought you outside myself, and in my deformity searched for you there and ran after the beauties that you made. You were with me, but I was not with you. The beauties that kept me away from you had no existence except in you. You called and shouted and broke into my deafness. You flashed and shone and dispelled my blindness. You sent forth fragrance, and I drew in my breath and panted for you. You touched me, and I burnt for your peace.

The heavenly city, while sojourning on earth, calls citizens out of all nations, and gathers together a society of pilgrims of all languages, without any scruples about diversity in the manners, laws and institutions whereby earthly peace is sought and maintained, neither abolishing nor undermining anything in them but, rather, keeping and preserving them: because, although they are different in different nations, all are intended for the same end of earthly peace, only providing that no impediment is put in the way of the worship of the one supreme and true God. The heavenly city on her pilgrimage makes use of earthly peace, and in what belongs to the mortal nature of mankind, seeks a common agreement of human wills, where piety and religion is kept in safety, and seeks to make this earthly peace contribute to the peace of heaven; for this alone can truly be called the peace of reasonable creatures that consists, as heavenly peace does, in the perfectly ordered and harmonious enjoyment of God and of one another in God.

The heavenly city on its pilgrimage possesses this peace by faith; and by this faith it lives righteously when every good action towards God and man refers to that peace, since the life of the city is social.

August 29   THE BEHEADING OF ST JOHN THE BAPTIST

Martyrdom as a universal vocation: red and white

Besides outward martyrdom there is also a secret martyrdom, about which the apostle speaks: 'This is our boast – the martyrdom of our conscience; for we have lived among men with holiness and godlike sincerity' (2 Cor. 1.12).

ORIGEN

In times of peace the Lord will give to the victorious a white crown as a reward for their works, in times of persecution a red crown as a reward for their suffering.

ST CYPRIAN

Do not think that you have acquired virtue, unless you have struggled for it to the point of shedding your blood.

EVAGRIUS OF PONTUS

Give your blood and receive the Spirit.

THE SAYINGS OF THE DESERT FATHERS

August 31   JOHN BUNYAN   *1628–1688*

He fought on the parliamentary side in the Civil War and was imprisoned after the Restoration, spending most of the years from 1660 to 1672 in gaol. Best known for the *Pilgrim's Progress*, from which this passage is taken:

I saw now that they went on, till they came at the river that was on this side of the Delectable Mountains. To the river where the fine trees grow on both sides; and whose leaves, if taken inwardly, are good against surfeits, where the meadows are green all the year long, and where they might lie down safely.

By this river side, in the meadow, there were cotes and folds for sheep, a house built for the nourishing and bringing up of those lambs, the babes of those women that go on pilgrimage. Also there was here one that was entrusted with them, who could have compassion, and that could gather these lambs with his arm, and carry them in his bosom, and that could gently lead those that were with young. Now to the care of THIS MAN, Christiana admonished her four daughters to commit their little ones, that by these waters they might be housed, harboured, succoured, and nourished, and that none of them might be lacking in time to come. This Man, if any of them go astray, or be lost, he will bring them again; he will also bind up that which was broken, and will strengthen them that are sick. Here they will never want meat, and drink, and clothing; here they will be kept from thieves and robbers; for this Man will die before one of those committed to his trust shall be lost. Besides, here they shall be sure to have good nurture and admonition, and shall be taught to walk in right paths, and that you know is a favour of no small account. Also here, as you see, are delicate waters, pleasant meadows, dainty flowers, variety of trees, and such as bear wholesome fruit.

So they were content to commit their little ones to him; and that which was also an encouragement to them so to do, was, for that all this was to be at the charge of the King, and so was as an hospital for young children and orphans.

THE FINAL GLORY

The resurrection of the body

At the round earths imagin'd corners, blow
Your trumpets, Angells, and arise, arise
From death, you numberlesse infinities
Of soules, and to your scattred bodies goe,
All whom the flood did, and fire shall o'erthrow,
All whom warre, dearth, age, agues, tyrannies,
Despaire, law, chance, hath slaine, and you whose eyes,
Shall behold God, and never tast deaths woe.
But let them sleepe, Lord, and mee mourne a space,
For, if above all these, my sinnes abound,
'Tis late to aske abundance of thy grace,
When wee are there; here on this lowly ground,
Teach mee how to repent; for that's as good
As if thou hadst seal'd my pardon, with thy blood.

JOHN DONNE

Consider the man in whom there dwelt a legion of all kinds of devils (Mark 5.9); they were there though they were not recognized, for their army is of finer stuff and more subtil than the soul itself. That whole army dwelt in a single body.

A hundred times finer and more subtil is the body of the just when they are risen, at the resurrection: it resembles a thought that is able, if it wills, to stretch out and expand, or, should it wish, to contract and shrink: if it shrinks, it is somewhere; if it expands, it is everywhere.

The spiritual beings in paradise are so refined in substance that even thoughts cannot touch them.

ST EPHREM THE SYRIAN

The way of exchange

The Prince Immanuel gave a ball:
cards, adequately sent to all
who by the smallest kind of claim
were known to royalty by name,
held, red on white, the neat express
instruction printed: *Fancy Dress.*

One man arrives at the ball without fancy dress. Before being turned away
he is given a glimpse of those there:

He saw along
the Great Hall and the Heavenly Stair
one blaze of glorious changes there.
Cloaks, brooches, decorations, swords,
jewels – every virtue that affords
(by dispensation of the Throne)
beauty to wearers not their own.
This guest his brother's courage wore;
that, his wife's zeal, while, just before,
she in his steady patience shone;
there a young lover had put on
the fine integrity of sense
his mistress used; magnificence
a father borrowed of his son,
who was not there ashamed to don
his father's wise economy.
No he or she was he or she
merely: no single being dared,
except the Angels of the Guard,
come without other kind of dress
than his poor life had to profess,
and yet those very robes were shown,
when from preserval as his own
into another's glory given,
bright ambiguities of heaven.

CHARLES WILLIAMS

Putting on the glory of creation

We do not want merely to *see* beauty. We want something else which can hardly be put into words – to be united with the beauty we see, to pass into it, to receive it into ourselves, to bathe in it, to become part of it. That is why we have peopled air and earth and water with gods and goddesses and nymphs and elves – that, though we cannot, yet these projections can, enjoy themselves that beauty, grace and power of which Nature is the image. For if we take the imagery of Scripture seriously, if we believe that God will one day *give* us the morning star and cause us to *put on* the splendour of the sun, then we may surmise that both the ancient myths and the modern poetry, so false as history, may be very near the truth as prophecy. At present we are on the outside of the world, the wrong side of the door. We discern the freshness and purity of morning, but they do not make us fresh and pure. We cannot mingle with the splendours we see. But all the leaves of the New Testament are rustling with the rumour that it will not always be so. Someday, God willing, we shall get *in*. When human souls have become perfect in voluntary obedience as the inanimate creation is in its lifeless obedience, they will put on its glory, or, rather, that greater glory of which Nature is only the first sketch. We are summoned to pass in through Nature, beyond her, into that splendour which she fitfully reflects.

C. S. LEWIS

On the eternal enjoyment of God

Consider first, that although the Kingdom of heaven abounds with all that can be imagined good and delightful; yet there is but one sovereign good, in the enjoyment of which consists the essential beatitude of heaven, and that is God himself; whom the blessed ever see as he truly is, face to face; and see him in the very centre of their own souls; and by the eternal contemplation of his infinite beauty and truth, together with all his divine attributes and attractions, they are quite ravished, and set on fire with seraphic flames of eternal love: by means of this contemplation and love, they are closely united by a most pure and amiable union, with this sovereign and infinite good; and they eternally enjoy him: he surrounds and penetrates them on all sides with inexpressible delights; he fills their own souls with himself, the overflowing source of all good; he gives himself to them to be their joy, their treasure, their never-ending bliss; he transforms them in a manner into himself: as when brass or iron in the furnace is perfectly penetrated by fire, it loseth in a manner its own nature, and becomes all flame and fire. O happy creatures! What can be wanting to complete your joys; who have within, and without you, the immense ocean of endless felicity.

RICHARD CHALLONER

The life of the age to come

What the soul now has treasured up within it will be revealed at the Last Day and displayed outwardly in the body. Think of the trees that have survived the winter, how they are warmed by the invisible power of the sun and the winds, and put forth buds and clothe themselves with leaves and blossom and fruit; or think of the flowers of the field at that same season of the year, how they come out from the bosom of the earth, so that the earth and the fields are covered and decked as with raiment; as Christ said of the lilies, 'Even Solomon in all his glory was not adorned as one of these' (Matt. 6.29). These are all parables and types and figures of Christians at the resurrection. To all souls that love God, to all true Christians, there shall come a first month, as the month of April, and this will be the day of resurrection. Through the power of the Sun of Righteousness the glory of the Holy Spirit comes out from within, decking and covering the bodies of the saints – the glory which they possessed before, but hidden within their souls.

At the resurrection all the members of the body are raised: as Scripture says, not a hair perishes (Luke 21.18). All our limbs become full of light, they are all plunged in light and immersed in fire, and they are transformed: yet they are not, as some assert, dissolved and turned into fire, with nothing of their natural substance left. Peter is still Peter, Paul is Paul, Philip is Philip. Each one retains his own nature and personal identity, but they are all filled with the Spirit.

As the Lord's body was glorified, when he went up the mountain and was transfigured into the glory of God and into infinite light, so the saints' bodies are also glorified and shine as lightning. The glory that was within Christ was outwardly revealed in his body and shone forth; and in the same way with the saints the power of Christ that is within them will at the Last Day be poured forth outwardly upon their bodies. For even now in their intellect they share in his substance and nature. So it is written, 'He who consecrates and they who are consecrated are all of the same stock' (Heb. 2.11), and 'The glory which thou hast given me, I have given to them' (John 17.22). Just as many lamps are lit from one flame, so the bodies of the saints, being members of Christ, must needs be what Christ is, and nothing else.

THE HOMILIES OF ST MACARIUS

REFERENCES

Page

1 Norman Nicholson (1914–87), Anglican, poet and descriptive writer. *Sea to the West* (1981), p. 36; *Selected Poems* (1982), p. 68.

2 Fr George Florovsky (1893–1979), Russian Orthodox theologian, teaching first in Paris and then in the USA. 'Creation and Creaturehood' in *Collected Works*, vol. 3 (1976), p. 45.

3 Fr Alexander Schmemann (1921–83), Russian Orthodox theologian at St Vladimir's Seminary, New York. *For the Life of the World: Sacraments and Orthodoxy* (1973), p. 59.

4 Gerard Manley Hopkins (1844–89), Roman Catholic Jesuit priest and poet. *Poems* (1930), p. 30.

4 Louis Chardon (1595–1651), French Catholic Dominican priest. *La Croix de Jésus* (1647), p. 422.

5 W. H. Vanstone (1923–), Anglican priest. *Love's Endeavour, Love's Expense* (1977), pp. 60, 62. He writes on p. 63: 'This principle ... does not imply that the Creator works upon a "material" which is fundamentally alien or resistant to the shape which he would impose upon it.'

6 Austin Farrer (1906–68), Anglican theologian. *Saving Belief* (1967), p. 52.

7 Julian (see May 8), *Revelations of Divine Love* 5.

8 Kathleen Raine (1908–), poet and critic. *Collected Poems* (1981), p. 7.

8 *The Way of a Pilgrim*: the autobiography of an anonymous Russian peasant in the middle of the nineteenth century. He practised the Jesus Prayer and carried in his knapsack the collection of mystical texts known as the *Philokalia*. Trans. R. M. French (1954), p. 31.

9 Fyodor Dostoevsky (1821–81), Russian novelist. *The Brothers Karamazov* (1880), book 6, chapter 3.

10 R. S. Thomas (1913–), poet and Anglican priest of the Church in Wales. *Laboratories of the Spirit* (1975), p. 65.

10 William Blake (1757–1827), English poet, artist and visionary. *Poetry and Prose*, ed. G. Keynes (1948), pp. 148, 184, 187, 193, 652, 860.

11 Fr Sergius Bulgakov (1871–1944), Russian thinker, initially Marxist, later an Orthodox priest. 'Religion and Art' in E. L. Mascall (ed.), *The Church of God: an Anglo-Russian Symposium* (1934), p. 175.

12 *Letters* 1, 43 (*PL* 77.496).

12 Iulia de Beausobre (ed.), *Russian Letters of Direction* (1944), p. 87.

13 *Protevangelion of James* (one of the infancy Gospels), chapters 4, 5 and 6.

13 Mother Mary and Archimandrite Kallistos Ware (trans.), *The Festal Menaion* (1969), pp. 107, 119.

14 Archimandrite Sophrony, *Wisdom from Mount Athos* (1974), p. 33; *The Monk of Mount Athos* (1973), p. 32.

15 *The Unity of the Catholic Church*, Tracts 5.4.

15 *The Festival Menaion*, pp. 144, 152.

16 J. R. Green, *Short History*, ed. Alice Green (1878), vol. 1, p. 58.

References

Page

16 Dietrich Bonhoeffer (1905–45), German Protestant theologian and martyr. *The Cost of Discipleship*, Eng. trans. (1962), p. 35.

17 Nicolas Zernov (1898–1980), Russian Orthodox lay theologian, teaching at Oxford. *St. Sergius, Builder of Russia* (1939), p. 153.

18 *Devotions*, trans. Peter Hall (1830), pp. 62, 63, 66, 67.

20 R. F. Wilson (ed.), *Life of St Vincent de Paul* (1873), p. 311.

21 Francis Thompson (1859–1907), Roman Catholic poet. *Collected Poems* (1913), p. 349.

22 In Alexander Carmichael, *Carmina Gadelica* (a collection of folklore from the Scottish Highlands), vol. 1 (1928), p. 49.

22 Evagrius (*c.* 345–99), Greek ascetic and mystical theologian, living in Egypt in the Nitrian desert. *On Prayer*, 80, 81.

23 *Letter* 130 (*PL* 22.1107).

24 This comes from a manuscript of the seventh century that belonged to the Abbey of Reichenau in Germany. The Latin is in *Missale Gallicanum Vetus*, ed. L. O. Mohlberg (1958), p. 78; the translation in G. Every, *Basic Liturgy* (1961), p. 46.

25 Theophilus of Antioch (late second century), an apologist for the faith. *To Autolycus* 2. 24.

25 St Irenaeus (see June 28), *Demonstration of the Apostolic Preaching* 12.

25 Blake, *Poetry and Prose*, ed. G. Keynes, p. 182.

26 St Gregory of Nazianzus (see January 25), *Oration* 38, 11.

27 St Maximus the Confessor (see January 21), *Ambigua* (*PG* 91.1304).

28 Father Dumitru Staniloae (1903–), Romanian Orthodox theologian. 'The World as Gift and Sacrament of God's Love' in *Sobornost* 5.9. (1969), p. 665.

29 *Caedmon's Metrical Paraphrase*, ed. B. Thorpe (1832) with a modern translation. Later scholarship has shown that this is not by Caedmon, the father of Anglo-Saxon poetry in the seventh century, but later. It was known to Milton.

29 John Milton (1608–74), Puritan poet and politician, used the manuscript assigned to Caedmon here, in *Paradise Lost* 1.40.

30 Mother Mary and Archimandrite Kallistos Ware (trans.), *The Lenten Triodion* (1978), p. 175.

30 Henry Vaughan (1622–95), Anglican poet and physician. *Works*, ed. L. C. Martin (1957), p. 440.

32 Thomas Traherne (1637–74), Anglican priest, poet and devotional writer. *Centuries, Poems and Thanksgivings*, ed. H. M. Margoliouth (1958), p. 6.

33 Edwin Muir (1887–1959), Christian poet and man of action, born in the Orkney Islands, who worked for the British Council in Rome and in Prague. *Collected Poems* (1960), p. 227.

34 Paul Evdokimov (1901–70), Russian Orthodox lay theologian, teaching in Paris. *L'Orthodoxie* (1959), pp. 60, 72.

34 Søren Kierkegaard (1815–55), Christian philosopher in Denmark. *Journals*, trans. A. Dru (1938), 3.2 (1834), 1051 (1854).

35 Nicolas Berdyaev (1874–1948), Russian Orthodox philosopher, working in Paris. *Dream and Reality* (1950), p. 46.

36 Trans., by a Franciscan, in *Works* (1882), p. 146.

37 *The Obedience of a Christian Man* (1528), ed. in Christian Classics Series (1888), p. 174.

38 *Way of Perfection* 31.

References

Page

39 Canon H. B. Rawnsley (1850–1920), Anglican clergyman, Vicar of Crossthwaite, Cumberland. *The English Hymnal* (1906), no. 247.

40 *Spritual Counsels of Father John of Kronstadt*, ed. W. J. Grisbrooke (1967), pp. 6, 27, 78, 107, 189.

40 Graham Greene (1904–), Roman Catholic novelist. *The Comedians* (1966), p. 283.

41 *Luther: Letters of Spiritual Counsel*, in Library of Christian Classics 18 (1955), p. 96.

42 Metropolitan Anthony (Bloom) of Sourozh (1914–), Russian Orthodox bishop in London. *Sobornost incorporating Eastern Churches Review* 1.2 (1979), p. 8.

43 St Isaac the Syrian (seventh century), Bishop of Nineveh in Mesopotamia. *Mystic Treatises*, trans. A. J. Wensinck (1923), p. 308.

43 *A pious association of the devout servants of Christ crucify'd and of his consoling Mother the Blessed Virgin in the English Colledge of the Society of Jesus at St Omer's* (1726), p. 40.

43 E. N. Trubetskoy (1863–1920), Russian Orthodox religious philosopher. The 'royal doors' in an Orthodox church are the central doors in the icon screen, opened at the initial blessing in the Eucharist. See N. Arseniev, *Russian Piety* (1964), p. 90.

44 *The Lenten Triodion*, p. 128; *Service Book of the Holy Orthodox-Catholic Apostolic Church*, trans. I. F. Hapgood (1922), p. 387.

45 Gerard Manley Hopkins, *Poems* (1930), p. 22 (1876).

45 Fyodor Dostoevsky, *The Brothers Karamazov* 6.3.

46 Archimandrite Macarius Glukharev (1792–1847), Russian Orthodox missionary priest in Central Asia. S. Tyszkiewicz and T. Belpaire, *Écrits d'ascètes russes* (1957), p. 103.

46 *The Gelasian Sacramentary* came originally from Rome, but this is amongst the prayers introduced into it in France in the eighth century. See *The Study of Liturgy*, ed. C. Jones, G. Wainwright and E. Yarnold (1978), p. 226.

47 Archimandrite Sophrony, *The Monk of Mount Athos*, p. 71.

47 St Catherine of Genoa (1447–1510), a married lady who devoted herself to the service of the sick and poor. *Treatise on Purgatory* 2.

47 Dante Alighieri (1265–1321), Florentine poet and politician, in exile from 1302. *Paradise, Canto* 31, 79–90, trans. George Every.

48 Joseph Hall (1574–1656), Anglican divine, Bishop successively of Exeter and Norwich, who suffered much in his old age from the Civil War. *A Treatise of Christ Mystical*, chapter 7.3, in *Works*, ed. Peter Hall (1837), vol. 7, p. 261.

48 St Symeon (see March 12), *Centuries* 3.4; *Sources chrétiennes* 51 (1957), p. 81.

49 *Service Book*, trans. I. F. Hapgood, p. 152.

49 'Shorter Canon of Intercession', in *Orologion to Mega*, ed. Apostoliki Diakonia (1963), p. 549.

50 Alexis Khomiakov (1804–60), Russian Orthodox lay theologian, cited in W. J. Birkbeck, *Russia and the English Church* (1895), pp. 193, 216.

51 *Laws of Ecclesiastical Polity* 1.3.2.

52 *Menaion tou Noemvriou*, ed. Phos (1960), p. 93.

52 Origen (*c.* 185–*c.* 254), theologian and preacher at Alexandria, presbyter and teacher at Caesarea. *On Prayer*, 11.5; 31.5.

53 Titus Matthaiakis, *O Osios Nektarios Kephalas* (1955), p. 127.

54 *Letter* 12.4 (*PL* 54.650).

54 Sulpicius Severus (*c.* 360–*c.* 420), historian and hagiographer. *Life of St Martin*, chapter 10 (*PL* 20.166).

References

Page

55 *Discourses upon the Scriptures* 136, vol. 2 (1819–20), p. 209.

56 *Blessed Paisius Velichkovsky*, ed. St Herman of Alaska Brotherhood, Platina (1976), p. 131.

57 Bede (see May 25), *Ecclesiastical History of the English People* 4.23.

57 *The Festal Menaion*, p. 185.

58 John Dryden (1631–1700), Roman Catholic from 1686, Poet Laureate 1670–89, wrote this in 1687. *Poems and Fables*, ed. J. Kinsley (1962), p. 422; *Works*, vol. 11 (1808), p. 167.

58 Jonas, *Life of St Columban* 1.17, ed. Bruno Krusch (1905) in *MGHSgus* 35.

59 *Epistle to the Corinthians* 24.

59 A. Roberts and J. Donaldson (eds.), *Apocryphal Gospels, Acts and Revelations*, in Ante-Nicene Christian Library, vol. 16 (1870), p. 369, from a manuscript in the Bodleian Library, Oxford (Bodley MS Baroc, 180, f. 111b).

60 Jeremy Taylor (see August 13), *The Great Exemplar of Sanctity and Holy Life* (1657), add. sect. 10.3.

61 St Andrew of Crete (see July 4), *The Great Canon*, in *The Lenten Triodion*, pp. 390, 392.

61 John Goter or Gother (1650–1704), Roman Catholic priest, spiritual and contro-versial writer. *Prayers for Sundays and Feasts from Advent to Easter*, in *Spiritual Writings*, vol. 13 (1718), pp. 13, 15. These were reissued separately or together several times in the eighteenth century.

62 J. H. Newman (1801–90), leader of the Oxford Movement in the Church of England from 1833 to 1843, Roman Catholic from 1845, a Cardinal from 1879. *Parochial and Plain Sermons* (1839), vol. 4, p. 378.

63 Pierre Teilhard de Chardin (1881–1955), Roman Catholic, Jesuit priest and geologist. *Le Milieu divin*, (trans. 1960), pp. 148–52.

64 St Nilus of Ancyra (d. *c*. 430), Greek monastic writer. *Letters* 2. 36–7.

64 St Isaac of Nineveh, *Mystic Treatises*, trans. A. J. Wensinck, p. 84.

64 St Mark the Monk (fifth century?), Greek ascetic. *On the Spiritual Law* 4.

64 Metropolitan Philaret (Drozdov) of Moscow (1782–1867), Russian Orthodox theo-logian. 'Comparison of the Differences . . . betwixt the Eastern and Western Churches' in R. Pinkerton, *Russia* (1833), p. 41.

65 Bernard Blackstone (ed.), *The Ferrar Papers* (1938), p. 234 (spelling and punctuation altered).

66 *The Sparkling Stone* 9, trans. C. A. Wynschenk Dom (1916), p. 203.

67 *Letters* 3.7 (1596), p. 117.

68 *De Mysteriis* 9.52–3.

69 L. Ouspensky and V. Lossky, *The Meaning of Icons* (1952), p. 123.

70 *Depositions in the Cause*, trans. (1908), *point* 40, p. 194.

71 F. A. Golder, 'Father Herman, Alaska's Saint', in *The Orthodox Word* 1.1 (1965), p. 10.

72 *Ascent of Mount Carmel* 2.5, 17.

73 *To the Romans* 4–7.

74 These antiphons or anthems are sung before and after the Magnificat at Evening Prayer on December 17 and the days after in the Roman rite and those derived from it, with minor variations. Anglicans begin a day earlier on December 16. In the new Roman Missal they are now in the Mass for the same days between December 17 and Christmas Eve.

References

Page

75 *The Festal Menaion*, pp. 253–4.

76 See January 25. *Oration* 38.1, 2, 13.

77 Fr Sergei Hackel (1931–   ), Russian Orthodox priest. 'Some Russian Writers and the "Russian Christ"' in *Eastern Churches Review* 10 (1978), p. 48.

77 Nestorius (d. *c.* 451), Archbishop of Constantinople, deposed by the Council of Ephesus. *Bazaar of Heracleides*, trans. G. R. Driver and L. Hodgson (1925), p. 69.

77 St Gregory of Nyssa (see January 10), *Catechetical Oration* 24.

78 T. S. Eliot (1888–1965), Anglican from 1927, poet, critic and publisher. *Collected Poems, 1909–62* (1963), p. 177.

79 John Goter, *Instructions for the Whole Year* (1696), vol. 1, p. 80; *Spiritual Writings* (1718), vol. 4.

80 St Dorotheus of Gaza (sixth century), Greek spiritual writer. *Instruction* 6.

80 *Starets* Silouan (see September 11), in *Wisdom from Mount Athos*, pp. 27–30.

81 Jeremy Taylor (see August 13), *The Great Exemplar*, sect. 6.3, add. sect. 6.11.

82 Samuel Johnson (1709–84), Anglican, poet, critic, lexicographer. *Diaries, Prayers and Annals*, ed. C. L. McAdam (1958), p. 152.

82 Richard Rolle (*c.* 1300–49), hermit of Hampole in Yorkshire. *On the Song of Songs* in *Selected Works*, ed. G. C. Heseltine (1930), p. 81.

83 *Longer Rules* 3.1; 7.4.

83 Irina Gorainoff, *Seraphim de Sarov* (1973), p. 133.

84 W. H. Auden (1907–73), Anglican, poet and critic. *Collected Longer Poems* (1968), p. 171.

85 Evelyn Waugh (1903–66), Roman Catholic novelist. *Helena* (1950), p. 239.

86 Sidney Godolphin (1610–43), Cavalier poet, killed in the Civil War.

87–8 *The Festal Menaion*, pp. 298, 301, 354, 380, 381, 382.

89 St Ephrem (see June 19), *Hymn to Christ*, trans. R. Murray, *Eastern Churches Review* 3 (1970), p. 143.

89 St Nicolas Cabasilas (fourteenth century), Byzantine civil servant and lay theologian, author of works on sacraments. *Life in Christ* 2 (*PG* 150, 524, 532).

90 St Cyril of Jerusalem (see March 18), *Catechetical Lectures* 20, 4–5.

91 Austin Farrer, *The Triple Victory* (1965), p. 32.

91 V. Lossky (1903–58), Russian Orthodox lay theologian, working in Paris. *The Mystical Theology of the Eastern Church* (1957), p. 171.

91 St Kallistos and St Ignatius Xanthopoulos (fourteenth century), Greek spiritual writers. *Century* 4.

92 *The Life of St Macrina* 23.

93 *On the Trinity* 2.25.

93 *Works*, vol. 1, ed. W. Armistead (1852), p. 60.

94 St Athanasius (see May 2), *Life of St Antony* 10.

95 *Sayings of the Desert Fathers*, alphabetical collection, 'Macarius of Egypt', 18–19, 31–2.

96 *Centuries on Love* 3.3–4.

96 *Letters to Persons in the World*, trans. H. B. Mackey (1883), p. 90.

97 St John Chrysostom (see January 27), *On the Priesthood* 3.7.

97 *Sayings of the Desert Fathers*, 'Gregory', 2.

98 Socrates (*c.* 380–*c.* 450), church historian. *Ecclesiastical History* 6.3.

98 *Works*, Paris ed. (1871–80), vol. 32 (1879), p. 681.

References

Page
99 George Every.
100 G. Bonetti, *Don Bosco's early apostolate*, trans. (1908), p. 394.
101 George Herbert (see February 27), *Works*, ed. F. E. Hutchinson (1941), p. 51.
101 Tito Colliander (1904–   ), Orthodox writer belonging to the Swedish-speaking minority in Finland. *The Way of the Ascetics* (1960), pp. 71, 73, 75.
102 Evagrius, *On Prayer* 14–16, 31–3, 36, 98, 102–3, 153.
103 St Theophan the Recluse (1815–94), Russian Orthodox spiritual writer; in Igumen Chariton of Valamo, *The Art of Prayer: an Orthodox Anthology* (1966), pp. 52, 63.
104 E. B. Pusey (1800–82), Anglican theologian in the Oxford Movement. *Parochial Sermons*, vol. 3 (1869), p. 229, citing Isaac Barrow (1603–77), an older Anglican divine.
105 This is by Fr Lev Gillet (1892–1980), a French Orthodox spiritual writer, for many years chaplain of the Fellowship of St Alban and St Sergius. *On the Invocation of the Name of Jesus* (1950), p. 5.
106 Simone Weil (1909–43), French philosopher of Jewish origin who died in England during the Second World War. *Waiting on God*, trans. (1951), p. 128.
106 Colliander, *The Way of the Ascetics*, p. 79.
107 Metropolitan Anthony of Sourozh, *School for Prayer* (1970), p. 2.
107 Thomas à Kempis (*c.* 1380–1471), spiritual writer in the Low Countries. *On the Imitation of Christ*, 1.3.2.
108 *The Cloud of Unknowing* 6, the work of an anonymous English mystic of the fourteenth century.
108 Julian (see May 8), *Revelations of Divine Love*, 5.
109 In *A Manual of Eastern Orthodox Prayers*, ed. Fellowship of St Alban and St Sergius (1945), p. 6.
109 In *Carmina Gadelica*, vol. 1, p. 231.
110 Alan Ecclestone (1907–   ), Anglican priest and spiritual guide, in E. James (ed.), *Spirituality for Today* (1968), p. 34.
110 *A Manual of Eastern Orthodox Prayers*, p. 24.
111 Theophylact (*c.* 1050–1108), Byzantine monk, bishop and commentator, Archbishop of Ochrida in Macedonia from 1078. *The Four Evangelists* (1631), p. 319 (*PG* 123.729).
111 *Correspondence*, ed. S. N. Schoinas (1960), Answers 23, 35, 239.
112 George Every.
113 Margaret Ford, *Janani* (1978), p. 75.
114 *Martyrdom*, 14–15, in J. B. Lightfoot and J. R. Harmer (eds), *The Apostolic Fathers* (1898), pp. 194–5.
115 *Works*, ed. F. E. Hutchinson (1941), p. 165.
116 *Conferences*, 10.10.
117 Mother Maria (Skobtsova) (1891–1945), Orthodox nun in Paris, who died in the gas chambers in Ravensbrück. S. Hackel, *One of Great Price* (1965), p. 4.
117 H. B. Dehqani-Tafti, *The Hard Awakening* (1981), p. 113.
118 St Basil (see January 1), *On Fasting*, 1.10.
118 Monica Furlong in *The Church Times*, 4 March 1983.
119 Robert Herrick (1591–1674), Anglican parish priest and poet. *Poems* (1965), p. 391.
120 H. Berthold (ed.), *Makarios/Symeon, Reden und Briefe*, *Logos* B 33.2, 1, vol. 2 (1973), p. 29.

References

Page

120 St Augustine (see August 28), *Tracts on St John* 12.14.

121 Isaac, *Ta evrethenta askitika*, ed. N. Theotokis and I. Spetsieris (1895), p. 10. The true author is not Isaac of Nineveh but another Syrian, John of Dalyatha (eighth century). Note the parallels with the Latin prayer, *Anima Christi*.

122 St Gregory of Narek (*c*. 950–*c*. 1010), Armenian Orthodox monk-poet. *Lamentations of Narek*, trans. Mischa Kudian (1977), p. 64.

123 St Francis de Sales (see January 24), *On the Love of God*, Book 6, 1.

124 *Manual of Eastern Orthodox Prayers*, p. 58.

124 Dietrich Bonhoeffer, *Life Together*, trans. (1954), pp. 87, 92.

125 Fr Alexander Schmemann, *Great Lent* (1969), p. 14.

125 *The Lenten Triodion*, p. 23.

125 G. Megas, *Greek Calendar Customs* (1963), p. 73.

126 H. A. Williams (1909–   ), Anglican priest, formerly chaplain of Trinity College, Cambridge, since 1968 in the Community of the Resurrection at Mirfield. *The True Wilderness* (1965), p. 29.

127 Fr Alexander Elchaninov (1881–1934), Russian Orthodox parish priest in France. *The Diary of a Russian Priest* (1967), pp. 27, 70, 84, 135, 185.

128 Dogmatic Decree of the Seventh Council (787) in J.-D. Mansi, *Concilia* 13.377.

128 St John of Damascus (d. *c*. 749), a civil servant of the Caliph, who became a monk at Mar Saba near Jerusalem and an Eastern Father of the Church. *On the Holy Icons*, 1.16.

128 Fr Gervase Mathew (1905–76), Roman Catholic Dominican priest, teaching in Oxford. *Byzantine Aesthetics* (1963), p. 23.

129 Nicolas Zernov, *The Russians and their Church* (1945), p. 108.

129 St Theodore the Studite (759–826), Abbot of the monastery of Studios in Constantinople, imprisoned for his defence of the icons. *Antirrheticus* 3.2.5.

129 *Triads* 2.3.51; 1.3.18.

130 A. W. Wade-Evans (ed.), *Life of St David* (1923), p. 30, modified. This account was written in about 1094.

131 *Sermons and Addresses* (1911), p. 37.

132 *Hymns* 28.112–18, 157–67.

133 *Rule of St Benedict*, Prologue.

134 *Confession* 9 and 10 (*PL* 53.803); 'The Deer's Cry', trans. Lady Isabella Gregory in *A Book of Saints and Wonders* (1907), ed. E. Malins (1973), p. 76.

135 *Catechetical Lectures* 14.9.

135 *Protevangelion of James* 17, 18.

136 Bede (see May 25), *Ecclesiastical History* 4.27.

137 'Sermon preached in the King's Chapel at Whitehall in 1685' in *Prose Works*, ed. W. Benham (1889), p. 85.

137 Preface to 'the Great Bible' of 1540 in *Remains and Letters*, ed. J. E. Cox (1846), pp. 122, 124.

138 George Every, after the Ethiopian 'Anaphora of our Lady', in J. M. Rodwell, *Ethiopian Liturgies and Hymns* (1864).

139 *The Festal Menaion*, p. 460.

139 St Nicolas Cabasilas, *Homily on the Annunciation* 4–5 (*Patrologia Orientalis* 19.488).

140 Sermon on 'Primitive tradition recognized in Holy Scripture', in R. Nye (ed.), *The English Sermon*, vol. 3 (1976), p. 197.

References

Page

141 *The Ladder of Divine Ascent,* trans. C. Luibheid and N. Russell (1983), p. 137.

141 P. D. Garrett, *St Innocent, Apostle to America* (1979), p. 178.

142 *The Lenten Triodion,* pp. 469, 471.

142 R. S. Thomas, *Later Poems, 1972–1982* (1983), p. 172.

143 Elizabeth Jennings (1926–), Roman Catholic poet. *Selected Poems* (1980), p. 72.

143 *The Lenten Triodion,* pp. 497, 499.

144 Blaise Pascal (1623–62), French Catholic savant. *Thoughts,* trans. Kegan Paul (1890), p. 31.

145 David Gascoyne (1916–), Christian poet and visionary. *Collected Poems,* ed. Robin Skelton (1965), p. 42.

145 Stevie Smith (1902–71), sceptical poet with an Anglican background. *Collected Poems* (1975), p. 69.

146 St Melito (d. *c.* 190), Bishop of Sardis in Asia Minor. *On Pascha and Fragments,* ed. S. G. Hall (1979), p. 88.

147 Fr George Florovsky, *Ways of Russian Theology,* in *Collected Works,* vol. 5 (1979), p. 217.

147 Charles Causley (1917–), Christian visionary. *Collected Poems, 1951–75* (1975), p. 69.

148 Saunders Lewis (1893–1985), Roman Catholic Welsh nationalist poet. *The Oxford Book of Welsh Verse in English* (1977), p. 187.

149 *The Lenten Triodion,* pp. 623, 625, 627, 634.

149 *The Gospel of Nicodemus* 8 (24), in C. Tischendorf (ed.) *Evangelia Apocrypha* (1876), p. 330.

150 William Langland (*c.* 1330–86), a poet who was a married clerk in minor orders and 'sang for souls' in Westminster and Worcestershire. *The Vision of Piers Plowman, passus* 18, lines 372–8, 397–9, modernized. See A. V. C. Schmidt (ed.), *A complete edition of the B text* (1978), p. 32.

150 P. Evdokimov, 'Le monachisme intériorisé' in *Le Millénaire du Mont Athos 963–1963.* Éditions de Chevetogne, vol. 1 (1963), p. 339.

150 F. D. Maurice (1805–72), Anglican seer and theologian. *Theological Essays* (1853), p. 161.

151 *PG* 59. 721–4.

152 Francis Kilvert (1840–79), Anglican curate. *Diary,* vol. 3 (1960), p. 257 (16 April 1876).

153 John Heath-Stubbs (1918–), Anglican poet and critic. *Selected Poems* (1965), p. 69.

154 *Carmina Gadelica,* vol. 2 (1928), p. 74.

154 George Herbert (see February 27), *Works,* ed. F. E. Hutchinson (1941), p. 41.

155 *Life of St Richard* (1945) in *Lives of the English Saints,* p. 118. This is based on two accounts in the *Acta Sanctorum* of the Bollandists.

155 G. A. Maloney, *Russian Hesychasm, the Spirituality of Nil Sorskij* (1973), pp. 114, 128, 138, 156, 164, 262.

156 *Some animadversions upon Mr Trapp's late reply,* appended to *An appeal to all those who doubt or disbelieve the truth of the Gospel* (1742) in *Works* (1762), vol. 6, p. 206 (reprinted in facsimile, 1893).

157 Armand Ravelet, cited in Francis Thompson, *Life and Labours of St John Baptist de la Salle* (1911), p. 46.

157 *Proslogion* 25 (*PL* 158.240).

References

Page

158 G. K. Chesterton (1874–1936), Roman Catholic from 1922, poet, novelist, journalist. *Collected Poems* (1927), p. 150.

158 Alexander Solzhenitsyn (1918–), Russian Orthodox novelist, expelled from the Soviet Union in 1974. Nobel Prize speech (1970), in L. Labedz, *Solzhenitsyn: a Documentary Record* (1974), p. 314.

159 V. Borisov (1945–), Russian Orthodox church historian living in the Soviet Union. 'Personality and National Awareness', in A. Solzhenitsyn (ed.), *From Under the Rubble* (1975), pp. 204, 209.

159 Reinhold Niebuhr (1892–1970), American theologian and political thinker. *Moral Man and Immoral Society* (ed. 1960), p. 91.

160 Said Ibn Batriq (877–940), the Melkite (Catholic and Orthodox) Patriarch Eutychius of Alexandria from 933, a physician previously. *Annals*, Latin trans. Edward Pococke (1658), p. 328 (*PG* 111.982).

160 Trans. in A. T. Drane, *History of St Catherine*, col. 2 (1887), p. 506.

161 Dafydd Ap Gwilym (1340–70), Welsh poet best known for his love poems. *Oxford Book of Welsh Verse in English* (1977), p. 40.

162 William Temple (1881–1944), Anglican, Archbishop of Canterbury, philosopher and theologian. *Fellowship with God* (1920), p. 108.

162 A Monk of the Eastern Church, *L'An de Grâce du Seigneur*, vol. 2 (1972), p. 107.

163 Fr Paul Florensky (1882–1943), Russian Orthodox theologian and mathematician; most of his later life was spent in Soviet prison camps. *Stolp i utverzhdenie istini* (1914), Fifth Letter.

164 John Dryden, *Works* (1808), vol. 11, p. 190.

165 Richard Challoner (1691–1781), Roman Catholic Bishop of Debra and Vicar-Apostolic of the London district from 1741. *Meditations for every day in the year* (1767), vol. 1, p. 311.

166 G. Every. Norman Nicholson (ed.), *Anthology of Religious Verse* (1942), p. 42.

166 Léon-Joseph Suenens (1904–), Roman Catholic, Archbishop of Malines 1961–79, Cardinal 1962. *Come, Holy Spirit* (with Michael Ramsey, 1977), p. 68.

167 *Pentekostarion*, Rome edition (1884), p. 414.

167 St Gregory of Nazianzus (see January 25), *Oration* 31, 26–7.

168 A. W. Hare (1792–1834), Anglican parish priest. 'Holy Branches; or why was the Trinity revealed?' in R. Nye (ed.), *The English Sermon*, vol. 3 (1976), p. 119.

169 Richard of St Victor (*c.* 1108–73), a Scot who became an Augustinian canon of St Victor, outside Paris. *On the Trinity* 5.2 (*PL* 196.949).

169 St Thalassius the Libyan (seventh century), priest and abbot, friend of St Maximus the Confessor. *Centuries on Love and Self-control*, 4.93, 95, 98.

170 St Maximus (see January 21), *Centuries on Theology and the Incarnate Dispensation of the Son of God*, 2.1.

170 St Hilary (see January 13), *On the Trinity* 2.14.2.

171 *The Lenten Triodion*, p. 405; *Triodion Katanyktikon*, ed. M. Saliveros, pp. 167, 227.

171 Gerard Manley Hopkins, *Poems* (1930), p. 56.

173 Origen, *Against Celsus* 7.43.

173 Bishop J. A. T. Robinson (1919–83), Anglican theologian, teaching in Cambridge. *Honest to God* (1963), p. 77.

174 John Goter, *Instructions for Feasts* (1699), p. 306; *Instructions for particular states and conditions of life* 13.4 (1689), p. 288; in *Spiritual Writings* (1718), vol. 4 and vol. 10.

174 St Athanasius (see May 2), *On the Incarnation of the Word* 54.

References

175 *The Sayings of the Desert Fathers*, 'Arsenius', 1–2, 13, 15, 27, 29–30.

176 *Revelations of Divine Love* 56.

176 *Ecclesiastical Hierarchy* 5.5 (written *c.* 500). The reference to other writers shows that the author did not originally claim to be St Paul's disciple.

177 *Works* (1745), vol. 3, p. 45, cited in A. G. Ferrers Howell, *Life of St Bernardine* (1913), p. 283.

177 Evelyn Waugh, *Helena* (1950), p. 259.

178 John and Charles Wesley, *Selected Prayers, Hymns ... and Treatises*, ed. F. Whaling (1981), pp. 192–3.

179 Cited by Jean Mabillon in *Acts of the Saints of the Order of St Benedict*, vol. 3 (1734), p. 503.

180 Father Bacci, *Life of St Philip Neri*, trans. F. I. Antrobus (1902), vol. 2, p. 397.

180 *Protevangelion* 12.

181 *Epistle to Diognetus* 5, an apology of the second century, in J. B. Lightfoot and J. R. Harmer (eds.), *The Apostolic Fathers* (1898), p. 493.

182 A. Elchaninov, *The Diary of a Russian Priest*, pp. 87, 124.

182 J. H. Newman, *Parochial Sermons* (1839), vol. 4, p. 198.

183 St Peter Damiani (1007–72), Italian ascetic reformer. *The Book of the Lord be with you* 6, a letter to a hermit (*PL* 145.235).

183 St Symeon (see March 12), *Catechesis* 8: *Sources chrétiennes* 104 (1964), p. 90.

184 Fyodor Dostoevsky, *The Brothers Karamazov* 6.3.

184 Canon A. M. Allchin (1930–), Anglican priest. *The Dynamic of Tradition* (1981), p. 28.

185 F. E. Brightman (ed.), *Liturgies Eastern and Western* (1896), pp. 378, 393.

185 Anglican-Roman Catholic International Commission, *Final Report* 1.3, 7, 8 (1982), p. 15.

186 *Liturgies Eastern and Western*, p. 41.

186 Bishop Alexander (Semenoff-Tian-Chansky), *Father John of Kronstadt: a Life* (1978), p. 35.

186 St Augustine (see August 28), *City of God* 10.6; *Sermons* 272, 227, 229.

187 John Masefield (1878–1967), Poet Laureate 1930–67. 'The Everlasting Mercy', in *Collected Poems* (1923), p. 129.

187 *Liturgies Eastern and Western*, pp. 394, 330.

188 Ernest Raymond (1888–1974), a former Anglican priest who lost his faith and became a popular novelist. In later life he returned to the Church and wrote about this in *The Bethany Road* (1967), p. 204.

188 St Thomas (see January 28).

189 Nicholas Cabasilas, *Life in Christ* 4 (*PG* 150, 581, 593, 597, 625).

189 *Teaching of the Apostles (Didache)* (first–second century), 9.

189 C. A. Swainson (ed.), *The Greek Liturgies* (1884), p. 171.

190 *First Apology* 67.

190 Margery Perham, *Lugard, the Years of Adventure* (1958), p. 216.

191 *English Correspondence* 31, ed. E. Wylie (1911), p. 138 (*PL* 89.750).

191 §8, in J.-D. Mansi, *Concilia* 4.1007.

192 Adamnan, *Life of St Columba*, ed. J. T. Fowler (1894), 2.27.

193 S. Brock, *The Harp of the Spirit*. Studies supplementary to *Sobornost*, no. 4 (1975), p. 48.

193 Robert Murray (1925–), Roman Catholic, Jesuit priest, Syriac specialist, teaching

References

Page

in London. 'Mary, the Second Eve in the Early Syriac Fathers', in *Eastern Churches Review* 3 (1971), p. 384.

194 St. Thomas Aquinas (see January 28), 'Sermons for Feasts', in *Works* (1570), vol. 16, p. 37, recto.

194 1.2 (1573), p. 8; in *Works* (1557), p. 1143; (1976), vol. 12, p. 12.

195 *Treatise concerning the Fruitful Sayings of David* (1714), p. 78.

195 Bede (see May 25), *Ecclesiastical History* 1.7.

196 Dom Anscar Vonier (1875–1938), Roman Catholic Benedictine monk of German origin who came to England to join Buckfast Abbey at the age of fourteen and became abbot in 1906. *The Divine Motherhood* (1921), p. 10.

196 *Demonstration of the Apostolic Preaching* 33; *Against Heresies* 3.19.6; 5.21.1 (following Harvey's edition).

197 John Goter, *Afternoon Instructions* (1699), vol. 2, p. 375; *Spiritual Writings* (1718), vol. 7, p. 346.

198 Macarius, *Homilies*, Collection H, 16,13; 17.1.

198 Alcuin (*c.* 735–804), a native of York, counsellor to the Emperor Charles the Great from *c.* 780. *On the Divine Offices* 16–17 (*PL* 101.1205). The attribution of this to Alcuin is open to question.

198 St Paulinus (*c.* 353–431), Bishop of Nola in the South of France. *Letters* 23.36.

199 Cardinal Suenens in *Come, Holy Spirit* (with Michael Ramsey, 1977), p. 55.

200 Sydney Smith (1771–1845), Anglican clergyman with a reputation for wit and for no nonsense. A sermon preached to lawyers at York in 1824. *Works*, vol. 3 (1854), p. 180.

201 Agatha Christie (1891–1976), writer of detective stories. *An Autobiography* (1977), p. 150.

202 Samuel Johnson, *Sermons*, vol. 1 (1788), pp. 239–40.

203 G. R. Dunstan (1917–   ), Anglican moral theologian. *Theology* 76, no. 631 (January 1973), p. 1.

204 A. Elchaninov, *The Diary of a Russian Priest*, pp. 25, 211, 216, 218, 219, 220.

205 Jonathan Swift (1667–1745), Anglican, Dean of St Patrick's, Dublin. 'Letter to a young gentleman lately entered into Holy Orders', in *Satires and Personal Writings*, ed. W. A. Eddy (1932), p. 272.

206 St John Chrysostom (see January 27), *On the Priesthood* 4.3

207 Rose Macaulay (1881–1958), Anglican novelist. *The Towers of Trebizond* (1956), p. 287.

208 Thomas Merton (1915–68), Roman Catholic Cistercian priest in the USA. *Conjectures of a Guilty Bystander* (1968), p. 58.

208 J. H. Newman, *Parochial Sermons* (1839), vol. 2, p. 18.

209 *The Lenten Triodion*, pp. 408, 411.

210 'Silence over Mount Athos', *Orthodox Life*, Nov.–Dec. 1968, p. 33.

211 William of Malmesbury (*c.* 1090–1143), church historian. *Gesta Pontificum* (1870), 2.75, p. 161.

211 *The Goad of Divine Love*, trans. J. Lewis (1642), ed. W. A. Philipson (1907), p. 206.

212 *The Russian Primary Chronicle*, trans. S. H. Cross and O. P. Sherbowitz-Wetzor (1953), p. 116.

213 Saunders Lewis in *The Oxford Book of Welsh Verse in English* (1977), p. 185 (extracts).

214 Nicolas Zernov, *Moscow the Third Rome* (1937), p. 22.

215 St Leo, *Sermon* 51 (94) (*PL* 54.310).

Page
215 Fragment in *Coptic Apocryphal Gospels*, ed. F. H. Robinson (1896), p. 6.
216 *Practical View* (1797), p. 468.
217 These are in all editions of *The Spiritual Exercises*, but not always in the same order.
218 G. P. Fedotov (1886–1951), Russian Orthodox church historian, teaching in Paris and New York. *The Russian Religious Mind*, vol. 2 (1966), p. 321.
219 *Carillon de Beaupaire*, August 1893, cited in Francis Trochu, *The Insight of the Curé d'Ars*, trans. M. Leahey (1934), p. 62.
220 Metropolitan Anthony, 'Body and Matter in Spiritual Life', in A. M. Allchin (ed.), *Sacrament and Image: Essays in the Christian Understanding of Man* (1967), p. 40.
221 *The Festal Menaion*, pp. 476, 477, 495.
221 Macarius, *Homilies*, Collection H, 1.2.
222 See Simon Tugwell OP, *The Way of the Preacher* (1979), p. 62.
223 Published on 26 September 1255, trans. in L. de Chevance, *St Clare of Assisi* (1927), p. 231.
224 *The Great Exemplar of Sanctity and Holy Life according to the Christian institution: described in the History of the life and death of the ever Blessed Jesus Christ the saviour of the world* (1657), p. 516.
224 N. Gorodetzky, *Saint Tikhon Zadonsky, Inspirer of Dostoevsky* (1951), pp. 119, 130.
225 G. Every.
226 V. Lossky, 'Panagia', in E. L. Mascall (ed.), *The Mother of God* (1949), p. 34.
226 C. A. Swainson, *The Greek Liturgies*, p. 162.
227 *Sayings of the Desert Fathers*, 'Paul', 1.
227 Isaac of Nineveh, *Mystic Treatises*, p. 386.
227 C. S. Lewis (1898–1963), Anglican, Professor of English Literature. *The Problem of Pain* (1940), pp. 124, 126.
227 W. Hazlitt (ed.), *The Table Talk of Martin Luther* (1857), p. 322.
228 *On the Love of God*, trans. Coventry Patmore (1884), p. 147.
228 Rupert of Deutz (*c.* 1075–1129), Benedictine abbot in Germany. *On St John* (1564), 2, p. 36 (*PL* 169.273).
229 S. Christodoulidis, 'Life of St Cosmas', in Bishop Augustine Kantiotis, *Kosmas o Aitolos* (1971), pp. 56, 58.
230 Sieur de Joinville, *Memoirs of King Louis*, trans. James Hutton (1868), p. 200.
231 St Augustine (see August 28), *Confessions* 9.10.
232 *Confessions* 10.27; *City of God* 19.17.
233 Origen, *Exhortation to Martyrdom* 21.
233 St Cyprian (see September 12), *On Works and Alms, Tracts* 10.21.
233 Evagrius, *On Prayer* 136.
233 *Sayings of the Desert Fathers*, 'Longinus', 5.
234 Illustrated edition (1861), p. 339.
235 John Donne (1572–1631), Anglican poet and divine, ordained in 1615, Dean of St Paul's, London from 1621. Holy Sonnets 7 in *Poetical Works*, ed. H. J. C. Grierson (1929), p. 296.
235 St Ephrem (see June 9), S. Brock, *The Harp of the Spirit*, p. 23.
236 Charles Williams (1888–1945), Anglican poet and prophet. *Apologue on the Parable of the Wedding Garment* (December 1940) in *The Image of the City and other Essays*, ed. Anne Ridler (1958), p. 166.
237 C. S. Lewis, 'The Weight of Glory' in *Transposition and other essays* (1949), p. 31.
238 Bishop Richard Challoner, *Meditations* (1767), vol. 2, p. 79.
239 Macarius, *Homilies*, Collection H, 5.8–9; 15.10, 38.

INDEX OF NAMES

ACKNOWLEDGEMENTS

'Nobbut God' by Norman Nicholson, from *Selected Poems*, is reprinted by permission of Faber and Faber Ltd and David Higham Associates Ltd.

The extract from *For the Life of the World* by Alexander Schmemann is reprinted by permission of Darton Longman & Todd Ltd and St Vladimir's Seminary Press. U.S. copyright by St Vladimir's Seminary Press, Crestwood, New York.

'Pied Beauty', 'The Wreck of the Deutschland', and 'The May Magnificat' are reprinted from *The Poems of Gerard Manley Hopkins* (fourth edition 1967), edited by W. H. Gardner and N. H. MacKenzie, published by Oxford University Press for the Society of Jesus.

The extract from *Love's Endeavour, Love's Expense* by W. H. Vanstone is reprinted by permission of Darton, Longman & Todd Ltd.

The extract from *Saving Belief* by Austin Farrer is reprinted by permission of Hodder and Stoughton Ltd.

'Vegetation', from *Collected Poems* by Kathleen Raine, is reprinted by permission of George Allen & Unwin.

'Good' from *Laboratories of the Spirit* and 'Lazarus' (from 'Covenant') in *Later Poems 1972–1982* by R. S. Thomas are reprinted by permission of Macmillan, London and Basingstoke.

Extracts from *The Monk of Mount Athos* and *Wisdom from Mount Athos* by Archimandrite Sophrony are reprinted by permission of A. R. Mowbray & Co. Ltd.

The extract from *The Cost of Discipleship* (second edition) by Dietrich Bonhoeffer is reprinted by permission of SCM Press Ltd and Macmillan Publishing Co., Inc. Copyright © SCM Press Ltd 1959.

'The Guardian Angel', Blessing of the Kindling, and Easter Sunday from *Carmina Gadelica* by Alexander Carmichael are reprinted by permission of Scottish Academic Press Ltd.

The extract by Dr. Dumitru Staniloae from 'Sobornost' (1969) is reprinted by permission of the Fellowship of St Alban and St Sergius.

'One Foot in Eden', from *The Collected Poems of Edwin Muir*, is reprinted by permission of Faber and Faber Ltd and Oxford University Press, Inc.

The extract from *Journals* by Søren Kierkegaard, translated and edited by A. Dru, is reprinted by permission of Oxford University Press.

The extract from *Dream and Reality* by Nicolas Berdyaev is reprinted by permission of Collins Publishers.

The extract from *Spiritual Counsels of Fr John of Kronstadt*, edited by W. J. Grisbrooke, is reprinted by permission of James Clarke & Co., Ltd.

The extract from *Letters of Spiritual Counsel* by Martin Luther (LCC XVIII) is reprinted by permission of SCM Press Ltd and The Westminster Press.

The extract by Anthony Bloom from 'Sobornost, incorporating Eastern Churches Review' (1979) is reprinted by permission of the Fellowship of St Alban and St Sergius.

The extract from *Blessed Paisius Velichovsky*, edited by the St Herman of Alaska Brotherhood, is reprinted by permission of St Herman of Alaska Monastery.

Extracts from *The Divine Milieu* by Pierre Teilhard de Chardin are reprinted by permission of Collins Publishers and Harper & Row, Publishers, Inc. English translation copyright © 1960 by the publishers.

The extract from *The Ferrar Papers* by Bernard Blackstone is reprinted by permission of Cambridge University Press.

The extract by F. A. Golder from 'The Orthodox Word' (1965) is reprinted by permission of the St Herman of Alaska Monastery.

The extract by Fr Sergei Hackel from 'Eastern Churches Review' (1978) is reprinted by permission of the Fellowship of St Alban and St Sergius.

The extract from 'Choruses from "The Rock"' in *Collected Poems 1909–1962* by T. S. Eliot, is reprinted by permission of Faber and Faber Ltd and Harcourt Brace Jovanovich, Inc. Copyright © 1963, 1964 by T. S. Eliot.

Extracts from *Sermons* by Samuel Johnson, edited by J. Hagstrum and J. Gray, are reprinted by permission of Yale University Press.

The extract from *Selected Works* by Richard Rolle, edited by G. C. Heseltine, is reprinted by permission of Longman Group Ltd.

Extracts from 'At the Manger', from 'For the time being, a Christmas oratorio' in *Collected Poems* by W. H. Auden, are reprinted by permission of Faber and Faber Ltd and Random House, Inc. U.S. copyright 1944 and renewed 1972 by W. H. Auden.

Extracts from *Helena* by Evelyn Waugh are reprinted by permission of A. D. Peters and Co., Ltd and Little, Brown and Company. Copyright © 1950 by Evelyn Waugh; renewed © 1978 by Evelyn Waugh.

Extracts by Robert Murray from 'Eastern Churches Review' (1970, 1971) are reprinted by permission of the Fellowship of St Alban and St Sergius.

The extract from *The Triple Victory* by Austin Farrer is reprinted by permission of Faith Press.

Extracts from *The Way of the Ascetics* by Tito Colliander are reprinted by permission of Harper & Row.

The extract from *The Art of Prayer: An Orthodox Anthology* by Igumen Chariton of Valamo is reprinted by permission of Faber and Faber Ltd.

The extract from *Waiting on God* by Simone Weil is reprinted by permission of Routledge & Kegan Paul Ltd and The Putnam Publishing Group.

The extract from *Beginning to Pray* by Anthony Bloom is reprinted by permission of Darton, Longman & Todd Ltd and Paulist Press. Copyright © 1970 by Archbishop Anthony Bloom.

The extract by Alan Ecclestone from *Spirituality for Today*, edited by E. James, is reprinted by permission of SCM Press Ltd.

The extract from *Janani* by Margaret Ford is reprinted by permission of Marshall, Morgan & Scott Ltd.

The extract by Monica Furlong from the 'Church Times' (March 1983) is reprinted by permission of the publisher.

The extract from *Lamentations of Narek* by St Gregory of Narek, translated by Mischa Kudian, is reprinted by permission of Mashtots Press. Copyright © Mischa Kudian 1977.

The extract from *The True Wilderness* by H. A. Williams is reprinted by permission of Constable Publishers.

Extracts from *The Diary of a Russian Priest* by Fr Alexander Elchaninov are reprinted by permission of Faber and Faber Ltd.

Acknowledgements

The extract from *Sermons and Addresses* by Edward King is reprinted by permission of Longman Group Ltd.

The extract from *A Book of Saints and Wonders* by Lady Gregory is reprinted by permission of Colin Smythe Ltd, publishers of the Coole Edition of Lady Gregory's writings.

'Lazarus' from *Collected Poems* by Elizabeth Jennings is reprinted by permission of Macmillan Publishers and David Higman Associates Ltd.

'Lachrymae' by David Gascoyne, from *Collected Poems*, edited by Robin Skelton, is reprinted by permission of Oxford University Press. Copyright © Oxford University Press 1965.

'So to Fatness Come' by Stevie Smith, from *The Collected Poems of Stevie Smith*, is reprinted by permission of James MacGibbon, Allen Lane (Publishers), and New Directions Publishing Corporation. Copyright © 1972 by Stevie Smith.

The extract from *Melito of Sardis: 'On Pascha' and Fragments*, edited by Stuart George Hall, is reprinted by permission of Oxford Unversity Press. Copyright © Oxford University Press 1979.

'I am the great sun' by Charles Causley, from *Collected Poems*, is reprinted by permission of Macmillan Publishers Ltd and David Higham Associates Ltd.

'To the Good Thief' and 'Mary Magdalene', by Saunders Lewis from *Presenting Saunders Lewis* (1973; second edition 1983), edited by A. R. Jones and G. Thomas, are reprinted by permission of University of Wales Press.

The extract from *Kilvert's Diary*, edited by William Plomer, is reprinted by permission of Jonathan Cape Ltd and Mrs Sheila Hooper.

'Canticle of the Sun' by John Heath-Stubbs, from *Selected Poems*, is reprinted by permission of Oxford University Press and David Higham Associates Ltd.

The extract from *From Under the Rubble* by Vadim Borisov, edited by Alexander Solzhenitsyn, is reprinted by permission of the Harvill Press, Collins Ltd, and Little, Brown and Company.

The extract from *Moral Man and Immoral Society* by Reinhold Niebuhr is reprinted by permission of SCM Press Ltd and Charles Scribner's Sons. U.S. copyright 1932 Charles Scribner's Sons; renewed 1960 Reinhold Niebuhr.

'The Woodland Mass' by Dafydd ap Gwilym, from *Welsh Poems: Sixth Century to 1600* (translated by Gwyn Williams) is reprinted by permission of Faber and Faber Ltd.

The extract from *Fellowship with God* by William Temple is reprinted by permission of Dr David Carey.

Extracts from *Come Holy Spirit* by Léon-Joseph Suenens are reprinted by permission of Darton, Longman & Todd Ltd and Morehouse-Barlow Co., Inc. Copyright © 1977 by Darton, Longman & Todd Ltd, London, and © 1976 by Morehouse-Barlow Co., Inc., Connecticut.

The extract from *The Dynamic of Tradition* by A. M. Allchin is reprinted by permission of Darton, Longman & Todd Ltd and The Seabury Press, Inc. Copyright © 1981 by A. M. Allchin.

'O Christ who holds the open gate' by John Masefield, from *Collected Poems*, is reprinted by permission of The Society of Authors (as the literary representative of the Estate of John Masefield) and Macmillan Publishing Co., Inc.

The extract from *The Bethany Road* by Ernest Raymond is reprinted by permission of the author and A. P. Watt Ltd.

Extracts from 'The Harp of the Spirit' by Sebastian Brock, in *Studies Supplementary to Sobornost* (No. 4) are reprinted by permission of the Fellowship of St Alban and St Sergius.

The extract from *The Divine Motherhood* by Anscar Vonier is reprinted by permission of Verlag Herder, Freiburg.

The extract from *An Autobiography* by Agatha Christie is reprinted by permission of Collins Publishers and Dodd, Mead & Company, Inc.

The extract from *The Towers of Trebizond* by Rose Macaulay is reprinted by permission of Collins Publishers and A. D. Peters & Co. Ltd.

The extract from *Conjectures of a Guilty Bystander* by Thomas Merton is reprinted by permission of Burns & Oates Ltd.

The extract by Anthony Bloom from *Sacrament and Image: Essays in the Christian Understanding of Man*, edited by A. M. Allchin, is reprinted by permission of the Fellowship of St Alban and St Sergius.

The extract from *The Way of the Preacher* by Simon Tugwell is reprinted by permission of Darton, Longman & Todd Ltd and Templegate Publishers.

The extract from *The Mother of God* by Vladimir Lossky, edited by E. L. Mascall, is reprinted by permission of A. & C. Black (Publishers) Ltd.

Extracts from *The Problem of Pain* and *Transposition and Other Addresses* by C. S. Lewis are reprinted by permission of Collins Publishers (Fontana Paperbacks).

Extracts from 'Apologue on the parable of the wedding garment' by Charles Williams, from *The Image of the City and Other Essays*, edited by Anne Ridler, are reprinted by permission of Oxford University Press and David Higham Associates Ltd.